ART

AND THE INDUSTRIAL REVOLUTION

by Francis D. Klingender

EDITED AND REVISED BY ARTHUR ELTON

Reprints of Economic Classics
AUGUSTUS M. KELLEY PUBLISHERS
New York 1968

©1968 Winifred Klingender and Evelyn, Adams & Mackay Ltd.
First published in 1947. Revised and extended edition
first published 1968. All rights reserved.

Published in the United States by

AUGUSTUS M. KELLEY · PUBLISHERS

New York, New York 10010

Library of Congress Catalogue Card Number
68-17687

Printed and bound by W & J Mackay & Co Ltd, Chatham.
Colour blocks by Star Illustration Ltd. The text is
set in 'Monotype' Walbaum. Made in England.

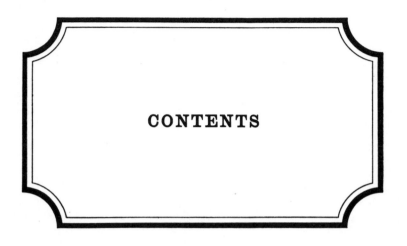

CONTENTS

FRANCIS DONALD KLINGENDER 1907–1955

The last time I met Francis Klingender, just after he had joined the staff of what is now Hull University, he explained that, to understand the attitude of the peoples of the USSR towards projects such as the Dnieperstroi Dam, then under construction, it was necessary to study the attitude of the peoples of Britain a hundred years before towards the feats of the great Victorian engineers. To prove his point, he compared illustrations in *Russia Today*, an English periodical sponsored by the USSR, with their equivalent from nineteenth-century issues of *The Illustrated London News*. The resemblance and identity of national enthusiasms were unmistakable. It was Francis Klingender's power of detailed, deep observation combined with associative leaps of the imagination, bringing into a single perspective events and ideas usually treated separately, that gives *Art and the Industrial Revolution* its permanent importance in the history of art.

Klingender was a dedicated Marxist, an historian and economist who loved to illuminate his scholarship by disparate flashes of observation. It was typical of him to choose for special study that area of art history neglected by both artists and historians, the region where art and technology meet and interpenetrate. Till his day, most art historians would have thought it a positive asset to be uncontaminated (as they might have put it) by industry and commerce. Most economic historians would have thought the study of the arts a frivolous interference with more serious preoccupations. From his expedition into the territory between the two Francis Klingender was to reap a rich intellectual reward and to put those who came after him in his permanent debt.

Francis Klingender's father, Louis Henry Weston Klingender, who claimed to be of Huguenot descent, was born in Liverpool in April 1861. Of his early life nothing is known, except that he must have migrated to Germany when a youth. For, by 1881, he was studying art in Düsseldorf under the celebrated painter of wild animals and the chase, Carl Friedrich Deiker (1836–92). Shortly afterwards Klingender himself became celebrated as a painter of wild life, specializing in anatomically detailed and minutely accurate studies of animals in conflict—boars attacking hounds, stags at bay, terriers harrying a fox, herds of animals in full flight. He was a frequent exhibitor at the Berlin Academy from the late eighteen-eighties, and later at the yearly exhibitions at Goslar in the Harz Mountains.

Louis Klingender prided himself on his realism as against the anthropomorphic sentimentality of Landseer, and remained all his life a fierce opponent of hunting and shooting, refusing to allow his work to be used to illustrate books on the chase. Though he roamed the game reserves of Count Henckel-Donnersmarck and Count Pless, and visited Russia and Turkey, he carried only a sketchbook and never a gun.

In 1902 he settled in Goslar with his English wife, Florence, *née* Hoette. Even today he is still remembered with affection, not only as a painter and sculptor of note, an intellectual and social leader, but also as a sportsman dedicated to swimming, athletics, and ski-ing. He devoted much time and energy to building up the Goslar Museum and collecting and arranging the exhibits in the fields of geology and natural history. Though he and his wife both spoke German without a trace of accent, it seems likely that he retained his British nationality and never took out German papers.

Francis Donald Klingender was born on 18 February 1907, at his parents' home in Ebertstrasse. The family led a happy, prosperous, busy life till the outbreak of war in 1914. Then, to his great distress, Louis Klingender was accused of spying and interned at Ruhleben, near Berlin. After a few months he was released, and returned to Goslar, where he had to report to the police each week, and was shunned as an enemy by most of his former friends. Though bitterly hurt by the reactions of his neighbours and in poverty, Louis Klingender managed not only to give his son a good classical education at the Goslar Gymnasium but to implant in him an enduring interest in art, something he always acknowledged with gratitude to the end of his life. Though Francis Klingender was taunted at school as an alien, and persecuted for his radical views, he matriculated with honours in 1925. Soon afterwards he and his mother and father, who had vainly interceded with British politicians in an attempt to ameliorate the terms of the Versailles Treaty, left Germany to settle in England.

There followed a period of privation, when Klingender had not only to complete his own higher education, in a language in which he was not completely fluent, but at the same time to support both himself and his mother and father, whose work, to his bewildered mortification, had become not only unfashionable but unsaleable. During this period his mother returned to Germany, where she died in 1944.

Soon after reaching London, Klingender took a job in an advertising agency, Rudolf Mosse Ltd, and enrolled as an evening student at the London School of Economics. At the former he was soon put in charge of a small market research unit; at the latter he studied under Hobhouse, Malinowsky and Ginsberg, and gained a first-class honours B.Sc. (Econ.) degree, with a special subject of sociology. Just before graduating he held briefly a marketing research appointment with Arcos Ltd, the Russian trading agency, which provided him with what he calls 'an illuminating insight into the conditions under which the more elementary levels of planning research were then conducted in a Soviet enterprise'.

After taking his degree, Klingender devoted himself to sociological fieldwork in connection with the *New Survey of London Life and Labour*, collecting material for the borough summaries under the guidance of Sir Hubert Llewellyn Smith. In 1930 he was awarded a two-year research studentship by the LSE, writing a thesis on *The Black-Coated Worker in London*, for which he was awarded his Ph.D. in 1934. Chapter XI in Volume VIII Section 111 of the *New Survey of London* is largely drawn from the material he collected for this thesis, as is his more extended monograph, *The Condition of Clerical Labour in Britain*, published in 1935 and his first book.

There followed a period of difficulty and frustration. Klingender's intellectual attainments made it difficult for him to accept a routine job, but his unswerving adherence to unpopular views made academic work for the moment difficult to secure. Continuing his 'theoretical and historical studies designed to elucidate the role of art as one of the great value-forming agencies in the social structure and social change', he turned to lecturing and writing, and was elected a member of the Executive Committee of the Artists International Association, becoming responsible for running the Association's Charlotte Street Centre.

In 1936, John Grierson invited him to undertake a financial study of the British film industry. This was published jointly with Stuart Legg in 1937 under the title *Money Behind the Screen*. It created a furore. Without relinquishing his association with Grierson and the documentary film movement, he was next engaged on a nation-wide series of interviews with agricultural experts for the Agricultural Research Council in an effort to establish the reasons for the lag between discoveries at the research stations and their application in the field. The substance of his report was embodied in the *PEP Report on Agricultural Research*. This led to a Leverhulme Research Fellowship in 1939–40, and his appointment as research secretary to a joint committee of PEP and the British Association charged, under the chairmanship of Julian Huxley, to conduct an inquiry into the social relations of scientific research. The outbreak of war brought this job to a stop.

Klingender's political opinions no doubt disturbed the authorities, and in any circumstances the poor health and asthma from which he had suffered since childhood are likely to have prevented his enrolment in the armed forces. Instead, as he observes dryly, his last experience in the applied field was gained during his wartime duties as a scientific officer at the Princes Risborough research unit of the Ministry of Home Security. Here he was attached to one of the statistical units, and took part in a survey of the social effects of bomb damage in Birmingham and Hull. However, he was still able to carry on his studies in a fragmentary way, organizing and preparing the catalogues of two exhibitions for the Artists' International—*Hogarth and English Caricature* (June 1943), and *John Bull's Home Guard* (January 1944). At this time he also published three monographs—*Russia —Britain's Ally, 1812–1942* (1942), a comparative study of the caricatures evoked in Russia by Napoleon and Hitler, with an introduction by Ivan Maisky; *Marxism and Modern Art* (1942), an approach to Socialist realism; and *Hogarth and English Caricature* (1944), developed from the AIA exhibition of the same title, and an important contribution to an understanding of the subject. He also wrote a number of articles for the *Burlington Magazine*, the *Architectural Review*, and other periodicals.

Towards the end of the war, and in the period immediately afterwards, Klingender began to study the subject that was to be his most important contribution to scholarship—*Art and the Industrial Revolution*, published in 1947 by Noel Carrington, printed by the Curwen Press, and dedicated to the students and tutors of the North Staffordshire Workers' Educational Association. Carrington's interest in the industrial revolution had been awakened by the Phillimore Collection on the history of railways, and he had already published Cyril Bruyn Andrews' *The Railway Age* (1937) in association with *Country Life*. His faith in Klingender's thesis and his foresight were alike remarkable.

In 1948 Sidgwick and Jackson published Klingender's *Goya in the Democratic*

Tradition from a manuscript completed in 1940.* It brought what was then a novel point of view to bear on a subject for generations overlaid and obscured by traditional attitudes. In the same year Klingender was appointed Lecturer in Sociology at University College, Hull. He subsequently represented the University of Hull on the British Universities Film Council. In 1950 old Louis Klingender died, at the age of 89.

Goya was Klingender's last major work to be published in his lifetime. It was succeeded only by a handful of relatively short essays and articles. His work in Hull led to a social study of small shopkeepers, published in *Current Affairs* under the title of 'The Little Shop' (No 127, 3 March 1951). 'Students in a Changing World' was spread over two issues of the *Yorkshire Bulletin of Economic and Social Research* (Vol. 6, Nos 1 and 2, February and September 1954). But perhaps of greater significance were two contributions he made in 1953 and 1954 respectively to the *Journal of the Warburg and Courtauld Institute* (Vol. 16, Nos 1 and 2), and the *British Journal of Sociology* (Vol. 5, No 2, June). The former was titled 'St Francis and the Birds of the Apocalypse', and the latter, 'Palaeolithic Religion and the Principle of Social Evolution'. Both were fragments of an altogether more profound study of the significance of animal forms in art, inspired perhaps by a sympathetic response to his father's lifelong preoccupation with wild life. He was completely absorbed by this subject during his last years and had completed, shortly before his death, the first draft of a manuscript entitled 'Animals in Art and Thought', which he considered might be his *magnum opus*. This manuscript is now being edited for publication by Mrs Frederick Antal.

In 1951, Francis Klingender married Winifred Margaret Kaye, a student of Social Studies at Hull University, and for the first time in his life found tranquillity and happiness. It is a tragedy that, after struggles that would have daunted many a lesser man, he did not live long enough to enjoy the intellectual rewards of his scholarship. He collapsed suddenly and died on 7 July 1955.

At this time his talent was scarcely recognized, and there appear to be only two obituaries, a factual one in the *Manchester Guardian*, and a more affectionate perceptive one in the Dutch paper *Kroniek*, which published many articles from his pen after the war.

*Letter from Klingender to Fred Uhlman. 14 August 1940.

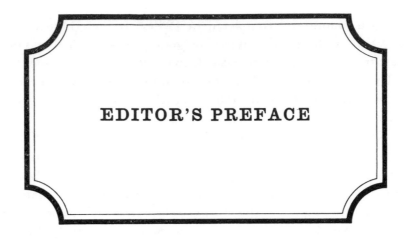

EDITOR'S PREFACE

The preparation of the text that follows has presented a great number of difficulties. Francis Klingender drafted it during and shortly after the war, when access to libraries was still difficult. So he was sometimes driven back on secondary sources, and placed too much reliance on the delightful but sometimes tendentious and inaccurate works of Samuel Smiles. I have traced all his sources back to the original, where necessary correcting them and, in many cases, amending, extending or adding to them.

Klingender's text bears some signs of hasty preparation, mainly because it was necessary to arrange for its publication to coincide with an exhibition at the Whitechapel Art Gallery to celebrate the centenary of the Amalgamated Engineering Union, an event in part dictating the content of his last chapter. In addition, the publisher was compelled to place a limit on its length. In consequence, parts of the original text are highly condensed and much essential knowledge is taken for granted. Many things he wanted to include had to be omitted, and he felt the time he had been able to spare for research inadequate. For this reason, I have expanded certain parts of the text, and have here and there clarified the flow of ideas. I have also added some sections, one defining eighteenth-century concepts of the sublime and the picturesque, terms used constantly by Klingender, who assumed a deeper familiarity with them than an ordinary reader could perhaps be expected to possess; and another defining and describing briefly the terms and techniques of wood-cutting, wood-engraving, line-engraving, mezzotint, stipple, aquatint, and etching.

A greater difficulty has been what to do about the mass of information on

Klingender's subject that has appeared in the past twenty years, and which he would certainly have incorporated had he lived to produce a revised edition himself. For example, at our meeting when he pointed out the resemblance between nineteenth-century British attitudes and twentieth-century Russian ones, we turned to an artist we both greatly admired—John C. Bourne. We agreed he was perhaps the greatest industrial topographer Britain has ever had, yet we reflected that his name appeared in no reference works and that we did not even know what the C. stood for. We resolved that, one day, we would find out. Since then I have been enabled to do the research that Francis Klingender would have taken such pleasure in pursuing and which was properly his. To my minor expedition into the life and works of Bourne must be added many works of great learning, among them, to mention only a few, the Abbey bibliographies of British illustrated books, J. T. Boulton's revealing edition of Burke on the Sublime, Robert Collison's work on Encyclopaedias, Desmond King-Hele's life of Erasmus Darwin, L. T. C. Rolt's account of Thomas Newcomen, Hugh Malet's life of the Duke of Bridgewater with the light it throws on Brindley, Elisabeth Beazley's life of William Alexander Madocks, another of Francis Klingender's heroes, and above all, the *History of Technology*, issued under the guidance and editorship of Charles Singer. Finally, it is certain that Francis Klingender would have been fascinated by the researches of von Heinrich Winkelmann, and of René Evrard and Jacques Stiennon of the Liège school of art history, and others, into the earlier phase of art and industry in the Erzgibirge, relatively unknown at the time he was preparing his text.

All these works support Francis Klingender's thesis of the interpenetration of art and technology. It seems to me clear, not only that Klingender would have drawn on their learning for any new edition of his book, but that, if this were not taken into account in a new edition, and the original were to be published as it stood, his reputation would not have been strengthened but weakened. For this reason, I have decided to add to Francis Klingender's text some of the material he would have incorporated himself, taking pains not to depart from and wherever possible to illuminate his attitude to the changing historico-economic situation. By doing this, it is my hope that Francis Klingender's reputation will be enhanced, that his originality will be the better appreciated, and that his work will find the place it deserves in the annals of the history of the arts and sciences.

Instead of an apparatus of notes and references, Klingender added a kind of running commentary to each chapter, embracing both general references to his sources and additional comments and afterthoughts. The result is that the references themselves are difficult to trace, and many of the comments and afterthoughts would have been better placed in the main text. I have therefore reverted to convention, supplying a running, numbered series of notes and references to each chapter, and bringing some of Klingender's comments back into the main text.

When *Art and the Industrial Revolution* was published, access to pictures was restricted and the selection available relatively meagre. My own collection, which Klingender drew on extensively, was much smaller and less representative than it is now. Accordingly, I have substituted some of the original illustrations by others affording better support to the text. Thanks in part to the Abbey bibliographies, I have been able to add detailed notes on the sources and iconography of the illustrations, with some additional notes on the artists and engravers.

AUTHOR'S ACKNOWLEDGEMENTS

In 1945, to celebrate its Silver Jubilee, the Amalgamated Engineering Union asked the Artists' International Association to arrange an exhibition, The Engineer in British Life. This first art exhibition sponsored by a British trade union suggested to me a wider study of the effect of the industrial revolution on the arts as a whole. I was greatly encouraged and helped in my work by discussions at week-end and summer schools at Barlaston Hall, and it is to the students and tutors of the North Staffordshire Workers' Educational Association that this book is accordingly dedicated. My thanks are also due for valuable information or the loan of material to Lady Trevelyan, Mrs Sacheverell Coke, Mrs Ivonne Kapp, Dr H. W. Dickinson, Dr N. Pevsner, Messrs Rhys Jenkins, A. Stowers, W. E. White, James Laver, Michael Robinson, C. A. M. Oakes, Arthur Elton, H. F. Clark, R. W. Robson, J. B. Jeffreys, Herbert Simon, Noel Carrington, Roger S. Darby, the Manager of Carron Company, the Directors of Hick, Hargreaves & Co. Ltd, Edgar Allen & Co. Ltd, and Ransomes, Sims & Jefferies Ltd, the Secretary of the Great Western and the Public Relations Officers of the other railway companies, and to all the other firms and individuals who answered my inquiries. I am no less indebted to the curators of the national and local museums, art galleries and public libraries who afforded me every assistance, despite difficulties of evacuation, shortage of staff and postwar rearrangement.

London, March 1947   F.D.K.

EDITOR'S ACKNOWLEDGEMENTS

For much help, advice and information, as well as for permission to reproduce various works in their collections, I am indebted to the Directors and staff of many Museums, Art Galleries and public or national institutions, notably: the British Museum; the Cyfarthfa Museum, Merthyr Tydfil; the Blackburn Public Libary and Art Gallery; the Institution of Civil Engineers; the Institution of Mechanical Engineers; the Kunstverein of Ludwigshafen am Rhein; the Laing Art Gallery, Newcastle on Tyne; the Manchester City Art Gallery; the British Railways Museum of Transport; the National Museum of Wales, Cardiff; the North-East Area Office of the National Trust; the Newport Art Gallery; the Pushkin Museum, Moscow; the Science Museum; the Sheffield Art Galleries; the State Hermitage Museum, Leningrad; Temple Newsam House, Leeds; the Walker Art Gallery, Liverpool; the Waterways Museum, Stoke Bruerne; the Victoria and Albert Museum. Messrs Carron Company, Shell-Mex and B.P., Christie, Manson and Woods, Sotheby, Maggs Brothers, the Parker Gallery and Frank T. Sabin have all been more than helpful. The text could scarcely have been written without the incomparable resources of the London Library.

For help of all kinds most freely given, I am indebted to Mrs Barnden of the Paul Mellon Foundation, Messieurs P. Colman and Jacques Stiennon of the Institute for the History of Art and Archaeology of the University of Liège, Dr Davidson and Mr R. J. Law of the Science Museum, Mr Charles Hadfield, Messrs Laurence Hallett and B. R. V. Hughes of the Royal Photographic Society, Mr Arnold Hyde, who was kind enough to allow me access to his collection on Manchester, Mr Christopher Hussey, on whose imaginative, revealing book, *The Picturesque,* both author and editor have drawn extensively, Mr Benedict Nicolson, Mr L. M. Oakes, Professor E. L. J. Potts of the University of Newcastle, Mr Graham Reynolds, Keeper of Prints and Drawings at the Victoria and Albert Museum, Mr L. T. C. Rolt, Sir John Summerson and Mr Ben Weinreb.

Separate acknowledgment is made in the notes after each title to each owner of a picture reproduced. However, I owe special thanks to Mr Edward Croft Murray and his staff at the British Museum Department of Prints and Drawings, for putting their learning most generously at my disposal and for affording valuable assistance at the photographic stage; to Mr Loraine Conran and Miss Elizabeth Johnston of the Manchester Art Gallery for much useful help and encouragement; to Mr Michael Diamond of the City of Sheffield Art Galleries for helping to trace pictures by Godfrey Sykes; to Mr John Scholes of the Museum of British Transport for allowing me access to the Bourne drawings; and to Messrs John Ingamells (now at York) and Peter Hughes of the National Museum of Wales at Cardiff for assembling material for the illustrations and for arranging for photographs. Viscount Lambton and Sir Edmund Bacon, Bt, kindly allowed me to have pictures in their collections photographed.

In my quest for details of the life of John Cooke Bourne I received much information from his son, Mr Henry Bourne, who died in 1962 at a great age, and from his wife, Jessie Tallack, from his grandsons, Messrs Eric, John and Gerald Bourne, and from Mrs Atkinson,

Mr J. G. S. Baker and Mr P. D. Ravenscroft. Mr Ivan Hooper gave me considerable help in unravelling the Bourne pedigree. Mme Larissa Doukelskaya, the learned Keeper of Prints at the Hermitage, Leningrad, made a search in Leningrad for Bourne's Kiev drawings. The Editor of *Country Life* has given me permission to reprint substantial parts of my article on Bourne.

Many people supplied me with biographical detail of Francis Klingender, and I must acknowledge the help I received from Mrs Frederick Antal, Professor J. D. Bernal, Messrs Mischa Black, Richard Carline, Noel Carrington, J. M. Richards, John Saville of the University of Hull, Fred Uhlman, who lent me some of Klingender's letters, and, not least, from Mrs Winifred Klingender, who allowed me to use a *curriculum vitae* prepared by Francis Klingender towards the end of his life. It is dated 1 February 1954, and I have drawn on it extensively. Dr Hillebrand, Archivist of Stadt Goslar, put me in touch with Herr Hans W. Ulrich also of Goslar, who knew the Klingenders before and during the first World War up to the moment they left Germany. He has allowed me to use an article on the elder Klingender that he contributed to the *Goslar Zeitung* on 23 November 1963, and in addition has set down all he could remember about the family.

My devoted secretary, Rosemary Wilkins, typed and retyped the manuscript and remained cheerful throughout its complicated course. My special thanks are due to the staff of FCP Studios and Laboratories, who were responsible for much of the colour and nearly all the black-and-white photography. My dear wife read the proofs and gave me much help and advice. She and my children suffered a steady erosion of family life with only a minimum of complaint while the manuscript and illustrations were being got ready.

To the above I must join the name of a friend of forty years' standing, Mr E. C. Kersley. Born on 6 November 1888, the son of a gardener, and partly brought up in an orphanage, he started work with a butcher at the age of 12, devoted his evenings and Saturdays to making sausages, and to doing other things he disliked. At 13 he joined the Scots Bridge Mill, which specialized in producing Boer War postcards and souvenirs and cigarette cards. At 14 he transferred to the Croxley Paper Mills. He made his first visit to the British Museum at the age of 15. In 1911 he emigrated to Canada.

Artist, Canadian lumberjack and cook, trade union organizer, pacifist, and a lifelong member of the Socialist Party of Great Britain, he became a dealer in pictures and prints in the old Caledonian Market after the First World War. He devoted his life to the acquisition of an enormous and diverse knowledge of many subjects, ballet, topography, portraiture, William Blake, engraving, lithography, watercolours and oil paintings. Aided by his intelligent wife, Nancy, with her strong and delicate mind, his generosity of spirit has been an encouragement to all who came in contact with him. His agile and informed eye enriched Francis Klingender's text. Without Ted Kersley, both editions of *Art and the Industrial Revolution* would have been the poorer.

London, October 1967   ARTHUR ELTON

ART AND THE INDUSTRIAL REVOLUTION

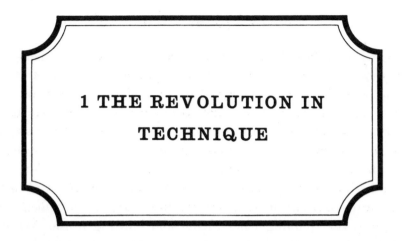

1 THE REVOLUTION IN TECHNIQUE

. . . every New View of Great Britain *would require a New Description; the Improvements that encrease, the New Buildings erected, the Old Buildings taken down; New Discoveries in Metals, Mines, Minerals; new Undertakings in Trade; Inventions, Engines, Manufactures, in a Nation, pushing and improving as we are; These Things open new Scenes every Day, and make* England *especially shew a new and differing Face in many Places, on every Occasion of Surveying it.*[1]

DANIEL DEFOE

THE ROOTS of the industrial revolution reach back to the Tudor period when England ceased to be a self-contained agricultural community, exporting her surplus wool to the manufacturing towns of the Continent. To become a great maritime and trading power, England had to develop her own industrial resources. She had to build and equip ocean-going ships, produce cloth and other finished goods for the new overseas markets, and supply the daily needs of the rapidly growing towns in which were concentrated her commerce and shipping, and the bulk of her new manufacturing enterprises.

Enriched by the dissolution of the monasteries and by colonial profits, aided by the grant of monopolies, a new class of adventurer emerged to direct the industrial expansion of the sixteenth and early seventeenth centuries. Foreign artisans, of whom many were refugees from religious persecution in their native countries, helped to train an efficient labour force for the new industries. Flemish weavers helped to establish the supremacy of the British woollen trade. Dutch engineers directed the first land-reclamation schemes in the Fens. German miners were brought in to exploit the deposits of metallic ores in Cumberland and Wales.

3

THE TIMBER CRISIS

When the Civil War began in 1642, Britain's industry had become, if not as powerful as those of the older industrial countries, at least as vigorous and up to date in its methods. But the slackening tempo of production that marks the second half of the seventeenth century was not so much due to the disturbed political state of the country as to a crisis in technique. Until the end of the last quarter of the eighteenth century by far the most important industrial raw material was wood. Apart from its uses as building material and domestic fuel, wood was required in ever-increasing quantities in the dockyards, mines, and factories. All the early machines were built of wood: windmills and waterwheels, cranes and winches, wagons, the spinning wheel, loom and knitting frame. Wood was also the foundation of the metal industries, for it was only by charcoal that all kinds of ore could be smelted. Charcoal was also an essential ingredient in the manufacture of gunpowder. As long as these technical conditions prevailed there was a limit to the growth of industry. It could develop only if the supply of timber could keep pace with its needs. Stagnation and eventual regression were inevitable as soon as demand for wood began to outstrip supply.

To find substitutes for wood was, therefore, one of the most urgent problems of the period, and the whole course of the industrial revolution may be described in terms of its progressive solution. The first step, taken in Tudor times, was the partial replacement of wood by coal as domestic fuel, especially in towns near the pits or accessible by sea. For this reason, the first English coalfields to be developed were those of Newcastle and Durham, the nearest by sea to the mouth of the Thames and the South Coast.

England's a perfect World, hath Indies too;
Correct your Maps, *Newcastle* is *Peru*.

So run the opening lines of *Views from Newcastle; Or, Newcastle Coal-pits*,[2] by the Cavalier poet, John Cleveland (1613–58). They were confirmed and amplified three-quarters of a century later when Daniel Defoe (1661–1731) described the Durham coalfield in his *Tour . . . of Great Britain*, first published in 1724–7:

From hence [Chester le Street] the Road to *Newcastle* gives a View of the inexhausted Store of Coals and Coal Pits, from whence not *London* only, but all the South Part of *England* is continually supplied; and whereas when we are at *London*, and see the Prodigious Fleets of Ships which come constantly in with Coals for this increasing City, we are apt to wonder whence they come, and that they do not bring the whole Country away;

so, on the contrary when in this Country we see the prodigious Heaps, I might say Mountains, of Coals, which are dug up at every Pit, and how many of those Pits there are: we are filled with equal Wonder to consider where the People should live that can consume them.[3]

Defoe also observed Lumley Castle just east of Chester le Street. Its park, he said, 'beside the pleasantness of it, has this much better thing to recommend it, namely, that it is full of excellent veins of the best coal in the country . . . This, with the navigable river [Wear] just at hand, by which the coals are carried down to Sunderland to the ships, makes Lumley Park an inexhaustable treasure to the family.' An otherwise unknown artist, Peter Hartover, made a painting of neighbouring Harraton House, Lumley Castle and the coal staithes on the Wear, amply supporting Defoe's amazement at the scale of the industry, and producing what must be the earliest view of an English industrial landscape (Fig. 1).

Though England's annual coal output increased fourteenfold, from about 200,000 tons in 1551–60 to nearly 3,000,000 tons in 1681–90,[4] it remained nearly stationary during the second half of the seventeenth century, or even threatened to decline. For, as the surface deposits were exhausted, deep pits had to be sunk, and many of these were susceptible to flooding. Wherever possible, the miners tried to cope with inroads of water by driving adits into the sides of the hills to drain the workings into lower-lying streams, or by installing pumps or bucket chains, driven by waterwheels, teams of horses, or even, in the smallest pits, by hand labour. But all these methods only touched the fringe of the problem. To work the new mines, and from them to find a substitute for the failing timber economy, a new power was required, and that power lay hidden within the coal itself. Hence, the most urgent technical problem of the time became the invention of an engine that would, in the words of David Ramsaye, 'Raise Water from Lowe Pitts by fire.'[5] Of the many ingenious inventors who tried to overcome this problem, the first to approach a practical solution was the Cornish mining engineer Thomas Savery (1650?–1715), whose steam engine, patented in 1698, acted as a combined suction and force pump.[6] The problem was finally solved by the more robust and elaborate engine developed shortly afterwards by the Dartmouth iron-monger, Thomas Newcomen (1663–1729) (Fig. 6).

The working of a Newcomen engine—wrote Samuel Smiles (1812–1904)—is a clumsy and apparently a very painful process, accompanied by an extraordinary amount of wheezing, sighing, creaking, and bumping. When the pump descends, there is heard a plunge, a heavy sigh, and a loud bump: then, as it rises, and the sucker begins to act, there is heard a creak, a wheeze, another bump, and then a rush of water as it is lifted and poured out.[7]

5

Clumsy as it was, the Newcomen atmospheric engine ameliorated the coal crisis. The first was erected at Huel Vor in Cornwall, followed by a second in 1712 at a coal-mine near Dudley Castle. Others were erected in the next few years in the Midlands and the North of England.[8] They represented an enormous advance. From about three million tons at the end of the seventeenth century the output of coal rose to five million tons in 1761–70, and to over ten million in 1781–90.[9]

Though the Newcomen engine's large fuel consumption tended to restrict it to sites near coal-mines and other places where cheap coal was available, J. R. Harris estimates that 60 were in use by 1733, and that at least a further 300 must have been put into commission by 1781.[10] Most of them were used to drain mines, but a number were erected in connection with the supply of water to London (Fig. 5).

The improvements of John Smeaton, F.R.S. (1724–92) progressively reduced the fuel consumption of the Newcomen engine, and the separate condenser patented by James Watt, F.R.S. (1756–1819) in 1769 brought it down by more than two-thirds for the same output of power. It was, therefore, in districts where the cost of coal was an important consideration, especially in Cornwall, that James Watt and his partner, Matthew Boulton (1728–1809), found their main market for the new engines they began to produce in 1775 at their Soho Manufactory near Birmingham. At first the reciprocating motion of the Watt engine was not converted to rotary motion by a crank or other means, so it could not be used to drive machines. For this reason almost all the sixty-six engines Boulton and Watt erected in Britain during the first decade of their partnership were for pumping or for working the bellows of blowing engines at ironworks. To drive their machines, the new factories continued to rely on water power. They jostled each other along the river valleys of Lancashire and Yorkshire in their efforts to secure a head of water.

Dr William Brownrigg, F.R.S. (1711–1800), the Whitehaven physician, and one of the leading experts of his day on mines and mining, described what the new power meant in one of the notes he contributed to a poem on the mines of Whitehaven, composed by the Rev. John Dalton (1709–63) in 1755:

It appears, from pretty exact calculations, that it would require about 550 men, or a power equal to that of 110 horses, to work the pumps of one of the largest fire-engines now in use (the diameter of whose cylinder is seventy inches) . . . And that as much water may be raised by an engine of this size kept constantly at work, as can be drawn up by 2520 men with rollers and buckets, after the manner now daily practised in many mines, or as much as can be borne up on the shoulders of twice that number of men, as is said to be done in some of the mines of Peru.—So great is the power of the air in one of those engines.[11]

The amount of water raised, when all four engines at the Whitehaven mines were working together, at a speed of thirteen strokes, was 1,228 gallons a minute or 1,768,320 gallons in twenty-four hours.

In the same year Smeaton established a rough method of calculating the efficiency or 'duty' of a steam engine by relating the amount of water raised to the weight of coal consumed. Thus the duty of one of the original Newcomen engines was about 4.3 million pounds of water raised one foot high for every bushel of coal burnt. Taking the bushel as equal to ninety-four pounds, the coal consumed raised 46,000 times its own weight of water by one foot.

From the 1760s onwards the efficiency of the pumping engine increased rapidly:[12]

Date	Type of engine	Duty [in million pounds weight]
1718	Newcomen engine	4.3
1767	Newcomen engine improved by Smeaton	7.4
1774	Newcomen engine improved by Smeaton	12.5
1779	Watt engine	22.6
1792	Watt improved engine	39.0
1816	Woolf compound engine	68.0
1828	Improved Cornish engine	104.0
1834	Improved Cornish engine	149.0

By 1780 the situation was beginning to change. The market for pumping and blowing engines had become saturated, and Boulton and Watt were looking for new outlets. Water power was becoming insufficient for the growing scale of industry. So Watt turned his attention to adapting his engines for use in factories, a development that was soon to revolutionize the whole face of manufacture, blackening the skies over the great industrial towns with smoke. In June 1781, Boulton wrote to Watt: 'The people in London, Manchester and Birmingham are *steam mill mad*. I don't mean to hurry you but I think . . . we should determine to take out a patent for certain methods of producing rotative motion from . . . the fire engine.'[13] In October of the same year Watt patented a number of devices for 'applying the reciprocating motion of steam-engines to procure a circular motion round an axis, for working mills and other machinery'. Lord estimates that rather over 100 of the engines the partners delivered between 1781 and 1800 were rotatives for the textile trade,[14] a figure to be treated with reserve as likely to be too low.

By the end of the eighteenth century the steam engine, invented to ensure the output of a raw material with, originally, only a limited industrial use, had become a universal motor destined to transform the whole economy.

IRON

Not only did the steam engine hurry on the replacement of wood by coal in the production of iron. It also made that replacement necessary. Its full powers could not be released until there was an abundant supply of iron, nor could it develop beyond its first cyclopic form until its makers had learnt to fashion iron with accuracy into any shape required. The technical changes in iron-making, engine-building, and engineering were thus closely interlocked, and the development of each usually had the same general pattern in which a slow period of transition taking up most of the eighteenth century was followed by a spectacular advance in the nineteenth.

The attempts made during the seventeenth century to substitute coke from coal for charcoal in the production or processing of iron were unsuccessful. So, as the forests shrank, the indigenous iron industry ceased to expand or even declined. By 1720 the ironmaster William Wood claimed that more than two-thirds of the iron used in Britain was being imported.[15]

At the beginning of the eighteenth century iron-making was still a rural industry scattered over the Sussex Weald, the Forest of Dean, and along the mountain streams of Yorkshire, Derbyshire, Shropshire, and Wales, where wood and water power were available in combination. The ore was first smelted with lime and charcoal in a blast-furnace, the bellows of which were generally worked by a waterwheel. To produce malleable iron for the use of the blacksmith, after fourteen days of firing the molten metal was allowed to run from the furnace into furrows of sand to form pig-iron, subsequently 'fined' by alternate reheating and hammering under a huge tilt-hammer worked by water power. The art of casting developed a little later, when the melt was run into moulds to produce finished goods of cast iron, from garden rollers and cooking pots to cannon.[16] The first man successfully to smelt iron with coke was Abraham Darby (1668–1717),[17] a Bristol Quaker who had taken over the lease of an old ironworks in the Shropshire Valley of Coalbrookdale on the River Severn (Fig. 2). From 1718 onwards cast-iron cylinders for the new steam engines were produced by this process. Although by 1750 the second Abraham Darby (1711–63) was able to use coke to produce pig-iron suitable for forging, charcoal was still indispensable in the forge itself, until

8

Henry Cort (1740–1800) revolutionized the method of producing malleable iron by the process of puddling and rolling, which he patented in 1783 and 1784.

Cort's inventions completed the pioneering stage of the revolution in iron-making. By the last quarter of the eighteenth century the old sites in the southern counties had mostly been abandoned, and the leading ironworks were situated in the coalfields of the Midlands, South Wales, and Scotland, where the Carron Iron Company started work in 1760. But the iron industry had not yet lost its picturesque character. Still surrounded by romantic scenery, the great ironworks, with their smouldering lime kilns and coke ovens, blazing furnaces and noisy forges, had a special attraction for eighteenth-century admirers of the sublime.

Pig-Iron Output in Great Britain[18]

Date	Tons
1720	25,000
1788	68,000
1796	125,000
1806	250,000
1825	703,000
1838	1,348,000

MACHINES AND FACTORIES

Newcomen's first engines had a wooden beam, a copper boiler of the kind used by brewers, a brass cylinder and lead pipes (Fig. 6). Its separate parts could be produced by carpenters, coppersmiths and plumbers working in their traditional manner but adapting their joint efforts to a new purpose. Newcomen succeeded where Savery had failed because the making and servicing of a Savery engine presupposed a degree of skill that had yet to be acquired by a long process of gradual innovation. John Theophilus Desaguliers (1683–1744), writing in 1744, stated that he had known Savery 'make Steam eight or ten times stronger than common Air; and then its Heat was so great as to blow open several of the Joints of his Machine: so that he was forc'd to be at the Pains and Charge to have all his Joints solder'd with Spelter or hard Solder. These Discouragements stopp'd the Progress and Improvement of this Engine, till Mr Newcomen . . . brought it to the present Form. . .'[19]

That the mastering of the principles of mechanical construction was slow is shown by James Watt's experience in the 1760s and '70s. His first attempt to build his new engine at the Carron Iron Works failed because the Scottish iron-workers were not yet able to make a steam-tight cylinder. It was only the superior skill of the workers in the Colebrookdale area that enabled John Wilkinson (1728–1808), the great rival of the Darbys in the Severn Valley, to solve this problem with the help of a boring mill he patented in 1774 for the manufacture of cannon. (Skilled men were so scarce that, even as late as the early nineteenth century, rival firms of engineers went to unbelievable lengths to entice key workers from their competitors. In 1802, for example, the younger James Watt (1769–1848) went to Leeds to try to recapture a number of skilled men who had deserted Soho to join Matthew Murray (1765–1826), one of the leading engineers of the day. The letters in which he describes his adventures read like a secret service plot.[20])

Apart from engine-making, the growing demand for all kinds of millwork stimulated the development of mechanical skill in the eighteenth century, and the millwright is the true ancestor of the modern engineer. Travelling over a wide area from his small workshop in the countryside, he had long been accustomed to build millraces, waterwheels and other working gear for the country miller. But in the seventeenth and eighteenth centuries the range of the millwright's activities was greatly widened, and he had to adapt his traditional skill to countless new purposes. He was called on to regulate river navigations, to erect waterworks for the new towns, to install pumps and heavy lifting-gear in the mines, and to adapt millwork for textile factories and the preparatory operations of the pottery trade.

The outstanding quality of the millwright of the later eighteenth century was his versatility. '. . . a good mill-wright', said Sir William Fairbairn (1789–1874), recalling his early experiences at a lecture in Derby, 'was a man of large resources; he was generally well educated, and could draw out his own designs and work at the lathe; he had a knowledge of mill machinery, pumps and cranes, and could turn his hand to the bench or the forge with equal adroitness and facility.'[21] William Murdock (1754–1839), who, early in his career, became Watt's principal engine erector in Cornwall, started life as a millwright. Thomas Telford (1757–1834) was a mason. James Brindley (1716–72), the great canal engineer, was also a millwright. From 1742 onwards he built grist, silk, and paper mills in the neighbourhood of Leek, where he had set up his workshop. He also designed flint mills for the potteries, installed drains and pumps in coal-mines, and erected Newcomen engines. Though he never learned to spell, was nearly illiterate, and spoke in broad Derby, even at the height of his fame, his versatility and inventiveness earned him the nickname of 'The Schemer'.[22]

One of the earliest millwrights to become a great engineer was George Sorocold (*fl.* 1690–1720). He built waterworks in many provincial towns at the end of the seventeenth century, and installed new pumping plant on London Bridge in 1704. He was consulted by the projectors of river navigation and dock schemes, and invented rope-making and sawing machines. But his most important achievement was the erection of the first large manufactory in England—a silk mill on an island in the Derwent near Derby, built between 1718 and 1722 for John and Thomas Lombe (1693?–1722; 1685–1739).

According to Defoe, he was 'flipt into the River', when showing the mill to some visitors. He was carried into the mill race and under the turning waterwheel, which he jammed till one of the blades broke. 'Upon which the Wheel went again, and, like *Jonah's* whale, spewed him out, not upon dry land, but into that Part they call the Apron, and so to the Mill-Tail, where he was taken up, and received no Hurt at all.'[23]

The mill itself is described in some detail in the third, greatly enlarged edition of Defoe's tour, published in 1742:

Here is a Curiosity of a very extraordinary Nature, and the only one of the Kind in *England*: I mean those Mills on the Derwent, which work the three capital *Italian* Engines for making Organzine or Thrown Silk, which, before these Mills were erected, was purchased by the *English* Merchants with ready Money in *Italy*; by which Invention one Hand will twist as much Silk, as before could be done by Fifty, and that in a much truer and better Manner. This Engine contains 26,586 Wheels, and 96,746 Movements, which work 73,726 Yards of Silk-thread, every time the Water-wheel goes round, which is three times in one Minute, and 318,504,960 Yards in one Day and Night. One Water-wheel gives Motion to all the rest of the Wheels and Movements, of which any one may be stopt separately. One Fire-engine, likewise, conveys warm Air to every individual Part of the Machine, and the whole Work is govern'd by one Regulator. The House which contains this Engine is of a vast Bulk, and Five or Six Stories high.[24]

Every schoolboy knows the story of how John Lombe went to Savoy to steal the secret of the silk-throwing engines at the risk of his life; how he fell a victim to the revenge of the cheated Italians, who followed him to Derby and killed him by slow poison; and how his half-brother, Sir Thomas Lombe, was rewarded by Parliament for his enterprise with a grant of £14,000 when the original patent expired in 1732.[25] But, as Professor G. N. Clark has pointed out, the Lombes could have saved themselves a great deal of trouble, expense, and danger if they had consulted Vittorio Zonca's *Teatro Nuovo di Machine et Edificii*, published at Padua in 1607, and available on the open shelves of the Bodleian since 1620. For in that book the secret they went to such pains to discover is explained and illustrated.[26]

Though the use of steam power and the growing need for standardization made the replacement of wood by iron increasingly necessary, most of the tools of the contemporary engineer were, in fact, the old tools of the woodworker, rendered capable of handling metal instead of wood through the application of mechanical power and automatic control. Indeed, until very nearly the end of the eighteenth century, wood remained the chief material from which the machines themselves were made, though iron began to be introduced for vital parts from the 1750s onwards. Smeaton constructed a windmill with an iron shaft in 1754, and used an iron gear wheel in a mill in 1769. In 1760 the Carron Iron Works began to replace wooden cog wheels by cast-iron gear wheels. The improved spinning machines which Sir Richard Arkwright (1732–92) installed in 1775 at Cromford and Belper, near Derby, were made partly of iron. But the first large-scale all-iron plant was the Albion Flour Mills in Southwark, designed by John Rennie (1761–1821), opened in 1784, and burnt to the ground in 1791.

COTTON

Many of the silk mills built at Derby, Stockport, Macclesfield, and elsewhere after 1732 were later converted into cotton mills. Whereas silk had been one of the most profitable commodities while international trade was still confined to small cargoes of high value, the new powers of mechanized production could only be developed fully if applied to cheap articles suitable for mass consumption at home and abroad. The key inventions in the textile trade, which culminated with the invention of James Hargreaves' spinning jenny in 1767, Arkwright's water frame in 1768, and Crompton's spinning mule in 1775, all related to the spinning of cotton. Hargreaves' jenny, which was specially adapted for the finer counts of yarn, could be installed at small cost by individual craftsmen. For example, when the father of Samuel Bamford (1788–1872), the radical weaver and poet, grew tired of school-teaching, he borrowed money and hired a jenny to start as a cotton spinner, though he had to give it up again because his creditor grew jealous of his success and demanded the immediate repayment of his loan. Bamford's story illustrated the fever of expansion that swept over Lancashire in the 1790s, and presented great opportunities even to those without resources of their own. For it is characteristic of this whole period that, at least until the end of the eighteenth century, mechanical inventions favoured the small man as well as the large capitalist.

However, Arkwright's water frame and Crompton's mule necessitated mass production on a factory scale. For this reason, the cotton mill Arkwright built in 1771 at Cromford, near Derby, with the backing of the stocking manufacturer, Jedediah Strutt (1726–97), became one of the first storm centres of industrial unrest.

Though spinning was revolutionized by the new inventions, the last decades of the eighteenth century were the golden age of the handloom weaver, whose efficiency had been much increased by the fly-shuttle John Kay patented in 1733. In consequence, the power loom, though invented by Edmund Cartwright, F.R.S. (1743–1823), and covered by a series of patents from 1785 to 1788, was bitterly opposed by the handloom weavers. It was, in fact, impracticable until W. Radcliffe and William Horrocks of Stockport improved it from 1803 onwards.

The same contradictory development of handicrafts and mass production occurred in the metal trades. While the mining and smelting of iron and copper were carried out by large-scale capitalist firms who even formed price rings and made monopolistic marketing agreements, the secondary metal trades, such as lock-, chain-, and nail-making, the Birmingham 'toy' trade and the Sheffield cutlery and plating trades, were mainly conducted by small masters who retained a measure of independence, even if they worked for a capitalist. The great Soho Manufactory Matthew Boulton opened in 1765, though of the greatest importance as a model of capitalist organization, was an exception, as was the great enterprise for the production of all kinds of iron goods which Ambrose Crowley (1635–1721) established in the late seventeenth century near Newcastle on Tyne.[27]

John Dyer described the growing industrialization of the cotton industry where 'all is here in motion, all is life', in engaging, enthusiastic verse in *The Fleece*, published in 1757:

> th' echoing hills repeat
> The stroke of ax and hammer; scaffolds rise,
> And growing edifices; heaps of stone,
> Beneath the chissel, beauteous shapes assume
> Of frize and column. Some, with even line,
> New streets are marking in the neighb'ring fields,
> And sacred domes of worship. Industry,
> which dignifies the artist, lifts the swain,
> And the straw cottage to a palace turns,
> Over the work presides . . .
> So appear
> Th' increasing walls of busy Manchester,
> Sheffield, and Birmingham, whose redd'ning fields
> Rise and enlarge their suburbs. Lo, in throngs,
> For ev'ry realm, the careful factors meet,

> Whisp'ring each other. In long ranks and bales,
> Like war's bright files, beyond the sight extend.[28]

How the city of Birmingham appeared to a young man of 18 on his first visit in 1741 is vividly described by William Hutton (1723–58): 'I was surprized at the place but more so at the people: They were a species I had never seen: They possessed a vivacity I had never beheld: I had been among dreamers, but now I saw men awake: Their very step along the street shewed alacrity: Every man seemed to know and prosecute his own affairs. . .'[29]

CANALS AND ROADS

Industry could not expand beyond very narrow limits as long as the transport of goods in bulk and even passenger travel remained impossible over large tracts of Britain for months at a time. The industrial revolution therefore implied a revolution in transport, and gave a powerful impetus to the building of canals and roads.

In England the navigation schemes of the seventeenth and early eighteenth centuries had been confined mainly to the improvement of natural rivers on which the traffic was hampered by swift currents and floods or droughts. The idea of canals, striking across country, piercing the hills by tunnels, crossing valleys by embankments and rivers by aqueducts, and climbing to their summits by flights of locks, had its origin in France in the Briare and Languedoc canals. The former, joining the Loire to the Seine, was opened in 1642. The latter, opened in 1681 and joining the Garonne near Toulouse to the Aude near Carcassonne, put the Mediterranean into direct communication with the Bay of Biscay. Regarded by A. W. Skempton as the greatest feat of civil engineering in Europe between Roman times and the nineteenth century, it was visited in 1754 by the young Francis Egerton (1736–1803), later the third Duke of Bridgewater. It made an indelible impression on him, and there can be little doubt that it inspired him to commission James Brindley to build the first great English summit-level canal from his mines at Worsley to Manchester, in order to free himself from the uncertainties of packhorses and the River Irwell Navigation.[30] From the beginning, Brindley and the Duke were determined to make the new canal independent of both. 'Pray . . . what then do you think is the use of navigable rivers?' Brindley was asked, when giving evidence before the House of Commons. 'To make canal navigations, to be sure,' was his reply.[31] To him, rivers were not means of communication in themselves, but a source of water to replenish his reservoirs.

The Bridgewater Canal was opened in 1761. At the Worsley end the canal penetrated about a mile underground into the workings of the mine itself, providing both easy transport and drainage. On its route to Manchester it was carried across the River Irwell by the Barton Aqueduct, of which Arthur Young (1741–1820) wrote after his visit in 1768: 'The effect of coming at once on to *Barton Bridge*, and looking *down* upon a large river, with barges of great burthen towing along it; and *up* to another river hung in the air, with barges sailing upon it, form altogether a scenery somewhat like enchantment. . .' (Fig. 20). At the time of Arthur Young's visit the extension of the Bridgewater Canal westward to Liverpool had not yet been completed, but Brindley's plan for carrying a branch across the Mersey struck that writer as the 'greatest undertaking (if executed) that ever yet was thought of, and will exceed the noblest work of the *Romans*, when masters of the world; or the legendary tales even of *Semiramis* herself'. . . . 'The number of foreigners who have viewed the Duke of Bridgewater's present navigation is surprising'—Young continued—'what would it be if his Grace was to extend it over a boisterous arm of the sea;—To exhibit a navigation afloat in the air, with ships of an hundred tons sailing full masted beneath it. What a splendid idea!'[32]

Though such a project was never realized, it fired the imagination of the physician, author and topographer, Dr John Aikin (1747–1822). As late as 1795, he did not find the idea too fanciful to persuade one of the most versatile artists and illustrators of the day, Thomas Stothard, R.A. (1755–1834), to delineate a navigation afloat in the air on a vignette on the engraved frontispiece of his *A Description of the Country . . . round Manchester* (Fig. 21).[33] He also devoted a large section of his book to canals in general.

An even greater scheme than the Bridgewater Canal was the Trent and Mersey (Grand Trunk) Canal, begun by Brindley in 1766 and completed in 1777, five years after his death. His aim was to carry his canals over the longest possible stretches on the same level. Wherever possible, he concentrated his locks at one point, like flights of steps, until he reached a level that could be maintained for many miles of dead water. To do so often involved huge works of engineering. Rising 395 feet to its summit at Harecastle, where it passed through a tunnel nearly 3,000 yards in length, the Trent and Mersey Canal was just over ninety-three miles long, or about 140 miles long including the junctions with the Birmingham Canal and the River Severn. There were thirty-five locks west of the Harecastle Tunnel and forty on the east side. Altogether there were five tunnels, five major aqueducts and about 155 minor ones. Josiah Wedgwood (1730–95), anxious to provide cheap transport to and from the Potteries, was its supporter and became its treasurer. It marked the beginning of the great era of canal construction that continued, through the speculative canal mania of the 1790s, until about 1830, when some 3,000 miles of canals were open in England and Wales.[34]

The same period was also the great age of roadmakers and of the mail coach. Ralph Allen (1694–1764), a self-made West Country capitalist, largely instrumental in making the Avon navigable from Bristol to Bath and an early railway builder, made a fortune out of organizing the cross- and by-posts in the early eighteenth century. John Palmer (1742–1818), the son of a Bath theatre proprietor, persuaded Pitt to allow him to convey letters by stage coach in 1785 and so inaugurated the age of the mail coach. It is a symptom of the speed with which the industrial revolution transformed the life of Britain that for Dickens, writing in the 1830s and '40s, this revolution in transport had already become a symbol of the good old times, a view supported by innumerable popular artists, including Henry Alken (1774–1850) and James Pollard (1797–*post* 1859).

The roads, too, had their triumphs of engineering and their heroes, of whom the most romantic was John Metcalf (1717–1810), known as Blind Jack of Knaresborough, sportsman, fiddler, carrier, soldier in the Duke of Cumberland's army during the Jacobite rebellion, and the first scientific roadmaker since Roman times. Blind since the age of 6, according to Smiles, he built 180 miles of excellent roads in Yorkshire, Lancashire, Derbyshire, and Cheshire between 1765 and 1792, and lived to the age of 93.[35]

Metcalf's work was continued on a far greater scale by Telford (who was also a great canal builder) and by James Loudon McAdam (1756–1836). But the convergence of the revolutions in transport and industry is most striking in the great cast-iron bridges, the first of which still crosses the Severn with a span of 100 feet at Colebrookdale (Figs. 25 and 26). Designed by Thomas Farnolls Pritchard, a Shrewsbury architect, and cast and erected by Abraham Darby III (1750–91), it was opened in 1779. An even more splendid bridge at Sunderland was completed in 1796 (Fig. 34). It was cast at Walker's foundry at Rotherham to the design of Rowland Burdon, M.P. for Sunderland. Though Tom Paine (1737–1809) exhibited a model of an iron bridge in London in 1789, Smiles' statement that he designed the Sunderland Bridge is a gross exaggeration.[36]

These two bridges were perhaps the first manifestation of the industrial revolution deeply to impress itself on the popular artists of the day. They found in them something both moving and classical, something in their simplicity and strength perhaps even reassuring to their clients, much disturbed by the wars and revolutions of the period. Though it inspired a spectacular aquatint by Wilson Lowry, F.R.S. (1762–1824), pioneer of steel engraving, after Thomas Malton (1748–1804), one of the finer topographical artists of his day, Telford's proposal to replace London Bridge by a single six hundred foot span of cast iron came to nothing (Fig. 35). 'By such noble undertakings is the present age peculiarly distinguished', Arthur Young had written in 1770, and he summed up the achievements of the heroic phase of the industrial revolution in these words: 'When agriculture, manufactures, and commerce flourish, a nation grows rich and great, and riches cannot abound, without exciting that general industry, and spirit of improvement, which at last leads to performing works, which, in poorer times, would be thought wonders.'[37]

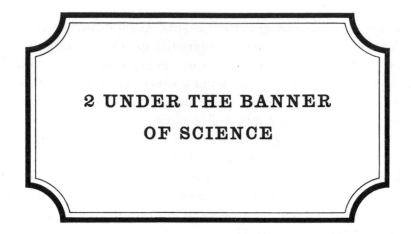

2 UNDER THE BANNER OF SCIENCE

O Sacred, Wise, and Wisdom-giving Plant,
Mother of Science, Now I feel thy Power,
Within me cleere, not onely to discerne
Things in their Causes, but to trace the wayes
Of highest Agents, deemd however wise.[1]   JOHN MILTON

ARTHUR YOUNG'S enthusiasm for the great engineering works of his time was shared by many of his contemporaries. Their confidence in the boundless possibilities of technical progress is typified by Young's criticism of old-fashioned methods he saw at Abraham Crowley's ironworks at Swalwell, a few miles from Newcastle upon Tyne.

Deploring that so much work was executed by manual labour, he was disgusted to see 'eight stout fellows hammering an anchor', turning it laboriously by hand. 'There are no impossibilities in mechanics,' he observed. 'An anchor of 20 tons may, undoubtedly, be managed [by machine] with as much ease as a pin.'[2] But not everyone was so enthusiastic. Samuel Johnson, so acute an observer of the disintegration of feudal society in the Scottish Highlands, did not bother to accompany Boswell when the latter inspected Boulton's Soho Manufactory during their visit to Birmingham in 1776. When they visited Derby in the following year Boswell went by himself to see Lombe's famous silk mill.

POEMS OF INDUSTRY

It is tempting at first sight to regard a poem, written in 1710 by the Rev. Thomas

18

Yalden (1670–1736), and describing the mines at Neath belonging to Sir Humphrey Mackworth (1657–1727), as an early anticipation of Young's enthusiasm for great works of engineering.[3] After describing how the mountains on the black and rugged coast of Wales were heaved up by the treasures they concealed, Yalden shows the miner cutting his way with 'pointed Steel' through rocks and subterraneous lakes to invade 'the Courts of *Pluto*',

> Drawing, in pestilential Steems his Breath,
> Resolved to conquer tho' he combats Death.

The poet then addresses the following lines to Sir Humphrey:

> Thy fam'd Inventions, *Mackworth*, most adorn
> The Miner's Art, and make the best Return:
> Thy speedy Sails, and useful Engines show,
> A Genius richer than thy Mines below.
> Thousands of Slaves unskill'd *Peru* Maintains,
> The Hands that labour still exhaust the gains:
> The Winds thy Slaves, their useful Succours joyn,
> Convey thy Oar [*sic*], and labour at thy Mine;
> Instructed by thy Arts a Power they find
> To vanquish Realms, where once they lay confin'd.

'Sails' in the third line refers to Mackworth's 'Sailing-wagons' in which, in favourable winds, his coal was propelled along rails laid from his pits near Neath to the waterside at Aberavon. William Waller, Mackworth's mine steward, describing them in 1698, states: 'And, I believe, he is the first Gentleman, in this part of the World, that hath set up Sailing-engines on Land, driven by the Wind, not for any curiosity, or vain Applause, but for real profit. . .'[4]

In spite of his apparent enthusiasm, it is doubtful whether Yalden's somewhat vague description of his hero's mines and inventions was based on first-hand knowledge: he is much more likely to have taken it from Waller, and when the circumstances in which the poem was written are considered its inspiration appears in a new light. Sir Humphrey Mackworth, M.P. for Cardiganshire on and off from 1700 to 1713, was a Tory lawyer who became a great capitalist when he married an heiress and developed collieries and copper-smelting works at Neath. In 1698 he became one of the founders of the Society for the Promotion of Christian Knowledge, and in the same year acquired the controlling interest in the late Sir Carbery Price's mines for £15,000. He formed 'The Corporation of the Governor and Company of the Mine Adventurers of England'. During the next ten years

19

funds raised by means of a lottery were used for the construction of canals, quays and docks in the Neath area. In 1709, when their capital had been expended, the company got into difficulties. Waller was discharged, and Mackworth himself accused of peculation. In 1710 the House of Commons voted him guilty of frauds and violation of the company's charter. Only the fall of the Whig ministry saved him from the results of this vote.[5] In his crisis Mackworth's Tory friends came to the rescue with a spate of pamphlets. Yalden's poem was part of their campaign. After a pointed reference to the grievous costliness of the war, it concludes:

> No greater Vertues on record shall Stand,
> Than thus with Arts to grace, with Wealth inrich the Land.

Political motives may also have inspired an article in *The Weekly Journal* on 18 December 1725, expressing the opposite view of technical progress, on the occasion of the erection of Savery's steam pumps at the York Buildings Water Works in London. It was probably put out by his long-established rival, the New River Company, a great undertaking supplying water to London by a canal to Sadlers Wells, completed by Sir Hugh Middleton (1560?–1631) more than a century earlier. Its title is : The York-Building Dragons; *or, A full and true Account of a most horrid and barbarous Murder, intended to be committed next Monday, on the Bodies, Goods, and Name of the greatest Part of his Majesty's Liege Subjects, dwelling and inhabiting between Temple-Bar in the East, and St James's in the West; and between Hungerford-Market in the South, and St Mary la Bonne in the North, by a Sett of evil-minded Persons, who do assemble twice a week, to carry on their wicked Purposes, in a* private Room *over a stable, by the Thames-side, in a remote Corner of the Town.*[6]

When fed with live coals, by 'a *Lancashire* wizzard, with long black Hair, and grim Visage . . . and a *Welchman*, bred on the top of *Penmanmaur*, the dragon will clap his Wings several Times successively, with prodigious Force, and so terrible will be the Noise thereof, that it will be heard as far as Calais, if the Wind set right'. He will then suck from the Thames 'such a prodigious Quantity of Water, that Barges will never more be able to go thro' Bridge'; then, being 'of a *huffing, snuffing* Temper, he will dart out of his Nostrils perpendicularly up to the Skies two such vast dense, and opagne Columns of Smoak, that those who live in the Burrough will hardly see the Sun at Noon-day'; finally he will poison the populace with the venomous effluvia he will draw from the river 'Through a long *Proboscis*, something like an Elephant's Trunk.'

At about the same time The New River Company was also chosen as the subject of a long and enthusiastic poem, *New-River*, by a certain William Garbott.[7] The even greater feat of engineering, the reclamation of the Fens, had already been celebrated in verse by Sir Jonas Moore (1617–79), Charles II's Surveyor-General of the Ordnance. Published posthumously in 1685, the second verse runs:

> I sing Floods muzled, and the Ocean tam'd,
> Luxurious Rivers govern'd, and reclam'd
> Waters with Banks confin'd, as in Gaol,
> Till kinder Sluces let them go on Bail;
> Streams curb'd with Dammes like Bridles, taught t'obey,
> And run as strait, as if they saw their way.[8]

Here indeed it seems safe to assume that the engineer's pride in his achievement was the main source of poetic inspiration. This is also true of a Prize Ænigma in *The Ladies' Diary* of 1725, which begins:

> I sprung, like Pallas, from a fruitful Brain,
> About the Time of CHARLES the *Second's* Reign

and ends

> On mighty Arms, alternately I bear
> Prodigious Weights of Water and of Air;
> And yet you'll stop my Motion with a Hair. . .

The answer to the enigma appeared in 1726: *Description of the Invention and Progress for raising Water out of Mines by the Force of Fire*.[9] The author was Henry Beighton, F.R.S. (1686–1743), the editor of *The Ladies' Diary*, who had already set his readers an even more mysterious puzzle in 1721, when he printed the first table of calculations ever to be produced on the powers of the steam engine.[10] A man of wide interests, Beighton lived at Griff, near Coventry, where Newcomen had erected one of his earliest pumping engines. He was the first scientist to study the Newcomen engine and to publish an engraving of it in 1717 (Fig. 6). He also erected one himself at Newcastle in 1718 and supplied his friend, Desaguliers, with the information on steam engines which he incorporated in the second volume of his *A Course of Experimental Philosophy*, published in 1744. Beighton also contributed to the *Philosophical Transactions*, and took part in a survey of the antiquities of Warwickshire.

The next writer of verse about a coal-mine also addressed the ladies. Although some of its images are taken from Yalden, the Rev. John Dalton's '*A descriptive Poem, addressed to two Ladies, at their Return from Viewing the Mines near*

Whitehaven', published in 1755, is unmistakably authentic in recording the impression created by the underground workings on the author's mind. It is also remarkable as one of the earliest equally authentic descriptions of the romantic mountain scenery near Keswick. The author first describes the ladies' descent:[11]

> But on you move thro' ways less steep
> To loftier chambers of the deep,
> Whose jetty pillars seem to groan
> Beneath a ponderous roof of stone.
> Then with increasing wonder gaze
> The dark inextricable maze,
> Where cavern crossing cavern meets,
> (City of subterraneous streets!). . .

Passing through narrow galleries, the ladies come to a fault where a 'massy rock' once opposed the miners' progress. Though perhaps influenced by Yalden, this passage shows how much more conscious Dalton was of the hardship of the miners' lives:

> Dissever'd by the nitrous blast,
> The stubborn barrier burst at last.
> Thus, urg'd by Hunger's clamorous call,
> Incessant Labour conquers all.

The road the ladies follow leads finally:

> Down to the cold and humid caves,
> Where hissing fall the turbid waves.
> Resounding deep thro' glimmering shades
> The clank of chains your ears invades.
> Thro' pits profound from distant day
> Scarce travels down light's languid ray.
> High on huge axis heav'd, above,
> See ballanc'd beams unweary'd move!

After struggling to explain the mechanics of the steam engine in octo-syllabic couplets, helped out by Brownrigg's notes, the author addresses himself to Savery:

> Man's richest gift thy work will shine;
> Rome's aqueducts were poor to thine!

This part of the poem ends:

> These are the glories of the mine!
> Creative Commerce, these are thine!

Judging by the reviews of the period, Dalton's poem created a considerable stir, and his first-hand account of industrial processes was much appreciated. But the clearest evidence for the penetration of industrial themes into the classical conventions of the period is provided by John Dyer's poem *The Fleece*, from which a few lines have already been quoted. A country parson who had started life as an artist, Dyer was already a well-known literary figure when he published *The Fleece* in 1757. Through his earlier poems *Grongar Hill* (1726) and *The Ruins of Rome* (1740), he had done much to awaken interest in the picturesque. It was therefore of great significance that a writer, so sensitive to new currents of thought and feeling, should have chosen the working processes of a great industry, from raw material to the final sale of the finished product overseas, as the subject for a long, didactic poem.

At the time Dyer was writing, cotton was still an exotic product serving, like silk, to furnish 'gauds and dresses, of fantastic web, to the luxurious'. In contrast, *The Fleece* describes the 'kinder toils' of combing, spinning and weaving wool, supplying 'cloathing to necessity'.[12] Its conception of trade reflects the stage of development which preceded mass production with the aid of machinery:

> . . . The pow'rful sun
> Hot India's zone with gaudy pencil paints,
> And drops delicious tints o'er hill and dale,
> Which Trade to us conveys. Nor tints alone,
> Trade to the good physician gives his balms;
> Gives cheering cordials to th'afflicted heart;
> Gives, to the wealthy, delicacies high;
> Gives, to the curious, works of nature rare;
> And when the priest displays, in just discourse,
> Him, the all-wise Creator, and declares
> His presence, pow'r, and goodness, unconfin'd,
> 'Tis Trade, attentive voyager, who fills
> His lips with argument. To censure Trade,
> Or hold her busy people in contempt,
> Let none presume.[13]

But Dyer was also excited by the technical improvements which were beginning to transform the economy. The most significant passages of his poem express the hopes such changes inspired in his contemporaries. Venerable tools, like the distaff Paris gave to Helen, are still widely used for spinning wool,

> But patient art,
> That on experience works, from hour to hour,
> Sagacious, has a spiral engine form'd,
> Which, on an hundred spo[o]ls, an hundred threads,

> With one huge wheel, by lapse of water, twines,
> Few hands requiring; easy-tended work,
> That copiously supplies the greedy loom.
>   Nor hence, ye nymphs, let anger cloud your brows:
> The more is wrought, the more is still requir'd:
> Blithe o'er your toils, with wonted song, proceed:
> Fear not surcharge; your hands will ever find
> Ample employment. In the strife of trade,
> These curious instruments of speed obtain
> Various advantage, and the diligent
> Supply with exercise. . .[14]

In his day John Dyer had no thought of technological unemployment or a surplus population. Elsewhere he declares:

> But chief by numbers of industrious hands
> A nation's wealth is counted: numbers raise
> Warm emulation: where that virtue dwells,
> There will be traffick's seat; there will she build
> Her rich emporium. Hence, ye happy swains,
> With hospitality inflame your breast,
> And emulation: the whole world receive,
> And with their arts, their virtues, deck your isle.[15]

He also recommended the employment of paupers in 'houses of labour'—workhouse-factories, one of which, situated in the Vale of Calder, he describes in glowing terms. He closes the passage with a detailed description of Lewis Paul's multiple spinning machine, patented in 1738, explaining that, even though it is designed for spinning cotton, it can also be used to spin fine carded wool. It is, Dyer explains,

> A circular machine, of new design,
> In conic shape: it draws and spins a thread
> Without the tedious toil of needless hands.
> A wheel, invisible, beneath the floor,
> To ev'ry member of th'harmonious frame
> Gives necessary motion. One, intent,
> O'erlooks the work: the carded wool, he says,
> Is smoothly lapp'd around those cylinders,
> Which, gently turning, yield it to yon cirque
> Of upright spindles, which, with rapid whirl
> Spin out, in long extent, an even twine.[16]

'How can a man write poetically of serges and druggets?' demanded Dr Johnson. 'Yet you will hear many people talk to you gravely of that excellent poem, "THE FLEECE".'[17]

NEW LIFE IN THE PROVINCES

The poets' interest in trade and engineering was only one of many symptoms of a shift that was taking place in the intellectual life of Britain. The most progressive currents of thought were no longer emerging in the metropolis, but in countless provincial areas, where mining, industry and farming[18] were being remodelled on scientific lines. Even the Royal Society, once the organizing centre of applied research, lost some of the initiative in this field during the eighteenth century.

A symptom of the intellectual awakening of the provinces is the topographical literature of the period. First becoming important in the seventeenth century, it grew ever more voluminous as the eighteenth century advanced, and culminated in the decades around 1800. It expressed a new attitude to nature and to history. With ever-increasing zeal, scientific men and local worthies drawn from all classes explored the mineral wealth, the soils, the plant and animal life of each locality. They described the dress and customs of the people, their methods of husbandry and their trade. Local dialects and folk-songs were recorded. And, with intense pride in the latest achievements of art and industry, there emerged a no less fervent enthusiasm for local history and archaeology.[19] Nor was this new attitude purely intellectual: it gradually produced a new romantic response to the beauties and charms of nature.

How intimately this change in outlook was linked up with the practical changes that were taking place at the time in agriculture and industry, and how rapidly it occurred, is illustrated by a passage from the preface to John Dalton's *Descriptive Poem*:

When we behold rich improvements of a wild and uncultivated soil, in their state of maturity, without having observed their rise and progress, we are struck with wonder and astonishment, to see the face of Nature totally changed. It carries an air of enchantment and romance: and the fabulous and luxuriant description, given us by the Poet, of yellow harvests rising up instantaneously under the wheels of the chariot of Ceres, as it passed over the barren deserts, hardly seems, in the midst of our surprise, too extravagant an image to represent the greatness and seeming suddenness of such a change. . .

But how great and rational soever the pleasure of such a sight may be, it is still surpassed by that arising from the extraordinary increase of a trading Town, and new plantations of Houses and Men. Such was the satisfaction the author felt at the appearance of the town and harbour of Whitehaven, after an absence of somewhat less than thirty years. The Mines near that place are remarkable for so many singular circumstances, that they are generally esteemed to be well worth the observation of travellers. . .[20]

A similar contrast emerges if Defoe's England of 1725 is compared with that described by Arthur Young in 1768. Defoe's *Tour* reads like a voyage of exploration into strange parts, where people lead busy but relatively changeless lives remote from the centre of affairs. Young's England resembles a gigantic laboratory. Everywhere exciting experiments are in progress; engineering feats undreamed of since Roman times are being carried out; a new sense of power is stirring in the north.

In contrast again, twenty-one years later, an inquisitive, dyspeptic Tory, the Hon. John Byng (1742–1813), later fifth Viscount Torrington, took the whole thing for granted, in the voluminous, revealing diaries he kept of his travels about England between 1781 and 1794. By stage coach, post-chaise, and on horseback, he moved in a state of relative comfort till recently unattainable. 'But a few years since'—he wrote in 1787—'travellers were scarce in this country, and post-chaises unknown; now, the country in these southern parts [of Wales] is become an high road to Ireland; Newton [Newport?] and Swansea are bathing places; and the strolling players, with all other mischiefs, will get, nay have got, among them.'

Preoccupied with the state of the inns that had sprung up to serve the new traffic, he looked sourly at the changes wrought by industry to country and town alike. 'As a sportsman'—he states in another passage—'I hate enclosures, and, as a citizen, I look on them as the greedy tyrannies of the wealthy few, to oppress the indigent many.' Exceptionally, he admired Sir Herbert Mackworth, a descendant of the Mackworth to whom Yalden had addressed his adulatory verse, perhaps because he had somehow managed to incorporate his coal-mines at Neath in a kind of gentleman's park. After an encomium in his honour, Byng adds with the cold-bloodedness of a Commissioner in Charity: 'The colliers, here, do not earn more than 1s 4d per diem, notwithstanding their labour, and danger; many of them being frequently burnt to death, by the foul air taking fire. There is an harper at Neath, (a blind one,) but . . . I sent not for him.'[21]

The flourishing intellectual life in the provinces was only, of course, in part due to the growing influence of the industrial middle classes. Much of it was linked with the revolution in farming and with the cultural interests of the great land-owners, especially their architectural activities and their landscape gardening. Estate poems and descriptions of gentlemen's seats occupy a prominent place in the topographical literature of the period.[22] Part of the nation-wide culture of the ruling aristocracy reinforced by the established Church, this side of provincial life was largely determined by the classical tradition preserved at the universities and by the fashions set during each season in the metropolis. Even in this sphere, however, the metropolitan influence to some extent overlapped with the more locally conditioned industrial interests. Some of the great proprietors in the north, whose land was rich in mineral deposits, became industrial magnates as well: for example, the Lowthers at Whitehaven, the Londonderrys at Seaham, the Howards in Northumberland, and later, the Duke of Bridgewater. But in the main manufacturing areas, and especially in the new industrial towns, the metropolitan influence was far less pronounced. The new industrialists were still regarded as an inferior class by the old landowning and merchant families, and they were also cut off from the official culture of the ruling classes by the fact that many of them were Nonconformists. Debarred from the universities, they had to provide their own education, and so could adapt it to the needs of the time. Hence the Nonconformist academies were the most advanced educational establishments in eighteenth-century England.[23] Joseph Priestley (1733–1804), for example, was a tutor of languages at the Warrington Academy from 1761 to 1767; John Aikin, whose *Description of Manchester* has already been quoted, was appointed tutor in Divinity and Classics in 1779. John Dalton (1766–1844) was Professor of Mathematics and Natural Philosophy at New College, Manchester, from 1793 to 1799.

The intellectual life of the towns was focused in the literary and philosophical institutions, many of which were founded in the last quarter of the eighteenth century, those of Newcastle upon Tyne, for instance, in 1775, Manchester in 1781, and Derby in 1784.[24] The range of their discussions and interests was wide. At Liverpool, the banker William Roscoe (1753–1831) studied botany and tried to reclaim part of Chat Moss, later the scene of a brilliant feat of engineering when George Stephenson carried the Liverpool and Manchester Railway across it. In 1773 he became one of the founders of a Liverpool Society for the Encouragement of the Arts of Painting and Design, which organized the first exhibition of pictures in any English provincial town. He wrote biographies of Lorenzo de Medici and Pope Leo X, and collected what is now the nucleus of the Old Masters section in the Walker Art Gallery. The discourse he delivered at the opening of the Liverpool Royal Institution, of which he was elected first President in 1817, one year after the failure of his bank, was entitled, 'On the Origin and Vicissitudes of Literature, Science and Art, and their Influence on the Present State of Society'.[25] His son, Thomas Roscoe (1791–1871), was the author of a number of excellent guide-books and railway histories, including *The Book of the Grand Junction Railway* (1839) and *The London and Birmingham Railway* (c. 1838).

As soon as it was founded the Newcastle Philosophical Society elected the young socialist schoolmaster, Thomas Spence (1750–1814), for a phonetic alphabet he had designed, but expelled him hastily in the same year for delivering a lecture advocating the abolition of private property in land.[26] But the interpenetration of scientific and artistic perspective is, perhaps, most striking in the case of Manchester. In the 1790s, on the eve of the great expansion of industrial capitalism based on steam power, both Robert Owen (1771–1858), the father of British Socialism, and John Dalton (1766–1844), the reviver of atomic theory, were members of the Philosophical Society of that city.

There were two centres in particular where the new outlook achieved its greatest success in the second half of the eighteenth century—industrial Scotland, based on Glasgow and Edinburgh, and the area between Derby, Stoke-on-Trent, Shrewsbury, and Birmingham, the heart of the industrial Midlands.

THE WEALTH OF NATIONS

The foundation for the rapid economic development of Scotland was laid in 1707 by the Act of Union, which opened English colonial trade to the Scottish sailors and merchants. From a sleepy university and cathedral town, Glasgow became one of the main centres of the trade with America, by 1771 handling more than half the total British imports of tobacco. Manufactories producing all kinds of consumption goods for export sprang up round the growing port. Heavy industry of the most modern type appeared with the opening of Carron Iron Works in 1760, and with the development of the mines associated with that great enterprise. Flax-growing and linen-making assumed importance in the eastern districts of Scotland, to be followed later by cotton manufacture in the west. From the middle of the eighteenth century lowland agriculture rapidly emerged from its primitive backwardness.

It was this background of progressive activity, reinforced by an exemplary system of general education and cheap universities, that conditioned the exceptional brilliance of Scottish intellectual life in the eighteenth century. In close touch with continental thought, Scotland occupied a leading position in philosophy, aesthetics, medicine, and the natural sciences. But its outstanding contribution was a new approach to history and a new science of society. Distinguished both from the abstract rationalism of the social contract theories and from the conservative traditionalism of Edmund Burke (1729–97), the Scottish historical school, represented in Glasgow by Adam Smith (1723–90) and John Millar (1735–97), and in Edinburgh by William Robertson (1721–93) and Adam Ferguson (1723–1816), based its theory of social development on a study of the changing forms of production. In this way it was able to give a scientific account of the origin and functioning of the new industrial civilization.

'It cannot be very difficult to explain'—wrote Adam Smith—'how it comes about that the rich and powerful should, in a Civilized society, be better provided with the conveniences and necessaries of life than it is possible for any person to provide himself in a savage and solitary state. It is very easy to conceive that the person who can at all times direct the labours of thousands to his own purposes, should be better provided with what he has occasion for, than he who depends upon his own industry only. But how it comes about that the labourer and the peasant should likewise be better provided, is perhaps not so easily understood. In a Civilized Society the poor provide both for themselves and for the enormous luxury of their Superiors. The rent, which goes to support the vanity of the slothful landlord, is all earned by the industry of the peasant. The monied man indulges himself in every sort of ignobel [sic] and sordid sensuality, at the expense of the merchant and the Tradesman, to whom he lends out of his stock at interest. All the indolent and frivolous retainers upon a Court, are, in the same manner, fed cloathed and lodged by the labour of those who pay the taxes which support them. Among savages, on the contrary, every individual enjoys the whole produce of his own industry.'[27]

According to Smith, even the labourer in civilized society is better accommodated than 'many an African king, the absolute master of the lives and liberties of ten thousand naked savages',[28] because of the enormous increase in productivity, due to the division of labour, when production for a market replaces communal production based on hunting, pasturage, or farming. Both the optimism and the radicalism of Smith's thought are underlined by the first passage quoted above, which is taken from an early, unpublished draft of *The Wealth of Nations*, dictated in 1763, shortly before he left Glasgow for France. This draft also shows more clearly than the final text, first published in 1776, how largely Adam Smith's vivid picture of the new society was based on his first-hand experience of industry and commerce gained during the thirteen years of his Glasgow professorship, from 1751 to 1763. For example, the final published text reads: '. . . every body must be sensible how much labour is facilitated and abridged by the application of proper machinery. *It is unnecessary to give any example*'.*[29] Yet the draft contains a long discussion on the evolution of mills and millwork, which shows how

* Klingender's italics.

29

intimately Smith was acquainted with what was then the most important branch of engineering. It is known also that he made a thorough study of industry while in Glasgow and he, too, is said to have had a ducking when he slipped off a plank and fell into a tanner's pit 'while demonstrating the division of labour'. He was a member both of the Political Economy Club and of another, patronized by the most important merchants of the city, and headed by Glasgow's greatest provost, Andrew Cochrane, an eminent merchant who was the first man to recognize Smith's economic ability.

Even more interesting is Adam Smith's reference to the steam engine in the original draft: 'It was a real philosopher only who could invent the fire engine, and first form the idea of producing so great an effect, by a power in nature which had never before been thought of. Many inferior artists, employed in the fabric of this wonderful machine may afterwards discover more happy methods of applying that power than those first made use of by its illustrious inventor.'[30] While Smith was dictating those lines, his friend, Joseph Black (1728–99), who had recently announced his discovery of the principle of latent heat, was encouraging the young instrument maker, James Watt, in the experiments he was making under the same college roof to improve the steam engine.

It is, indeed, Smith's discussion of the role of the 'philosopher' which is most relevant in the present context, for it defines the position of the artists as well as the scientists and intellectuals generally in the new industrial civilization. In the first place Smith affirms that the difference 'between a philosopher and a common street porter, for example, seems to arise not so much from nature, as from habit, custom and education'. It is an historical result of the division of labour, for 'without the disposition to truck, barter, and exchange, every man must have procured to himself every necessary and conveniency of life which he wanted. All must have had the same duties to perform, and the same work to do, and there could have been no such difference of employment as could alone give occasion to any great difference of talents.'[31]

In the original draft, Smith extends the principle of the division of labour from physical to intellectual work. 'In opulent and commercial societies, besides'—he states—'to think or to reason comes to be, like every other employment, a particular business, which is carried on by a very few people, who furnish the public with all the thought and reason possessed by the vast multitudes that labour.' Only a very small part of any ordinary person's knowledge has been the produce of his own observation or reflection. 'All the rest has been purchased, in the same

30

I PITMEN PLAYING AT QUOITS (*c. 1840*) *Henry Perlee Parker*

manner as his shoes or his stockings, from those whose business it is to make up and prepare for the market that particular species of goods.' That particular species of goods includes, as Smith is careful to explain, 'all his general ideas concerning the great subjects of Religion, morals & government, concerning his own happiness and that of his country'.[32]

In 'civilized society', therefore, religion, morals, philosophy, science and art have become commodities, to be bartered in the market-place, like shoes and stockings. Far from being a disadvantage, in Adam Smith's view, this was the only means of keeping the intellectual in tune with his time. Their rich endowments enabled the greater number of universities only too often to become 'the sanctuaries in which exploded systems and obsolete prejudices found shelter and protection, after they had been hunted out of every other corner of the world'. On the other hand, in the poorer universities, the teachers, 'depending upon their reputation for the greater part of their subsistence, were obliged to pay more attention to the current opinions of the world'.[33]

Smith recognized that, as a result of the division of labour, the labouring poor, that is, 'the great body of the people', whose working lives are reduced to the monotonous repetition of a few simple operations, would necessarily tend to become 'as stupid and ignorant as it is possible for a human creature to become'. He therefore demanded that the State should intervene to prevent this evil by providing universal education.[34]

Moreover, specialization does not stop at the separation of intellectual from manual labour. Philosophy, like every other trade, 'is subdivided into many different branches, and we have mechanical, chemical, astronomical, Physical, Metaphysical, moral, political, commercial and critical philosophers. In philosophy, as in every other business, this subdivision of employment improves dexterity and saves time.' In Smith's days, however, the process of specialization had not yet advanced far enough to destroy that other main quality of the philosopher he also emphasized, namely the urge 'to observe every thing' and the capacity 'of combining together the powers of the most opposite and distant objects'.[35] It was their habit of ranging over the widest field of knowledge and relating their studies to practical needs that distinguished not only Adam Smith's circle, but also their philosophical friends elsewhere, and which accounts for the extraordinary brilliance of the intellectual life of the time.

Smith's economic studies form part of a much wider programme, including literary criticism, philosophy, ethics, and jurisprudence, which he first expounded in his lectures to the Edinburgh Philosophical Society from 1748 to 1751. He dealt with ethics in his *Theory of Moral Sentiments*, published in 1759, and his posthumous philosophical essays include fragments on aesthetics. One of Adam Smith's colleagues at Glasgow, John Anderson (1726–96), apparently found no difficulty in exchanging the chair of Oriental Languages for that of Natural Philosophy and in conducting experiments in ballistics, instead of teaching Hebrew. An improved gun he invented towards the end of his life was accepted by the French Revolutionary Government as 'the Gift of Science to Liberty', after it had been rejected by the British authorities.

The Scottish medical schools first achieved their great and lasting reputation under the influence of such men as William Cullen (1710–90), and the brothers John and William Hunter (1728–93; 1718–83). Joseph Black was at various times Professor of Medicine, Anatomy and Chemistry at Glasgow and Edinburgh. John Roebuck (1718–94), the son of a Sheffield cutler, who founded the Carron Company in 1760, had been trained as a medical student at Edinburgh, where he became the lifelong friend of David Hume (1711–76), and William Robertson. James Hutton (1726–97), the father of modern geology, and, with Black, Adam Smith's closest friend during his later Edinburgh period, also started with medicine before turning to industrial chemistry and geology. The practical basis of his work is underlined by his first book, published in 1777 and titled *Considerations on the Nature, Quality and Distinctions of Coal and Culm*.

In another sphere the humanism that distinguished the Scottish intellectuals at this period is illustrated by the two eminent judges, Lords Monboddo and Kames. James Burnet, Lord Monboddo (1714–99), applied the historical approach to the study of linguistics in his book *On the Origin and Progress of Language* (1773–92), and startled his contemporaries with his assertion that the early ancestors of man must have had tails. Henry Home, Lord Kames (1696–1782), one of the sponsors of Adam Smith's first lectures at Edinburgh, attacked the classical conception of authority in his *Elements of Criticism*, published in 1762, and directed aesthetic thought in Britain into the channels of psychology and even physiology. Since so much of a lawyer's work is concerned with the passions and affections of men, and with the problems arising from their daily occupations, Lord Kames also considered that students of law should spend a great deal of their time 'in the acquisition of general knowledge, the elements of the sciences, as Physics and Natural History, the principles of Mechanics and Mathematics, and in the elegant studies connected with Belles-Lettres and Criticism.'

The University of Glasgow, too, sponsored the fine arts. At the time when it was giving house-room to James Watt, it was also accommodating the brothers Andrew and Robert Foulis (1712–75; 1707–76), distinguished printers, whose types were designed on its premises by Alexander Wilson (1714–86), the professor of astronomy. The Foulis brothers, in turn, established one of the earliest Academies of Art in Britain, and from 1761 to 1775 arranged annual exhibitions of paintings in the rooms of the College, and even out of doors in the Quadrangle. The collection of pictures bequeathed to Glasgow University by William Hunter in 1783 included works of the schools of Salvator Rosa and Guido Reni, Dutch landscapes and genre pieces, and three exquisite Chardins, and probably typifies the taste of this circle. Although Hunter moved to London in 1740 he remained all his life in close touch both with his university and with the Scottish intellectuals generally.

The trial of one of the earliest steamboats, on Dalswinton Loch in 1788, affords another significant glimpse of Scottish intellectual life during the last years of Adam Smith. Inspired by Patrick Miller (1731–1815), Scottish banker, industrialist and a large shareholder in the Carron Company, it was designed by Alexander Nasmyth (1758–1840), painter, engineer, designer of cast-iron roofs and bridges, and the father of James Nasmyth (1808–90), the inventor of the steam hammer.

The vessel was not only one of the first to be driven by steam, but one of the first to have an iron hull—a double one constructed of tinned iron plate. The engines were built by William Symington (1763–1831), who had, at about the same time, demonstrated a model steam carriage in Edinburgh.

The trial on Dalswinton Loch was watched from the bank by young Henry Brougham (1778–1868), the great Scottish Lord Chancellor. On board were not only Patrick Miller and Alexander Nasmyth, but Miller's tenant, Robert Burns.[36]

When Burns passed by the Carron Works one August Sunday morning in 1787, and was refused admission by the doorkeeper, he scratched the following lines on a window pane:

> We cam na here to view your warks,
> In hopes to be mair wise,
> But only, lest we gang to Hell,
> It may be nae surprise;
> But when we tirl'd at your door,
> Your porter dought na hear us;
> Sae may, should we to Hell's yetts come,
> Your billie Satan sair us.[37]

This extraordinary society is illuminated by one source which no one should neglect who wishes to study it—the delightful *Original Portraits* by John Kay (1742–1826).[38] In the copious biographical notes that accompany them the philosophers and their friends appear, as it were, 'in an undress'. Kay, who was a barber turned caricaturist, stalked his quarries in the streets, in the lecture room, at their desks, and in their favourite haunts, the countless social, literary, and scientific clubs. Surrounded by lairds and lawyers, doctors and divines, shop-keepers and tradesmen, common street porters and fishwives, the philosophers appear, each sharply outlined for a brief instant, to be swallowed up in the next in the throng of picturesque characters among whom they spent their lives. Kay loved them for their foibles, no less than for their attainments: the professors fighting over the elephant's skeleton at the gate of Robert Adam's new college building; Lord Justice Eldon reading the Riot Act to his rebellious cats; Hutton and Black accidentally renting a room for a learned society in a house of ill-fame. It is a fascinating medley of intellectual candour, simple living, hard drinking and small-town gossip.

THE BOTANIC GARDEN

In 1765, shortly after Adam Smith had left Glasgow, another Scottish scientist, Dr William Small (1734–75), who had resigned his post of Professor of Natural Philosophy at Williamsburg, Virginia, called on Matthew Boulton at Birmingham with a letter of introduction from Benjamin Franklin. As a result he joined Boulton's great engineering enterprise at Soho, which had been open for three years. He probably saw James Watt when the latter first passed through Birmingham in the spring of 1767, for they kept up a regular correspondence with each other during the years that followed. It was Small who prepared the ground for the negotiations that led, in 1775, to the partnership between Boulton and Watt, after John Roebuck (1718–94), founder of the Carron Company and Watt's first patron, had gone bankrupt. Small, who had great social as well as scientific gifts, appears to have brought together that remarkable group of men of the most divergent temperaments and experiences known as the 'Lunar Society'. They met at each other's houses once a month, on the Monday nearest to the full moon, to foster their common enthusiasm for science. Founded in about 1776, for more than a quarter of a century the Lunar Society represented the vanguard of scientific thought in England.[39] Its members were in constant communication with the leading scientists in Scotland, America, France, and other continental countries. Closely concerned with the practical application of knowledge, it formed a kind of scientific general staff for the industrial revolution. The majority of its members were themselves industrialists: Boulton and Watt, and, until his premature death in 1775, Dr William Small; Samuel Galton, F.R.S. (1753–1832); James Keir (1735–1820), who, after an adventurous military career, started a chemical manufactory, and became partner and manager of a Birmingham glassworks in 1772; those landowners, philanthropists, and enthusiastic amateur mechanics, Richard Lowell Edgworth, F.R.S. (1744–1817), and Thomas Day (1748–89), author of *Sandford and Merton*; the Derby clockmaker and geologist, John Whitehurst (1713–88); the animal breeder and chemist, Dr William Withering, F.R.S. (1741–88), a celebrated physician noted for his botanical studies; and, from 1780, when he settled in Birmingham as a Nonconformist minister, Joseph Priestley, F.R.S. (1733–1804). Though he was not a member of the Lunar Society, Josiah Wedgwood was in close touch with the group. John Wilkinson occasionally attended the meetings.

The patriarch and leading spirit of the Lunar Society was Dr Erasmus Darwin, F.R.S. (1731–1802), a busy country doctor at Lichfield. To quote Ernst Krause, his first serious biographer, he was the first thinker 'who proposed and consistently carried out, a well-rounded theory with regard to the development of the living world.'[40] On the other hand, his famous grandson, Charles Darwin (1809–82), seems to have done less than justice to his scientific prescience in the field of evolution.[41] An ardent scientific propagandist, Erasmus Darwin founded both the Lichfield Botanic Society, which published translations of the works of Linnaeus, and the Derby Philosophical Society after moving to that city in 1782. His roving interest in mechanics is shown by his construction of a 'speaking machine' and his designing of a flint mill for Wedgwood. He shared Watt's secret of the separate condenser before the latter obtained his first patent. He was abreast of all the most advanced scientific thought of his time, and his foresight was such that his scientific prophecies could not but appear fictitious to most of his contemporaries. But the importance of Erasmus Darwin for the intellectual history of the last decade of the eighteenth century rests on his didactic poems, published in the later years of his life. In them he transmitted to educated readers, wherever the English language was understood, that enthusiasm for science and the belief in the perfectability of human affairs which inspired the members of the Lunar Society.

The first and most influential of Darwin's poems was *The Botanic Garden* issued in two parts—Part I, *The Economy of Vegetation*, and Part II, *The Loves of the Plants*. Part II was published first, in 1789, with a second edition in 1790. Part I appeared belatedly in 1791, and thenceforward the two parts were issued together, with a combined title-page.[42]

Darwin opened his Advertisement to the combined work with the words: 'The general design of the following sheets is to inlist Imagination under the banner of Science; and to lead her votaries from the looser analogies, which dress out the imagery of poetry, to the stricter, ones which form the ratiocination of philosophy.' There can be no question of Darwin's contemporary success. Until 1798 the reception accorded his poem was uniformly enthusiastic. '*The Triumph of Flora*,' said Horace Walpole in 1792, referring to the opening passage of Part I of *The Botanic Garden*, 'is most beautifully and enchantingly imagined: and the twelve verses that by miracle describe and comprehend the creation of the universe out of chaos, are in my opinion the most sublime passage in any author, or in any of the few languages with which I am acquainted.'[43] Among the dedicatory poems from admirers, prefixed to the later editions, there is a charming one from William Cowper. As late as 1803 the *Edinburgh Review* could write that Darwin's fame would rest on his merit as a poet, while 'his reveries in science have probably no other chance of being saved from oblivion, but by having been "married to immortal verse" '.[44] But since some modern readers are apt to regard *The Botanic Garden*, with its mingling of technical description and classical allegory, as a ludicrous performance,* it is worth analysing the conditions which made this marriage between science and art a brilliant if short-lived success.

At first sight the form of Darwin's poem seems to differ in no way from the classical convention adopted by the general run of didactic poets in the eighteenth century. There seems little to choose between the passages quoted earlier in this chapter from Dalton, Dyer and Yalden and, for example, the lines with which Darwin begins his description of the steam engine:

> Nymphs! you erewhile on simmering cauldrons play'd,
> And call'd delighted Savery to your aid;
> Bade round the youth explosive steam aspire
> In gathering clouds, and wing'd the wave with fire;
> Bade with cold streams the quick expansion stop,
> And sunk the immense of vapour to a drop.—
> Press'd by the ponderous air the Piston falls
> Resistless, sliding through it's iron walls;

* An attitude that, in part thanks to the author, is now rapidly changing to one of respect for Darwin's thinking and poetry alike.—*Ed*.

> Quick moves the balanced beam, of giant-birth,
> Wields his large limbs, and nodding shakes the earth.[45]

But on closer analysis Darwin's nymphs reveal a graceful charm and a mis-chievous propensity for unexpected metamorphoses into machinery, plants or elemental forces of nature, incompatible with the dignity of the muse who guides the reader through the terrors of the mine in the poems of Yalden or Dalton or, to cite another art, of 'Apollo and muses' who 'sing great George's praise' in Thorn-hill's Painted Hall at Greenwich. Darwin, in other words, used classical imagery in a new and already romantic way: 'The Rosicrucian doctrine of Gnomes, Sylphs, Nymphs and Salamanders', he writes in the Apology which opens Part 1, 'was thought to afford a proper machinery for a Botanic poem; as it is probable, that they were originally the names of hieroglyphic figures representing the elements.' He explains further this curious theory of classical mythology, which he had derived from Bacon, by adding: 'The Egyptians were possessed of many discoveries in philosophy and chemistry before the inventions of letters; these were then expressed in hieroglyphic paintings of men and animals; which after the discovery of the alphabet were described and animated by the poets, and became first the deities of Egypt, and afterwards of Greece and Rome.'[46] Thus Darwin felt he was only restoring the deified natural processes embodied in the classical myths to their original, natural functions by using them as poetic illustrations of the latest scientific theories. For example, he sees 'Venus rising from the sea [as] an hiero-glyphic emblem of the production of the earth beneath the ocean', or takes the 'Mythological interpretation of Jupiter and Juno . . . as an emblem of the composition of water from two airs.'[47]

This use of allegory was justified, moreover, by Darwin's own theory of the arts which he explains in the three 'Interludes' in Part II—*The Loves of the Plants*. . . . 'Poetry'—he writes—'admits of very few words expressive of perfectly abstracted ideas, whereas Prose abounds with them. And as our ideas derived from visible objects are more distinct than those derived from the objects of our other senses, the words expressive of these ideas belonging to vision make up the principal part of poetic language. That is the Poet writes principally to the eye.' '. . . Science is best delivered in Prose, as its mode of reasoning is from stricter analogies than metaphors or similes.' In conjuring up his poetic visions before the reader's inner eye, the poet aims to achieve that same complete absorption which is experienced in dreams, where no extraneous objects or previous experiences are allowed to intrude upon the flow of images. To achieve this, 'The matter must be

37

interesting from its sublimity, beauty, or novelty: this is the scientific part; and the art consists in bringing these distinctly before the eye . . .' The representations of poets and artists need not, therefore, correspond with nature. On the contrary: 'Nature may be seen in the market place, or at the card-table; but we expect something more than this in the play-house or picture-room.' With this he opens the door wide to fantasy: 'The further the artist recedes from nature, the greater novelty he is likely to produce; if he rises above nature, he produces the sublime; and beauty is probably a selection and new combination of her most agreeable parts'. While Rubens produces ridiculous effects by combining in one canvas allegorical figures with natural ones, Reynolds makes even portraits sublime. We admire persons in his portraits whom, in reality, we should have passed by unnoticed. Angelica Kauffman 'attracts our eyes with beauty, which I suppose no where exists; certainly few Grecian faces are seen in this country', while 'the daring pencil of Fusseli [*sic*] transports us beyond the boundaries of nature, and ravishes us with the charm of the most interesting novelty. And Shakespeare, who excells in all these together, so far captivates the spectator, as to make him unmindful of every kind of violation of Time, Place, or Existence.'[48] Not content with praising him, Darwin selected Henry Fuseli (1741–1825) to make two of his illustrations, which were engraved by William Blake (1757–1827).

The artists he lists, and the addition of Shakespeare, typify Darwin's combination of romantic feeling with classical imagery, and explain the Midsummer-Night's-Dream mood of his poem. It is a series of cameos in which, as in Ovid's *Metamorphoses*, images, now 'sublime', now 'beautiful', now 'novel', are suddenly transmuted into natural objects, scientific theories, or even industrial processes. Here, for example, is Darwin's description of Arkwright's cotton mill at Cromford:

> So now, where Derwent guides his dusky floods
> Through vaulted mountains, and a night of woods,
> The Nymph, Gossypia, treads the velvet sod,
> And warms with rosy smiles the watery God;
> His ponderous oars to slender spindles turns,
> And pours o'er massy wheels his foamy urns;
> With playful charms her hoary lover wins,
> And wields his trident,—while the Monarch spins.
> —First with nice eye emerging Naiads cull
> From leathery pods the vegetable wool;
> With wiry teeth *revolving cards* release
> The tangled knots, and smooth the ravell'd fleece;
> Next moves the *iron-hand* with fingers fine,

Combs the wide card, and foams the eternal line;
Slow, with soft lips, the *whirling Can* acquires
The tender skeins, and wraps in rising spires;
With quicken'd pace *successive rollers* move,
And these retain, and those extend the *rove*;
Then fly the spo[o]les, the rapid axles glow;—
And slowly circumvolves the labouring wheel below.[49]

Darwin's poetic imagery was exactly what appealed to his contemporaries, who were just as enchanted, for example, by *The Shakespeare Gallery* published by John Boydell (1719–1804), or by the imagery of Mozart's *Magic Flute* (1791). They were thus content to follow him through the 'looser analogies' of his poetic embellishments to the stricter ones of his philosophy, where his real importance became apparent. For the range of *The Botanic Garden* is far wider than the title implies. It embraces the whole field of knowledge and its industrial application, and even today there is no better way of ascertaining the state of science in 1789–90, or a more agreeable one, than by consulting the text of Darwin's poems and his voluminous notes. He is equally well-informed and inspiring, whether he is dealing with the latest theory of the origin of the earth or the latest stage in the development of the steam engine. While in the text, for example, he mentioned the steam-driven machinery of the Albion Flour Mills, opened in 1784 and completed in 1788, he had just time, in a supplementary note, to regret its destruction by fire in 1791, 'Whence London has lost the credit and the advantage of possessing the most powerful machine in the world!'[50] The passage on the steam engine concludes:

Soon shall thy arm, UNCONQUER'D STEAM! afar
Drag the slow barge, or drive the rapid car;
Or on wide-waving wings expanded bear
The flying-chariot through the fields of air.
—Fair crews triumphant, leaning from above,
Shall wave their fluttering kerchiefs as they move;
Or warrior-bands alarm the gaping crowd,
And armies shrink beneath the shadowy cloud.[51]

'As the specific levity of air is too great for the support of great burthens by balloons,' Darwin explains elsewhere, 'there seems no probable method of flying conveniently but by the power of steam, or some other explosive material; which another half century may probable [*sic*] discover.'[52]

He expresses himself in similar terms when discussing Priestley's experiments for producing oxygen from various minerals. This discovery, he writes, might soon 'enable adventurers to journey beneath the ocean in large inverted ships or diving balloons'.[53] He adds in a further note, 'it is probable in another half century it may be safer to travel under the ocean than over it . . .' And he describes the 'huge sea-balloons' or, 'diving castles, roof'd with spheric glass, ribb'd with strong oak, and barr'd with bolted brass', in which Britannia will be drawn by obedient sharks through her new realm beneath the main, exploring the bottom of the sea 'Beneath the shadowy ice-isles of the Pole.'[54] But Erasmus Darwin's grasp of the interconnexion of all things in nature, and his faith in the boundless perspectives of science, were most strikingly expressed when he wrote in explanation of his bold hypotheses: 'Extravagant theories . . . in those parts of philosophy, where our knowledge is yet imperfect, are not without their use; as they encourage the execution of laborious experiments, or the investigation of ingenious deductions, to confirm or refute them. And since natural objects are allied to each other by many affinities, every kind of theoretic distribution of them adds to our knowledge by developing some of their analogies.'

Nor was the author of *The Botanic Garden* interested only in science. His philosophical speculations and descriptions of engines, mills and forges alternate with references to Howard's campaign for prison reform, or to that for the abolition of slavery, and he hails the revolutions in America and France. And all these serious topics are capriciously interspersed with allusions to nymphs and naiads, the great Egg of Night, Venus visiting the Cyclops, Jupiter and Semele, Mrs Delany's paper-garden, Miss Crew's drawings, the Portland Vase, Mr Fusseli's Night Mare, Witches, Imps and Sorcerers, the Cave of Thor, Nebuchadnezzar and Moses, Tender Husbands, Harlots and Giants, Dejinira in a Lion's Skin, a Turkish Lady in an undress, Parched Deserts of Africa, Ice-scenes in Lapland, a Lady saluted by a Swan, and a hundred others[55] for the reader to contemplate 'as diverse little pictures suspended over the chimney of a Lady's dressing-room, *connected only by a slight festoon of ribbons.*'[56]

'Lo,' the good doctor addresses the reader in his Proem to *Loves of the Plants*, 'here a CAMERA OBSCURA is presented to thy view, in which are lights and shades dancing on a whited canvas, and magnified into apparent life!—if thou art perfectly at leisure for such trivial amusements, walk in, and view the wonders of my INCHANTED GARDEN.'[57]

It is not difficult to imagine the success of such an appeal in that first year of the French Revolution, when the dreams of the philosophers seemed on the verge of fulfilment, in that dawn, when it was bliss to be alive, 'but to be young was very heaven'. How deeply Wordsworth himself was stirred by the profound substance if not by the form of Darwin's message is shown by the following lines which he wrote in 1794, when he was 24 years old, and which he intended to add to his poem, 'An Evening Walk', written in 1788–9. After asking sadly, 'are there souls whose languid powers unite no interest to each rural sound or sight . . . ?' he continues:

> How different with those favoured souls who, taught
> By active Fancy or by patient Thought,
> See common forms prolong the endless chain
> Of joy and grief, of pleasure and of pain;
> But chiefly those to whom the harmonious doors
> Of Science have unbarred celestial stores,
> To whom a burning energy has given
> That other eye which darts thro' earth and heaven,
> Roams through all space and unconfined,
> Explores the illimitable tracts of mind,
> And piercing the profound of time can see
> Whatever man has been and man can be,
> From him the local tenant of the shade
> To man by all the elements obeyed.
> With them the sense no trivial object knows,
> Oft at its meanest touch their spirit glows,
> And proud beyond all limits to aspire
> Mounts through the fields of thought on wings of fire.[58]

With its tension between content and form, and with the engaging charm which is the outcome of that tension, *The Botanic Garden* perfectly expressed the mood of the moment in 1789. It was essentially a moment of transition. New energies were bursting through the soil of an age-old civilization, and the old forms still clung to them, like protective sheaths, till a younger generation of poets succeeded in transmuting 'the language really used by man' into a form of poetry that was 'the spontaneous overflow of powerful feelings'. Wordsworth affirmed that the poet must be 'ready to follow the steps of the Man of science', and to be at his side 'carrying sensation into the midst of the objects of the science itself'.[59] Nevertheless, after the publication of *Lyrical Ballads* in 1798, the kind of poetical imagery Darwin had used, and the whole classical convention that was the heritage of a privileged minority, no longer sufficed to voice the aspirations expressed in *The Botanic Garden*.

In the same year, an attack was launched on Darwin from a quarter that cared nothing for poetic form. George Canning (1770–1827) and his friends were consumed by hatred of the philosophy that was the inspiration equally of the older and the younger poets. No longer content merely to persecute booksellers, Nonconformists, and Radicals, reaction prepared itself to tear out by the roots the whole system of dangerous ideas, the faith in science. It is testimony to the influence of Darwin's poem that Canning should have singled out *The Loves of the Plants*, almost ten years after it was first published, for an attack in *The Anti-Jacobin* under the title *The Loves of the Triangles*, savagely inscribed to Dr Darwin:

> Debased, corrupted, groveling, and confined,
> No Definitions touch *your* senseless mind.

The poem was an easy target, for where the faith is lacking the form becomes ridiculous:

> Lo! where the chimney's sooty tube ascends,
> The fair Trochais from the corner bends!
> Her coal-black eyes up-turn'd incessant mark
> The eddying smoke, quick flame, and volant spark;
> Mark with quick ken, where flashing in between,
> Her much-loved *Smoke-Jack* glimmers thro' the scenes;
> Mark, how his various parts together tend,
> Point to one purpose,—in one object end;
> The spiral *grooves* in smooth meanders flow,
> Drag the long *chain*, the polish'd axles glow,
> While slowly circumvolves the piece of beef below:
> The conscious fire with bickering radiance burns,
> Eyes the rich joint, and roasts it as it turns.[60]

How quickly the mood of enchantment with its temporary union between art and science was dispelled may be seen from Francis Horner's comment on the continuing influence of the Lunar Society, when he visited Soho in 1809: 'The impression which they made is not yet worn out, but shows itself, to the second and third generation, in a spirit of scientific curiosity and free enquiry, which even yet makes some stand against the combined forces of Methodism, Toryism, and the love of gain.'[61]

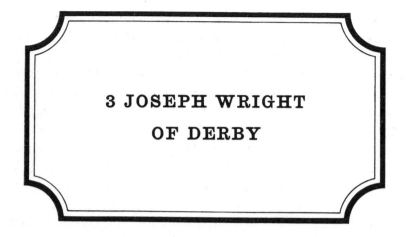

3 JOSEPH WRIGHT
OF DERBY

So **Wright's** *bold pencil from Vesuvio's hight*
Hurls his red lavas to the troubled night;
From Calpe starts the intolerable flash,
Skies burst in flames, and blazing oceans dash;—
Or birds in sweet repose his shades recede,
Winds the still vale, and slopes the velvet mead;
On the pale stream expiring Zephirs sink,
And Moonlight sleeps upon its hoary brink.[1]

ERASMUS DARWIN

INDUSTRIAL DESIGN

THE TYPICAL product of the Staffordshire potteries till well into the eighteenth century was the heavy red or brown slipware, often called Toft ware, with its bold criss-cross pattern, naïvely drawn figures and crude lettering. On the other hand, after about 1769 even the ware made by Wedgwood for common use was specially designed by artists, while a large proportion of his output consisted of purely ornamental cameos, medallions, vases, and other *objects d'art*.[2] Similarly, one of the original products of the ironmasters in the old forest foundries of Sussex was the cast-iron fire-back with its delightful unselfconscious decoration in relief. In the end it was driven out by the exquisite grates produced by manufacturers such as the Carron Company, which was closely associated with many of the fashionable designers and artists of the day, including the brothers Adam, of whom John was a partner.[3] In the case of both these industries, what might be called 'peasant art' came to be replaced by 'industrial design'. In effect, the revolution in taste brought about by the industrial pioneers was as profound as the revolution they wrought in the organization and technique of production.

The change was general throughout the industrial field. Matthew Boulton achieved an international reputation as a producer of elegant buckles, buttons, sword-furniture, and other 'toys' long before he engaged in the engine business.[4] The Sheffield and London manufacturers of plate and cutlery were his close rivals in excellence of design and craftsmanship.[5] In the cotton industry, Samuel Oldknow (1756–1828) made his fortune with high-quality muslins before he built his great spinning mill at Marple and turned to the manufacture of coarse yarns for mass consumption.[6]

What happened in all these spheres is an excellent illustration of Adam Smith's principle of the division of labour. Goods which had previously been made from start to finish by a single craftsman were now produced by specialists in stages which 'improved dexterity and saved time'. Perhaps the most fundamental division was that between designing and making. Once design became the specialized task of the 'artist', who did not himself actually work at the wheel or bench or lathe, the spontaneous taste of the craftsman was inevitably undermined. Instead, his inventiveness showed itself in the solution of technical problems of execution. Hence the division of labour resulted, not only in marked changes in the level of design, but also in changes in the level of manufacturing technique.

The main stages of the development can be followed fairly clearly in the case of the pottery trade, particularly in Staffordshire. The first improvement over the traditional English slipware was made in 1672, when John Dwight of Fulham (1637–1703), took out a patent for making salt-glazed stoneware—that is, pottery fired at a high temperature to the point of great hardness and vitrification, and glazed by throwing salt into the kiln when the fire is at its hottest. Though the process was already well known on the Continent, it does not appear to have been practised before this time in England. A little later, the Wedgwoods started the manufacture of stoneware in Burslem at the instigation of John and David Elers, Dutchmen who had followed William of Orange to England.[7]

Some eighty years later John Elers's son asked Josiah Wedgwood to inscribe a medallion to his father as the inventor of English pottery, something Wedgwood declined to do. In a letter of 19 July 1777 to his partner, Thomas Bentley (1730–80), he doubts the validity of Elers's claim to have introduced salt-glazing, but credits him with the improvement of refining the common red clay of the district, 'by casting it in plaister moulds, & turning it upon the outside upon Lathes, & ornamenting it with the Tea branch in relief, in imitation of the Chinese manner of ornamenting this ware.'[8] After the Elerses had left the district, Wedgwood goes on to say, the firm had introduced white stoneware, using pipe clay mixed with powdered calcined flint, in yet another attempt to imitate Chinese porcelain.

As a result of his enterprise and his inventiveness Josiah Wedgwood was the first English potter to attain a European reputation. Less a craftsman than an entrepreneur, he became one of the great capitalists of the eighteenth century, combining resources of imagination with a lively power of administration. According to W. B. Honey, 'his actual achievement was a contribution to amenities rather than to art. His cream-coloured ware was not only cleaner and more durable in use than anything as cheap that had preceded it, but in its forms it showed a practical intelligence that gave attention for the first time to the fitness for their purpose of spouts and strainers, handles and lids, securing at once an economical lightness and a "modern" efficiency . . . His notions of art as embodied in his decorative wares were largely those of his age; it was an "educated" taste, accepting what was fashionable, not a native sense of beauty or of traditional craftsmanship . . . His ideal of a minute mechanical perfection was entirely consonant with the taste he showed for pure and dry classical forms.'[9]

The desire to emulate more elegant foreign products turned the Staffordshire potters, led by Wedgwood, from their traditional methods and started them on the search for improved materials, techniques and standards of design. Other trades producing high-quality consumption goods followed suit. This trend led inexorably to the introduction of mass production for an international market in factories employing many hundreds of workers, a phase inaugurated by the opening of Matthew Boulton's Soho Manufactory in 1762 and Wedgwood's Etruria in 1768.

How immensely all problems of production and design were complicated by this development may be seen from the correspondence between Wedgwood and Bentley, who was in charge of the London sales office of the firm until his death in 1780. Special clays, imported from Cornwall and other districts, including small quantities from America, were used for different kinds of ware, and the completion of the Trent and Mersey Canal in 1777 made production all but independent of local supplies of raw material. Gradually, all the preliminary processes, such as the grinding of flints and the sifting and mixing of clays, were mechanized. Finally, the actual making of pottery, which could not then be mechanized, was subdivided, specialized throwers, turners, moulders, decorators, setters and their numerous assistants taking the place of the former all-round potter. Production problems such as these stimulated the systematic organization of scientific research. Wedgwood himself was made a Fellow of the Royal Society in 1783 for his invention of a pyrometer.

In the sphere of design, the urge to emulate or surpass the best products of past or distant civilizations continued unabated. The chinese models imitated earlier in the century were replaced by the 'Etruscan' ware and by the ancient medals, cameos and reliefs which the taste of the later part of the eighteenth century proclaimed as the finest products of the potter's or sculptor's art. Wedgwood ransacked the most famous collections of the time for models. The trouble he took to reproduce not only the design but also the texture of the Portland Vase with his new materials shows his eagerness to rival the noblest works of the ancients. More important than such direct copies, however, was the drive for a continuous supply of original designs, which were produced both by artists employed as wage-earners in the factory itself and by free-lance designers. It is interesting how many of the problems, familiar to industrial designers today, concerning conditions of employment or the artists' property in their ideas, already occur in the Wedgwood-Bentley correspondence.[10] Both partners were constantly on the look-out for unknown talent, and had a flair for recognizing it. Among the well-known sculptors of the late eighteenth century both John Flaxman (1755–1826) and John Bacon (1740–99) owed much to Wedgwood.

But the most serious problem introduced by the increased scale of production arose from the need 'to truck, barter and exchange'—in short, marketing—which Adam Smith recognized as the essential concomitant of the division of labour. '*Fashion*', Wedgwood wrote in 1779, 'is infinitely superior to *merit* in many respects; & it is plain from a thousand instances that if you have a favorite child you wish the public to fondle & take notice of, you have only to make choice of proper sponcers'.[11] Although the creators of fashion, Wedgwood, Boulton and the other manufacturers of luxury goods, especially silk fabrics, were also its slaves. Already in the second half of the eighteenth century the real arbiter of taste was no longer the designer or even the manufacturer, but the salesman, whose business it was both to sense every fluctuation in the public mood and, if possible, to anticipate change and to motivate fashion by a ceaseless flow of 'novelties'.

It is not difficult to understand why the improvement of design and craftsmanship, which was the immediate effect of the division of labour, proved to be short-

II LOCOMOTIVE ENGINE (*1848*) *John Emslie*

lived and was followed by the catastrophic debasement of both in the nineteenth century. Competition, and the progress of technique, forced the manufacturers to produce on an ever larger scale. To sell their increased output they had to aim at cheapness and no longer primarily at quality. They had to find a market precisely among those former craftsmen, now turned wage labourers, whose natural sense of design had been destroyed by the division of labour. But as 'taste' became the exclusive attribute of an ever narrower circle of specialists, the appreciation of design vanished as rapidly among the middle and upper classes as among the workers. Hence the salesman's search for indications of public 'taste' became a scramble for 'selling points'. These developments did not, however, become decisive in the period now under review. Indeed, the experience of the later eighteenth century is particularly significant today, because it proves that, given certain conditions, industrial technique is not incompatible with the highest levels of design. But that the tendency to debasement was present even at that early period is shown by Matthew Boulton's ceaseless struggle to eradicate the taint attached in the public mind to 'Brummagem' ware.

(So Klingender, writing in 1946–7. It is certain that, were he revising his text today, he would have modified his views about the worth of Victorian taste and culture. For there is now abundant evidence that, in the nineteenth century, mass production and the new industrial processes stimulated popular art forms no less vigorous and attractive than the 'peasant' art preceding mechanization. With its soaring nave and transepts of iron and glass, the Crystal Palace of 1851, one of the great architectural monuments of Britain, was at once the product of mass production and of standardization, and a reflection of popular taste (Figs. 99–102). The things of common use, from the cast-iron detail of a station roof to locomotives, resplendent in brass and bright paint, from lamp standards to garden seats, from furniture to fabrics, from steel engravings to chromolithographs, often had a grace, delicacy and functional beauty Wedgwood himself would have admired.

It is true, of course, that large sections of the middle and upper classes lost their appreciation of design. Appalled by the industrial landscape, and at the same time enriched by the squalor it engendered, they retreated into parlours and drawing-rooms stuffed with bric-a-brac. To separate themselves from the new proletariat of the cities they erected a sterile system of privilege and gentility derived from the aristocratic principles of the previous century. A literate, dedicated minority, represented on one side by William Morris and on the other by the art-for-art's-sake movement of Oscar Wilde, himself appalled by the poverty surrounding his

47

own luxury, tried to find its way out of the impasse by a retreat to earlier modes of work and thought.

Between the two great wars of the present century a proportion of the middle classes, led by Bloomsbury, attempted with ephemeral success to create a personal haven of cultural exclusiveness by the systematic denigration of Victorian art and culture. The Second World War swept them away, and left behind a kind of vacuum of taste which every petty mercantilist and speculative builder has hastened to fill, to the enduring detriment of our age.)

That Wedgwood, like Boulton and other manufacturers of the time, should have adopted the classical forms fashionable in the second half of the eighteenth century was inevitable in view of his dependence on the international luxury market. But that he produced portraits of Newton, Franklin and Priestley in the manner of ancient cameos was not as incongruous as it might seem, for Wedgwood's classicism, like that of Erasmus Darwin, had a thoroughly modern twist. Quite apart from the elements that made the classical revival, sponsored by J. J. Winckelmann (1717–68), Denis Diderot (1713–84) and other intellectuals, an expression of the growing influence of middle-class 'enlightenment' in the latter half of the eighteenth century, Wedgwood had a special motive for emulating the ancients—the enterprising manufacturer's desire to excel the noblest works produced at any place or in any period.

The strength of this motive is shown by a letter in which Wedgwood appears, not as an employer of industrial designers, but as a patron of painters. It was written on 5 May 1778 to Bentley, who had urged him to buy a painting by a certain Joseph Wright (1734–97), who was exhibiting six pictures at the Academy for the first time.

'I am glad to hear'—Wedgwood wrote—'Mr Wright is in the land of the living, & continues to shine so gloriously in his profession. I should like to have a piece of this gentlemans art, but think Debutade's daughter would be a more apropos subject for me than the Alchymist though one principal reason for my having this subject would be a sin against the Costume, I mean the introduction of our Vases into the piece, for how could such fine things be supposed to exist in the earliest infancy of the Potters Art.—You know what I want, & when you see Mr Wright again I wish you could consult with him upon the subject. Mr Wright once began a piece in which our Vases might be introduced with the greatest propriety. I mean the handwriting upon the wall in the Palace of Nebucadnazer.'[12]

It was not its Gothic gloom that made Wedgwood reject the picture which

Wright painted in 1771 and called 'The Alchymist in search of the Philosopher's Stone, discovers Phosphorus, and prays for the successful conclusion of his operation, as was the custom of the Ancient Chymical Philosophers'. His principal reason for turning it down was that he was more anxious to publicize his achievement as a potter than his fame as a modern 'chymical' philosopher. Hence 'Debutade's Daughter' that Bentley had suggested as an alternative to the 'Alchymist' seemed more appropriate, for the mythical Debutade was supposed to have been connected with the earliest infancy of the potter's art at Corinth. His daughter 'invented' sculpture when she traced the outline of the shadow cast by her sleeping lover on a wall, and filled in the intervening space with clay. After much further discussion the subject that was ultimately commissioned, and duly carried out by Wright in 1782–4, was 'The Corinthian Maid', now in the Mellon Collection.

The story does not end here, for the claims of chemistry as a suitable subject for a picture were strengthened in Wedgwood's mind early in 1779, when Priestley's assistant, Warltire, came to Etruria and arranged a course of lectures and private instructions for the Wedgwood children and friends.[13] Their theme was just the kind of thing for which Wright was famous. But just then Wedgwood was particularly interested in George Stubbs (1724–1806), who had been experimenting since 1771 with a form of enamel painting. He had produced nineteen new fireproof tints, but he could not obtain copper tablets that were large enough for his purpose. After many fruitless trials he approached Wedgwood and Bentley with the suggestion that they should make him tablets of earthenware instead. Wedgwood took up the idea in the autumn of 1778 and obtained the first useful results by the following May. In a letter to Bentley, of 30 May 1777, he stated:

Mr Stubbs wishes . . . to do something for us by way of setting off against the tablets. My picture, & Mrs Wedgwoods in enamel will do something. Perhaps he may take your governess & you in by the same means. I should have no objection to a family piece, or rather two, perhaps, in oil, if he sho^d visit us this summer at Etruria. These things will go much beyond his present trifling debt to us.

The two family pieces I have hinted at above I mean to contain the children only, & grouped perhaps in some such manner as this.

Sukey playing upon her harpsichord, with Kitty singing to her which she often does, & Sally & Mary Ann upon the carpet in some employment suitable to their ages. This to be one picture. The pendant to be Jack standing at a table making fixable air with the glass apparatus &c; & his two brothers accompanying him. Tom jumping up & clapping his hands in joy & surprise at seeing the stream of bubbles rise up just as Jack has put a little chalk to the acid. Joss with the chemical dictionary before him in a thoughtful mood, which actions will be exactly descriptive of their respective characters.

My first thought was to put these two pictures into Mr Wright's hands; but other ideas took place, & remembering the labourers, & cart in the exhibition, with paying for tablets &c I ultimately determin'd in favour of Mr Stubbs. But what shall I do about having Mr S. & Mr W. here at the same time, will they draw kindly together think you?[14]

His anxiety may well have been justified, for Wright too aspired to work in enamel and in this connection proposed to visit Etruria at the end of 1779 to 'catch any help from its fires.'[15] However, everything went smoothly and Stubbs painted a charming conversation piece when he came to Etruria in 1780. Josiah and Mrs Wedgwood are sitting on a bench underneath a large oak in their park, his elbow resting on a small table on which one of the famous vases is displayed. In front of them are the four older children on horseback and the three little ones playing with a go-cart.

Both Stubbs and Wright remained on excellent terms with Wedgwood for the rest of their lives, painting further pictures for him and supplying him with designs and models for his pottery. Though Stubbs despised the Academy as much as Hogarth, he was not opposed to the classical idea as Wedgwood understood it, in spite of his view that nature was superior to art.[16]

GEORGE STUBBS[17]

Born in 1724, the son of a Liverpool saddler, from his earliest youth George Stubbs displayed a passionate interest in anatomy. He began studying bone structures at the age of 8. He worked for a time under Hamlet Winstanley (1800–61), a minor portrait painter and engraver, but broke away at the age of 22 to become a lecturer in anatomy to medical students at Hull. There he dissected the dead body of a pregnant woman, and engraved his own embryological drawings for Dr John Burton's *An Essay towards a Complete New System of Midwifery*, published in 1751. After short visits to Rome and Morocco, where he actually saw a lion attack a horse, he returned to England and spent the years 1756 to 1760 on a lonely Lincolnshire farm, dissecting horses and making a series of anatomical studies which he published in 1766 as *The Anatomy of the Horse*. Its scientific precision makes this work a landmark in the history of its subject. It won Stubbs the friendship of the greatest natural scientists of his day and the patronage of wealthy owners of horses and livestock. But his most ambitious project, started in 1795 when he was 72, was *A Comparative Anatomical Exposition of the Structure of the Human Body, with that of the Tiger and Common Fowls*. This was left unfinished at his death in

1806, but the text and those engravings he had completed were published post-humously in 1817. They have recently been issued in facsimile.

His particular qualities have been analysed by Geoffrey Grigson in a penetrating article in *Signature*.[18] Keeping 'nearer the scientific than the aesthetic tendencies' of his age, his tastes were those of an experimenter and observer. He avoided both the picturesque make-believe of Sir Uvedale Price (1747–1829) and the apocalyptic elements of Edmund Burke's conception of the sublime. In his paintings he succeeds in combining affectionate observation with a kind of cool lucidity.

Stubbs' excellence as a painter was grounded in his indefatigable research into anatomy and the structure of the living body. It expressed itself in his treatment of trees no less than in his studies of animals and man.

Stubbs' peculiar conception of the classical is best illustrated by his plaque of *Phaeton and the Chariot of the Sun*, showing Phaeton straining desperately to arrest the headlong descent through the clouds of a fiery team of English thoroughbreds while the axles of his chariot are bursting into flames. One version of this subject was exhibited in 1762, and another two years later. And in 1783 Stubbs designed yet a third 'Phaeton' as a black basalt plaque for Wedgwood. It is now in the Etruria Museum.

The bond of sympathy that tied Wedgwood both to Stubbs and to Wright was their passionate devotion to science.

JOSEPH WRIGHT OF DERBY[19]

Joseph Wright was the first professional painter directly to express the spirit of the industrial revolution. His portraits link the circle of Wedgwood, Darwin, and the Lunar Society with that of the first cotton lords, Arkwright, Strutt and Crompton. But Wright was not only a painter of natural philosophers and industrialists. He was also a natural philosopher himself, preoccupied with the problem of light, which was the subject of his ceaseless experiment. The cold light of the moon mingled with dim candlelight; the glow of phosphorus in a chemical laboratory; dark trees silhouetted against blazing furnaces and a star-lit sky; the glare of molten glass or red-hot iron in gloomy workshops; the flaming pottery ovens at Etruria. By studying effects such as these Wright achieved that distinct and personal style that marks his position in the history of art. As a painter of artificial and natural light effects, Wright links the chiaroscuro style of Caravaggio (1569–1609) and his followers, from Gerard von Honthorst (1590–1656) and Georges de la Tour (1593–1652) to Godfried Schalcken (1643–1706), with the romantic naturalism of the later English landscape school. That Wright's preoccupation with the problems of light was largely due to his own scientific temperament and to the influence of his environment is suggested by his isolated position among English artists.

The son of a Derby lawyer, he was born in 1734, some twelve years after the Lombes' silk mill had been completed. He studied under the portrait painter, Thomas Hudson (1701–79), Reynolds' master, from 1751 to 1753, and for a further fifteen months in 1756–7. In this way he acquired the sound craftsmanship which the English face painters of the early eighteenth century had inherited from the Dutch, and it was as a portrait painter that he started his career when he returned to Derby after completing his training.

One of the first of his studies of artificial light, 'Three Persons viewing the Gladiator by Candlelight', exhibited in 1765 at the Society of Artists, was probably painted under the influence of the Dutch 'candlelight' painters, especially Schalcken, who twice visited England and was a favourite of William III. In order to give the most natural effect to his candlelight pieces, Schalcken placed the object he intended to paint in a dark room. Looking through a small hole, he painted by daylight what he saw by candlelight. At first Wright painted in one room by daylight, posing his sitters in an adjoining room which had been darkened. Later, he invented a contrivance of panelled screens in the corner of his studio behind which he could pose his subjects in the dark. By opening one panel and then another, he could study them from different angles.[20]

Wright's handling of light and, in one or two instances, his themes, were anticipated by George de la Tour of Lorraine. Though it is almost certain that Wright did not know his pictures or even his name, there can be no doubt that the two painters had a common point of view towards their subjects. With a very few exceptions, all de la Tour's works were illuminated either by a shaft of sunlight or by the light of candles or torches, sometimes flaring nakedly, sometimes shielded by a hand or arm. Everything except the particular aspects he wishes to reveal is lost in deep shadow. Most of his subjects are Biblical or religious, but his treatment of them is one of dramatic actuality. His nativity, for example, is less a Biblical reconstruction than a study of a family in his native village of Lunéville. Cool, austere and undetailed, his pictures have a penetrating realism that puts them out of their epoch. They have little in common either with the grandeur and luxurious beauty of the works of the court painters of the day or with the bright, classical

52

imagery of his contemporary, Caspar Poussin (1613–1675), and still less with the secular elegance of such painters as Antoine Watteau (1684–1721). It was for this reason, perhaps, that de la Tour was scarcely recognized, even in his own day, and disappeared completely from the canon of French art, till his splendid talent was at last recognized by the art historians of the twentieth century.[21] To a lesser extent, both Stubbs and Wright suffered the same treatment. Perhaps the phrase, already quoted, used by Grigson of Stubbs, can be applied to all three. They suffered because they kept nearer the scientific than the aesthetic tendencies of their lifetime.

PHILOSOPHERS IN ART

In 1766 Wright exhibited one of his best and most original pictures at the Society of Artists—'A Philosopher giving that Lecture on the Orrery, in which a Lamp is put in the Place of the sun' (Fig. 31). In 1768 he repeated his success with 'An Experiment on a Bird in the Air Pump' (Fig. 32). Both were mezzotinted, the former in 1768 by William Pether (1731–95), the latter in 1769 by Valentine Green (1739–1813). Pether was a portrait painter of note and a skilled engraver. He was, respectively, cousin and father of two famous painters of moonlight scenes, Abraham and Sebastian Pether (1756–1812; 1790–1844). The former, known as Moonlight Pether, combined painting with science and mechanics, designing and constructing telescopes, microscopes, air pumps and scientific instruments. His moonlights are notable for their astronomical accuracy, and he painted also scenes of fire and volcanoes in eruption. Sebastian painted similar subjects, and is said to have invented the stomach pump. Green was one of the most celebrated and expert engravers in mezzotint of the eighteenth century, specializing in portraits after Reynolds, historical subjects, particularly after Benjamin West (1738–1820), and old masters. He built up an extensive connexion on the Continent and was almost ruined by the French Revolution.

Wright's essentially modern attitude is evident even in the one picture of his scientific series in which he was deliberately antiquarian, 'The Alchymist in search of the Philosopher's Stone, discovers Phosphorus. . .' Despite its Gothic setting and picturesque embellishments, this work is utterly opposed in spirit to most of its seventeenth-century predecessors. Without a trace of satire, its mood is as serious as that of the 'Orrery' and 'Air Pump'. Its purpose is not to ridicule the superstitions of the past, but to commemorate the birth of modern science from those superstitions. For it was the discovery of phosphorus that stimulated the research of Robert Boyle (1627–91) and his contemporaries into the nature of combustion, and marks the beginning of chemistry as a modern science.

Wright's philosophers differ profoundly, both in spirit and style, from the philosophers and alchemists dear to many Dutch and Flemish genre painters of the seventeenth century. In 'The Alchemist' by Adrian van Ostade (1610–85) or 'The Philosopher' by Cornelius Bega (1630–64), to take two pictures that can be studied in the National Gallery, London, or in 'The Alchemist' by David Teniers the Younger (1610–94) in The Hague, a skilfully diffused half-light casts a mysterious gloom over a jumble of objects, from stuffed crocodiles to alembics, traditionally associated with the search for the elixir of gold. The whole atmosphere, and also the dress of these fraudulent 'Philosophers', suggests that they are either quacks or else are living in a world of dreams, out of tune with their time. And, indeed, these northern sages and their cousins, the beggar-philosophers of Velasquez (1599–1660) and of Josef Ribera (1588–1656), can trace their descent from the 'portraits' of Aristotle and other ancient representatives of the Liberal Arts which the scholastic theologians included in their allegorical picture cycles.

Characteristically, however, de la Tour's 'Alchemist' shows a man studying a chemical reaction in a beaker with a serious intentness, unencumbered by the conventional trappings. In the same tradition, Joseph Wright used the half-light to evoke a mood of wonder, and to concentrate the attention on essentials. In his study of the group round the Orrery every superfluous detail is absorbed in the dark shadows of the background. The light reflected from the eager faces of the observers, each a sensitive psychological study, or from the intersecting circles of the Orrery, emanates from the focal point of the experiment. Rarely before had the excitement of scientific exploration been expressed as dramatically as this. 'The Anatomy Lesson' by Rembrandt (1607–1669), painted in 1632 and now at The Hague, was a noble tribute paid by art to science. 'The Astronomer' by Vermeer (1632–75), now at Frankfurt, foreshadowed the tense absorption of Wright's onlookers. But how original Wright was in terms of the English tradition may be seen by comparing his pictures with Hogarth's 'Anatomy' in the 'Four Stages of Cruelty', a sermon in the manner of the Dance of Death cycles. In contrast, Wright's 'Orrery', 'Air Pump' and 'Alchymist' are the first paintings to express the enthusiasm of the eighteenth century for science.

The work of Wright's early period, up to his journey to Italy in 1774, also illustrates the intimate association of science and industry in the minds of his contemporaries. The eight pictures he sent to the Society of Artists exhibition of

54

1771 included not only the 'Alchemist' but also 'A Blacksmith's Shop' (Fig. 33) and 'A Small Ditto, viewed from without'. In the following year he exhibited another 'Blacksmith's Shop', 'A Moonlight' and, even more important as a record of contemporary industry, 'An Iron Forge'. The exhibition of 1773 included 'An Earth Stopper on the Banks of the Derwent', a night-piece showing a man at work by the light of a lantern, and 'An Iron Forge, viewed from without'. (Fig. 19). The latter was acquired by Catherine the Great for £136 directly from his studio in 1774.[22] and is now at the Hermitage. Yet a further 'Smith's Forge' was shown in 1775. Two versions of a 'Glass-blowing House' were shown by a descendant of the artist at the memorial exhibition at Derby in 1883, while a 'Blast-furnace by Moonlight' was included in the bicentenary exhibition of 1934. The latter pictures may date from the later period, when he also painted a 'View of Cromford, near Matlock', of which there are several versions. They present a romatic view of Arkwright's great cotton mill, its windows blazing with lights, while the moon emerges from behind a bank of clouds (Fig. 28). 'These cotton mills, seven storeys high, and fill'd with inhabitants'—wrote Byng some eleven years later—'remind me of a first-rate man of war; and when they are lighted up, on a dark night, look most luminously beautiful.'[23]

THE 'ARTES MECHANICAE'[24]

In turning to industry for the subjects of so many of his major paintings, Wright was as much a pioneer as he was in glorifying science. Although art was intimately associated with productive labour in primitive society, and in the mural decorations in Egyptian tombs, labour plays only a subordinate role in the great tradition of European painting up to the time of the industrial revolution. This attitude is connected with the contempt for manual work which first appeared when industrial production, based on slave labour, began to replace small-scale craft production in classical antiquity. Craftsmen at work are depicted on the early black-figure pottery of Attica, and tablets of the same period from Boeotia contain the earliest surviving drawings of miners. But work-scenes are scarcely ever found on the red-figured vases of the classical era, except as illustrations of myths, such as the Labours of Hercules, Penelope at her Loom, or Vulcan at his Forge.

In principle, the Church was just as negative in its attitude to manual work as the ancient philosophers. Work was Adam's curse, the punishment inflicted on mankind for the first parents' original sin. It could occupy, therefore, only a

55

subordinate place in Christian art, as in the illustrations of Biblical texts and stories, such as the labours in the vineyard, the construction of the Ark or the building of the Tower of Babel, and in the representation of craftsman-saints like St Eloi, a farrier, or St Crispin, a cobbler. But more important than these occasional work-themes was the ancient peasant calendar, depicting the labours of each month, which the Church found it expedient to embody in its canon, together with other survivals of pre-Christian imagery.The cycle of the labours of the months, which can be traced in ancient times in Athens and Alexandria, occurs in countless variations as a symbol of the mutability of earthly life in medieval manuscripts and in the carved decorations and misericords of the great Romanesque and Gothic cathedrals. It culminated gloriously as one of the most fruitful subjects for the reawakening naturalism of the fourteenth century in the miniatures of the *Livres d'Heures* of the school of Burgundy.

In contrast to the ancient cycle of the rural occupations, the appearance of the urban craftsman in medieval art was a result of the growing power of the guilds. Since no less than forty-seven out of the 106 stained-glass windows of Chartres Cathedral, of which the earliest dates from A.D. 1194, were given by guilds, it is not surprising that they depict the occupations of their donors. Similarly, the power of the merchants and craftsmen of Venice is reflected in the splendid reliefs that illustrate their activities on the upper arch of the main porch of St Mark's, erected in the early thirteenth century. Miners and mining are a constant theme in the decorations of ecclesiastical and secular ceremonial plate associated with the Erzege-birge. This shift in the social relationships of medieval society also led to a modification of the doctrine of the Church. According to the Dominican theologian, Vincent of Beauvais, the *artes* were a means of mitigating the curse of original sin. Henceforth, the crafts became symbols of the *artes mechanicae* in the scholastic picture of the universe. As such, they appear in the reliefs on the campanile of Florence Cathedral, designed by Giotto (1266–1337) and executed after his death by Andrea Pisano and his assistants.

When the invention of printing created a vast new field for popular art, the scholastic theme of the *artes* was absorbed, in a modified form, in the specula or mirrors of human life. illustrating the occupations of all ranks and conditions of men. They were issued in many versions from the fifteenth century onwards. The Books of Trades, published in Britain until the middle of the nineteenth century, are the final offshoots of this tradition. While the illustrations in these series are objective records of secular life, their scholastic origin is often betrayed by the moralizing character of the captions, some of which have little direct bearing on the illustrations they are supposed to explain. They reflect the growing tension in industrial relations since the later Middle Ages, for they generally censure the idleness of journeymen and apprentices and exhort them to obey their masters. Hogarth's link with the medieval tradition of popular art is evident, for there is an important element of moral exhortation in his cycle 'Industry and Idleness' (1747). He chose the Spitalfields silk trade as his setting at a time of extreme friction between masters and men.

There are, however, two other developments that should be borne in mind in evaluating Wright's achievement—the tradition of technical illustration that sprang up independently in the sixteenth century with the invention of printing, the revival of learning and the growth of industry; and the first appearance, at about the same time, of industrial themes as subjects for the fine arts.

Joseph Wright's attitude to industry can be related to the illustrations added to scientific and technical treatises, such as that of Vitruvius, when they were printed for the first time. The art of technical draughtsmanship, of which the drawings by Leonardo da Vinci (1452–1519) are the outstanding example, spread quickly. It is splendidly represented in many of the great technical, military, architectural, and anatomical works of the sixteenth century, especially in *De Re Metallica* by Georg Agricola (1494–1555), published at Basle in 1556, and *Le Diverse et Artificiose Machine* by Agostino Ramelli (1531–90), printed in Paris in 1588. During the seventeenth and eighteenth centuries technical works and compendia appeared in ever-increasing numbers, culminating in Diderot's *Encyclopédie*, published in 1751–65, with its separate volumes of plates, and in the *Description des Arts et Métiers*, published by the Académie Royale des Sciences at Paris in twenty-seven volumes in 1761–82. Tilt-hammers of the type depicted by Wright are illustrated in both.

The first formal attempts by painters to introduce industrial scenes and themes into the fine arts occurred during the Reformation, when the struggle against Catholicism inspired landscapes and genre paintings designed to re-establish the common man in the face of the aristocratic absolutism of the Spanish rulers of the Low Countries.[25] The earliest is perhaps 'Paysage avec haut Fourneau' or Blast Furnace, painted in about 1520 by Joachim Patenier (*c.* 1480–1524), now in a private collection. It was followed by a number of mining landscapes of the Erzgebirge and the Liège industrial basin. Sometimes, as in an industrial altarpiece at Annaberg, painted in 1521 by Hans Hesse (*fl.* fourteenth to fifteenth century), the miners are associated with angels in evidence of better times to come in after-life. But often the detail of their life and work is shown with an objectivity unembellished by supernatural aid. These paintings are the first to foreshadow the concept that manual labour has a self-sufficient dignity and strength of its own. Something of the kind is evident in the splendid drawing of miners at work by the younger Holbein (1477–1543) in the British Museum. At Brussels there is a landscape by Lucas van Gassel (c. 1500–70), painted in 1544, depicting the surface workings of a mine in extensive sympathetic detail, and including one of the earliest known views of a mine truck on wooden rails. (The earliest of all is probably that in Der Ursprung Gemeyner, a textbook on mining published anonymously in about 1519.) The French artist, Henri met de Bles (c. 1490—c. 1550), who worked at Malines, interspersed a number of striking mining pictures among his religious paintings. There is one in the Uffizi and another at Prague. Most remarkable of all is an extraordinary series of industrial landscapes in the Liège basin by the brothers Lucas and Martin van Valckenborch (c. 1530–97; c. 1535–1622), two German Protestants who dedicated themselves to the struggle against Spain, and of whom Lucas was a pupil of Pieter Brueghel the elder (c. 1530–69).[26]

In the south, this movement is echoed by a striking series of industrial murals ordered by Vasari in about 1570 for the study of Francesco I de'Medici in Florence. Executed by such artists as Jan van de Straat (c. 1523–1605), they depict the life and work not only of alchemists but of jewellers, glass-workers and dyers, in a style partly heroic, partly realistic. They respresent a strange intrusion into a world not usually preoccupied with the springs of its own commercial success.[27]

With the rise of the Reformation and the defeat of Spain, a new and wealthy bourgeoisie established itself in the Low Countries. Industry and manual labour were virutally eliminated as serious themes for formal painting. Instead, there was a call for scenes illustrating the secure and prosperous lives of the merchants. The lower classes were kept severely in their place in innumerable village and tavern scenes of low life. If work scenes appeared at all, they usually came in mythological or allegorical disguise with the revival of classical themes from the fifteenth century onwards.

That such a retreat from industrial realism brought its strains and contradictions is illustrated by 'Venus at the Forge' by Pieter Brueghel's son, Jan (1568–1625), a contemporary of the van Valckenborch brothers. In this picture, in the Kaiser Friedrich Museum in Berlin, the nude figures of Venus, Cupid, and Vulcan occupy only a small part of a canvas dominated by the ruins of a Roman palace with

Mount Etna in the distance. The centre of the foreground is piled high with armour. A stall on the left displays splendid specimens of contemporary goldsmith's work, together with the tools of that craft, while the remainder of the composition is devoted to a minutely detailed record of the iron industry. Miners are raising and shifting ore in the foothills of Mount Etna; a mill installed on the bank of a stream drives a tilt-hammer and grinding wheels; the ruined palace contains a cannon foundry and boring mill of the type that continued in use until the days of John Wilkinson. The figure of Vulcan is in sharp, incongruous contrast to a group of blacksmiths in contemporary dress.

The clash between the mythological figures and the workers is heightened by the fact that the former were painted by Hendrik van Balen (1575–1632), either because Brueghel found it impossible imaginatively to bridge the two conventions, or, as his unkinder critics alleged, because his mastery of the human figure was weak. He evidently gave up the unequal struggle, and thenceforward directed his talent to a series of beautiful studies of the new fruits and flowers then being introduced to the tables of the wealthy, earning the nickname 'Velvet', apparently because of his sumptuous clothes.[28]

Jan Brueghel was not the only artist to find mythological themes incompatible with realism. In Velasquez' 'The Forge of Vulcan', painted at Rome in 1630 and now at the Prado, the mythological element, though still incongruous, is subordinate to the artist's interest in actual life. It is into a real smithy that the divine messenger is stepping. The smiths with their tools are rendered with dramatic realism, their work suspended with astonishment at the appearance of such an unaccountable visitor. Later, at the height of his power, Velasquez took the decisive step of abandoning the mythological theme entirely. His 'Tapestry Weavers' (*Las Hilanderas*), painted in 1657 and also at the Prado, is one of the earliest and will always be one of the greatest of factory paintings.

At about the same time the brothers le Nain similarly resolved the conflict between classical convention and realism.' Venus at the Forge of Vulcan' at Rheims, attributed to Mathieu le Nain (1607–77), is close in composition to 'The Forge' by his brother, Louis (1588–1648), at the Louvre. But in the latter Vulcan has been reduced to the role of onlooker, and Venus and Cupid replaced by the blacksmith's wife and child. It seems probable that the former picture is the original composition and the Louvre picture a brilliant variation.[29]

Joseph Wright tackled a similar theme in his 'Blacksmith's Shop' (Fig. 33), painted in 1770 or 1771. In this he combines classical and realistic elements, both

59

subordinated to a romantic mood that is new. While Velasquez and the le Nains chose a moment of rest, when work was suspended, Wright chose a dramatic moment, when the smiths are actually striking the iron.

Though Wright's figures are full of action, they are often placed in settings that can have only the remotest resemblance to an actual workshop. The 'Blacksmith's Shop', (Fig. 33) for example, is a ruined classical building where the smiths are working at night. Only the walls and some arches are standing, while a shelter of wood and thatch has been erected inside. This is the kind of setting that Italian painters of the sixteenth century often chose for pictures of the Nativity or Adoration. In fact, this picture echoes the stable in Veronese's 'The Adoration of the Magi', now in the National Gallery but in Wright's day still in San Silvestro in Venice. The resemblance between the two extends even to such details as the thatched shelter or the sculptured angels in the pendentives of the arch.

There is a marked similarity, too, between the old smith in the right-hand foreground of Wright's picture and the corresponding figures in both the forge paintings by the le Nains. In Mathieu's picture he is Vulcan, and therefore, with Venus, the main figure in the composition. In the pictures by both Louis le Nain and Wright he has been reduced to an onlooker, and it is difficult to believe that there is not a connexion between the two, even though in 1770 the former was not in the Louvre but still in the collection of the Duc de Choiseul. However, Wright may have seen an engraving of it. One appeared in a book of engravings after pictures in the Choiseul Collection, published in 1761, and there were others.

In 'The Iron Forge', exhibited in 1772, Wright abandoned the classical ruin. Although there is still an old man, echoing Vulcan, sitting in the foreground, the shed and the billet of iron under the water-driven trip-hammer give a good impression of a small forge of the period. The idyllic, sentimental element so characteristic of the circle that produced 'Sandford and Merton' is charmingly represented by the presence of a young mother, a baby in arms, and a young boy.

'The Iron Forge, viewed from without' which Catherine of Russia bought in 1773 has a new, almost theatrical, even mystical, intensity (Fig. 19). The *dramatis personae* consist of the smith, with a tall, youngish man on the left, leaning on a staff, an old man (who may be in charge of the furnace and the bellows), and a woman. They are housed in a kind of ruined Gothic barn, with one side broken away. The whole building stands like a stage set in a rugged landscape, fitfully illuminated by a moon glimmering behind a wrack of storm cloud. The smith, his back to the onlooker, is turning the workpiece on the anvil, his body silhouetted,

60

and shielding the glare of the white-hot metal. The classical reference has all but disappeared, though in another context the onlooker on the left might have been Vulcan and the woman Venus.

These three pictures, and others like them, with their disguised allusions to the classical and Christian myths, are the counterpart of *The Botanic Garden*. But what distinguishes Wright's industrial paintings from most earlier pictures with similar themes is his interest in the labour process as such. This is particularly striking, if his work is compared with the thousands of Dutch genre pictures of the seventeenth century depicting scenes from daily life, of which only a handful illustrate manual labour. There are a few pictures of farriers or blacksmiths by Philips Wouwerman (1619–68), Gabriel Metsu (1629–67), Jan Steen (1626–79), the brothers Adrian and Isaac van Ostade (1610–1685; 1621–49), and other artists. Gerard Ter Borch (1617–81) painted a knife-grinder, Quiryn Brekalenkam (1621–68) cobblers, and Cornelius Decker (*fl.* mid-seventeenth century) weavers. But the only kind of work that occurs sufficiently often to prove that picture buyers liked to see it on their walls is the domestic labour of women. The rich merchants of the Dutch Republic felt as superior to manual work as the slave-owners of classical Greece.

WRIGHT'S LATER WORK

Wright's later pictures blend classical, romantic and sentimental elements. Ancient mythology and motives taken from Shakespeare, Milton, Percy's *Reliques*, Beattie and Sterne share pride of place with 'The Siege of Gibraltar' and such subjects as 'The Old Man and Death', 'The Widow of an Indian Chief watching the Arms of her Deceased Husband', or 'The Dead Soldier'. Engravings after the last were so successful that Wright was urged to paint 'A Shipwrecked Mariner' as its companion.

But it was the play of light in nature that more especially fascinated Wright during the last twenty years of his life. The eruption of Vesuvius, which he happened to witness during his visit to Naples, provided a climax to the dramatic effects of his earlier work, and he continued to paint it repeatedly in later years. Catherine of Russia bought a splendid example for £300 in 1779.[30] It is now in the Hermitage. Though he became increasingly responsive to nature's lyrical moods as he grew older, he never lost the spirit of scientific curiosity. 'The water indeed is further advanced than ye rest of ye picture,' he wrote of a small view of Rydal which he was painting in 1795, two years before his death, 'for I was keen to produce an effect which I had never seen in painting of shewing pebbles at the bottom of the water with the broken reflections on its surface.'[31]

It was to the 'grand paintings of the eruptions of Vesuvius, and of the destruction of the Spanish vessels before Gibraltar, and to the beautiful landscapes and moonlight scenes' that Erasmus Darwin alluded in a note to the stanzas, added to later editions of *The Botanic Garden*, and quoted at the head of this chapter.

PEHR HILLESTRÖM AND LÉONARD DEFRANCE

Wright was not the only eighteenth-century artist who brought scientific and industrial themes into the orbit of the fine arts. The same thing happened at two other key centres of the industrial revolution, Sweden and Belgium. The Swedish court painter, Pehr Hilleström (1732–1816),[32] was born two years before Wright, and survived him by nineteen years. After working in the Stockholm tapestry factory on furnishings for the new royal palace, he went to Paris in 1757–8 and studied painting with François Boucher (1703–70). But the artist whose manner he adopted when he returned to Sweden was Jean Chardin (1699–1779). In 1776 Hilleström was appointed court painter by Gustavus III, but soon tired of the mock-medieval tournaments and theatrical displays his royal master ordered him to depict.

However, the sumptuous court of the ruler who had overthrown the constitutional liberties of his realm was not the only centre of culture in eighteenth-century Sweden. The dominant role the Swedes were able to play in European affairs during the seventeenth and early eighteenth centuries was based on their great mining and iron industry. Annual exports of bar-iron from Sweden exceeded 50,000 tons during the latter part of the century. Britain in particular, with its expanding industries, provided an inexhaustible market. There was thus great prosperity in the Swedish mining areas and a thriving bourgeois cultural life. Here Hilleström found a market more congenial than the court, although he did not abandon his official position. He paid his first visit to the famous copper-mine at Falun in 1781, and henceforth adopted industry as one of his main subjects. If a few pictures of blacksmith's shops he painted between 1773 and 1780 are included, the total number of his industrial paintings is 124. Apart from copper- and iron-mines, he painted smelting works, cannon foundries, forges, the Soderfors anchor factory, and the Kungsholm glassworks. Like Wright, he uses for illumination the glow of furnace and forge, the dazzling light of white-hot metal and the flame of torches. Though he is a painter of action, catching the men at work in striking attitudes, he is more of a reporter than Wright and less of a dramatist.

The other continental artist who painted modern industrial subjects at this period had a more adventurous career than either Wright or Hilleström. This was the Liègeois, Léonard Defrance (1735–1805).[33] After finishing his apprenticeship with a local painter he walked to Rome in 1753 and spent five years there, supporting himself by painting saints and portraits of popes for the dealers. Then he packed up his things again and walked, with a friend who was a doctor, to Naples, and thence by gradual stages by way of Montpellier, Toulouse and Bordeaux, back to Liège, which he finally reached in 1760. During the next thirteen years he had a hard struggle to support himself by doing portraits and routine pictures for the Church, a field he found restricted and frustrating, for he had made many friends in progressive circles during his travels through France. In 1773, therefore, he went to Holland, where he spent a year copying the minor Dutch masters for sale in Paris. From these, and from Jean Honoré Fragonard (1732–1806), who encouraged him in his work, Defrance acquired the light touch and brilliant colouring that distinguish his later pictures.

After returning to his native town in 1774 he chose his subjects by preference from popular life. Apart from market scenes, mountebanks, miners at an inn, and similar genre subjects, his pictures preserved in public and private collections in the Liège area depict a coal-mine, a rolling mill, a foundry, a cooper's shop and tobacco factories. It is interesting that the social comment so pronounced in the work of Constantin Meunier (1831–1905) and other Belgian and Dutch artists of the late nineteenth century already appears, a century earlier, in Defrance. In his pictures of a tobacco factory, for example, the ragged clothes of the children, sitting on the floor picking tobacco leaves, are contrasted with the smart silk frocks of ladies who are being shown round the factory by its owner. After his appointment as Director of the Liège Academy in 1778, Defrance paid an official visit to Paris every second year to attend the Salon. While he was there in 1789 he received the news that the revolution had started in Belgium. He returned at once and threw himself into the political struggle, playing a prominent part in the confiscation of Church property and other revolutionary measures during the following years. One of his pictures commemorates the suppression of the monasteries. Later, however, he returned to his academic duties, which he carried on until his death in 1805.

Although Wright was far less prolific, his influence as a painter of industrial subjects probably exceeded that of either Hilleström or Defrance, for his best pictures were engraved and published by print-sellers of the international standing of William Pether (1731–95) and the Boydells. Indeed, it is not impossible that, before they had begun to paint industrial scenes, both Hilleström and Defrance had seen the engravings after 'The Blacksmith's Shop', published in 1771, and 'The Iron Forge', published in 1773.

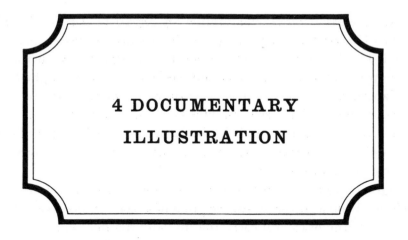

4 DOCUMENTARY ILLUSTRATION

Learn this ye painters of dead stumps,
Old barges, and canals, and pumps,
Paint something fit to see, no view
Near Brentford, Islington, or Kew—
Paint any thing,—but what you do.[1]

THE REV. JOHN EAGLES

SCIENCE AND the graphic arts were closely linked. Since the fifteenth century the development of woodcutting and of engraving on wood and copper, as of printing generally, was greatly stimulated by the revival of learning. In turn, the woodcutters, engravers and printers provided both the scientist and the artist with an immense new public.

LINE, AQUATINT AND LITHOGRAPH[2]

Woodcutting was the first method of duplicating designs and pictures. The wood is cut *with* the grain. Those parts of the design to appear white are hollowed out by a knife or gouge. The parts in relief hold the ink. The technique was originally used for printing fabrics, but was applied to paper as soon as this became readily available from about the middle of the fifteenth century. It was common for the artist to prepare his design on the face of the block, which was then cut by a craftsman, a very early example of the division of labour.

The woodcut lends itself to the production of broad, direct and powerful images, and the illustrations of mines and mining in Agricola's *De Re Metallica*, first published in 1556, are typical. Although in the hands of a master such as Albrecht Dürer (1471–1528) and his cutters a woodcut can display a wealth of detail and shading, the preparation of such elaborate blocks requires the highest skill and is extremely laborious. By the eighteenth century the woodcut had returned to the broad and coarse styles of the early Middle Ages and was used mainly to embellish the popular prints, broadsheets and chapbooks of the time. The technique petered out in the nineteenth century, except in the hands of a few masters such as Sir William Nicholson (1872–1949).

Wood engraving was introduced in the eighteenth century. It is essentially a line technique, using a graver *across* the grain of a block of boxwood. However, the raised portions of the block still carry the ink, and the lines cut in it print white. The art of wood engraving was perfected by Thomas Bewick (1753–1828). It was a great advance on the cruder woodcut, being simple, elegant, and cheap. The blocks could be cut relatively quickly. Though small they were durable and did not lose their quality, even after long printing runs. They could be used in combination with ordinary type to produce a page carrying both text and illustration. This made possible the production of cheap, illustrated periodicals, notably the *Penny Magazine* and the *Penny Encyclopaedia*, founded in 1832 and 1833 by that great popular educator, Charles Knight (1791–1873), and *Punch* and the *Illustrated London News*, founded in 1841 and 1842 respectively.

In a *metal* engraving, the metal itself is directly scored by the graver. The engraved lines carry the ink, while the surface of the plate prints white. In an etching, the metal plate is covered with a coating or waxes, gums and resins, called the etching ground. The artist draws on the coating with an etching needle, laying bare the metal beneath, which is then bitten by the application of acid.

Till well into the nineteenth century the metal plates used for engraving and etching were usually of copper, a soft metal from which it was impossible to take large numbers of prints without signs of wear. For this reason, copper engraving and etching could not be applied to the mass production of illustrated books. Engraving on steel was first practised in 1810 in America for the production of banknotes. Between 1815 and 1860 line engraving on steel almost completely superseded copper engraving for cheap book illustration.[3]

The process was often regarded with contempt, perhaps because of the very fact that it enabled reproductions of pictures and works of art to be circulated cheaply to rich and poor alike. This offended the exclusive attitudes of the well-to-do connoisseur, who was liable to dismiss steel engravings as being so coarse as to debase the whole art of engraving. Yet there can be no doubt that the process has a charm and delicacy of its own which is only now coming to be appreciated. In addition, the large, cheap editions of topographical works revealed views of English scenery to people previously cut off from enjoying them because of the relatively high prices of books illustrated in traditional ways. Just how large were some editions using the new process is apparent from the Address to *Westmoreland, Cumberland, Durham & Northumberland Illustrated*, published by Fisher, Son & Co. in 1832. (Reissued in an enlarged form, under the title *Picturesque Rambles in Westmoreland . . . etc*, in 1847.) Steel engravings reveal, states the Address, 'with Claude-like grace and effect . . . [the] . . . unequalled beauty of British Landscape', and have helped to produce 'a new era in the empire of taste'. So great a number of fine impressions can be taken 'that the treasures of art are sold at a price so trifling, as to place these beautiful productions within the reach of all who take an interest in them,—and who does not?' Fisher, Son & Co. claimed that they had spent on this work alone no less than £5,000 on artists and engravers, £2,750 on printing the steel plates, £2,750 on paper and paper duty, and £500 on the letterpress—£11,000 in all.

The *mezzotint* process of engraving, introduced in the second half of the seventeenth century, consists of traversing the whole plate with a 'rocker' having a serrated edge, which causes a uniformly indented surface. A print from a plate treated thus would be uniformly black. The plate is then worked over with a 'scraper', the indentation being smoothed away in varying degree where the light portions are to appear. The *stipple* process, introduced in the middle of the eighteenth century, depends on both engraving and etching. The plate is covered with an etching ground which is then perforated to produce great numbers of small points which are etched to give tone. The *aquatint* was introduced in France by Jean Baptiste le Prince (1734–81), and first used in England in 1775. The process depends on etching the plate through a porous ground of powdered resin or asphaltum. The plate is immersed in acid, which is left to bite as deeply as is required for the lightest parts, which are varnished to protect them from further attack. The plate is returned again to the acid for further and deeper biting. The next lightest portions are then varnished, and the process is continued till the darkest portion is reached.

Mezzotint, stipple, aquatint, and a number of variants were devised in order to convey gradations in tone as well as line. Mezzotint, in particular, was applied to the reproduction of paintings and portraits, aquatint to topographical scenes and descriptive illustrations of all kinds. The first British book to be issued in aquatint was *Views in Aquatinta . . . in South Wales*, by Paul Sandby (1725–1809), published in 1776 and reproducing wash drawings made in that and the previous year.

The process of *lithography* was invented by Johann Aloys Senefelder (1771–1834), of Munich, apparently by accident. The principle is simple. A flat surface of fine-grained absorbent limestone is polished. The design is drawn directly on to the stone with a greasy crayon. The surface of the stone is wetted. The water is absorbed except by those parts of the surface touched by the crayon. The stone is next inked, the ink being retained by the parts touched by the crayon, but rejected by the rest. The paper is then pressed on to the surface, and picks up the image in reverse.

Senefelder's first lithographs date back to about 1800. He attempted to keep the process secret, but it was much pirated, though he did not publish an account of it till 1818. The publisher, Rudolf Ackermann (1746–1834) issued a translation in English in 1819 under the title, *A complete Course of Lithography*, and, with the lithographer, Charles Joseph Hullmandel (1789–1850), did much to popularize the process. It was particularly attractive, not only because it was cheap and the stones durable, but because the artist could work on the stone directly without the intervention of copyist-craftsmen. Lithography revolutionized the art of reproducing pictures and, from about 1830, drove out almost all other techniques except mezzotint for reproducing portraits and paintings, steel engravings for cheap topographical and other books in long runs, and wood engravings for illustrating both periodicals and books. All of them were finally superseded by the various photo-mechanical processes of reproduction.

ILLUSTRATIONS IN COLOUR

From the Middle Ages to the end of the nineteenth century woodcuts, engravings and lithographs were issued in enormous numbers, either as book illustrations or independently, many of them in black-and-white, and some coloured by hand. (The number originally issued in colour today appears exaggerated owing to the practice adopted by unscrupulous dealers of colouring up prints and engravings to enhance their value.) But the art of true printing in colour, which had long been the cherished dream of the illustrators and picture-makers, was much more difficult to master. Until Newton's analysis of the spectrum supplied the theoretical foundation of colour printing by means of multiple plates, the only feasible method of producing coloured prints on a commercial scale was to tint or 'stain' the individual sheets by hand. The practical significance of Newton's theory to printing did not escape Erasmus Darwin, who devotes a good deal of attention to the primary colours in Part 1 of *The Botanic Garden*. He indulges in prophetic fantasies even more far-seeing in Part II, where he discusses the relation of painting and music.[4] After pointing out that Newton had observed that 'the breadths of the seven primary colours in the Sun's image refracted by a prism are proportional to the seven musical notes of the gamut', he suggests that this idea should be taken a step further by producing 'a luminous music, consisting of successions or combinations of colours, analogues to a tune in respect to the proportions above mentioned. This might be performed by a strong light, made by means of Mr Argand's lamps[5], passing through coloured glasses, and falling on a defined part of a wall; with movable blinds before them, which might communicate with the keys of a Harpsicord; and thus produce at the same time visible and audible music in uniform with each other. The execution of this idea'—he adds—'is said by Mr Guyot to have been attempted by Father Castel[6] without much success'. Erasmus Darwin then touches on experiments by his son, Dr Robert Darwin[7], to assess the relative degrees of pleasure or pain produced by exposing the eye to different colours in succession. He suggests his inquiries should be taken a step forward: '. . . if visible music can be agreeably produced'—he argues—'it would be more easy to add sentiment to it by representations of groves and Cupids, and sleeping nymphs amid the changing colours, than is commonly done by the words of audible music.'

Although Erasmus Darwin thus dimly foresaw the coloured sound film of the present age, he was shrewd enough to appreciate what was practicable in his own time, and did not pursue this tempting theme. Instead, he continued his note on Newton's observations on primary colours by stating that experiments based on them 'might much assist the copper-plate printers of calicoes and papers in colours; as three colours or more might be produced by two copper-plates. Thus suppose some yellow figures were put on by the first plate, and upon some parts of these yellow figures and on other parts of the ground blue was laid on by another copper-plate. The three colours of yellow, blue and green might be produced; as green leaves with yellow and blue flowers.'

Newton's theory had, in fact, already been applied on these lines to the art of printing many years before Darwin wrote *The Botanic Garden*. In 1719 James

69

Christopher le Blon (1667–1741), who had started experiments in 1704, took out an English patent for 'multiplying pictures and draughts by natural colours, with impression', using three plates for the primary colours and often a fourth for black. The process he used was mezzotint. In 1720 he formed a company in London for its exploitation. His invention failed as a commercial venture, just as Savery's steam engine had failed, and for the same reason: the special skill required to operate either invention was not yet sufficiently disseminated to enable them to be applied successfully on a commercial scale.[8] Instead, colour printing remained the jealously guarded secret of a small number of artists both on the Continent and in England. Not even Matthew Boulton, who in 1777–80 had entered into a partnership with the Birmingham engraver Francis Eginton (1737–1805) to exploit the latter's process of 'mechanical painting' with oil and water colours, could make the new technique a commercial success.[9] Indeed, printing in full colour in mezzotint or aquatint never became established on a large scale. In aquatint, however, it was common to use one plate for the design proper and another for a tint. The same principle was extended to lithography. In either case further colouring was often laid on by hand.

Colour printing on a large scale was not practised until well into the nineteenth century, when George Baxter (1806–67) introduced wood and steel engravings in colour, and Thomas de la Rue introduced chromolithography in 1832, using flat oil colours for the printing of playing cards. This process, of which the modern poster is a direct descendant, was first applied on a serious scale to book illustration by the architect Owen Jones (1809–1874) in *Plans, Elevation, Sections, and Details of the Alhambra*, published in two huge folio volumes in 1842 and 1845. It came into its own with the publications generated by the Great Exhibition of 1851.[10]

Until true colour printing had been mastered on a commercial scale the demand for coloured prints could only be met by colouring prints by hand. Printmaking came to be split up into three specialized but interdependent crafts: making the original drawing or 'design'; engraving; where required, tinting or staining.

During the first half of the eighteenth century line engravings formed the principal basis for making colour prints. Their style was perfectly adequate for the clean-cut architectural prospects and technical drawings of the period. But it was far less satisfactory for rendering the graded tones of painting or the chiaroscuro effects demanded by the growing taste for the picturesque. Mezzotint and aquatint were introduced primarily to meet this need. These enabled the whole tonal structure of a painting or drawing to be reproduced in sepia or black and white, so that only

70

the actual colours remained to be washed on by hand. The art of designing for the engravers was modified accordingly, and line drawings were gradually replaced by ink or sepia wash drawings in delicately graded tones of grey or brown.[11] Often enough the engravings from them were also issued in monochrome. For example, the early impressions of Paul Sandby's *Views . . . in South Wales* were in sepia. Colour was only applied to later, weak impressions of the plates. (Fig. 18).

The drawings after which coloured prints were to be made were tinted with a few light touches of transparent watercolour as a guide to the engravers and stainers. At first only parts of the engraving were tinted, the effect of the remainder depending entirely on monochrome tones. Though the tinting process was both subtle and important, it was often undertaken by children. Both Thomas Girtin (1775–1802) and Joseph Mallord William Turner (1775–1851) started their careers as engraver's colour-washers. Even in the last decade of the eighteenth century, when the whole surface of a drawing or engraving came to be coloured, the grey or sepia foundation remained until Girtin and Turner dispensed with it altogether in their designs and so created the technique of watercolour drawing as an independent art in its own right.[12]

While, therefore, the technique of designing for engravers developed from a subsidiary craft into the independent and essentially English art of watercolour drawing, the collaboration between designer, engraver and colour-washer produced a great tradition of coloured illustration that has never been surpassed. It flourished until about 1830, when it was rapidly replaced by the new techniques of lithography and steel engraving at a time when that jack-of-all-trades, the mill-wright, was being replaced by the mechanical engineer proper. The changes both in technique of illustration and in engineering are exemplified by the successive editions of a pamphlet by John Berkinshaw describing his epoch-making patent for making rails from wrought iron instead of cast iron. The first two editions of 1821 and 1822 are illustrated by a line engraving of a horse-drawn train of coal wagons; the third, 1824, edition has a line engraving of a train of coal wagons drawn by a Stephenson locomotive; the fourth, 1827, edition goes over to lithography with an illustration of a train on the Stockton and Darlington, drawn by a Stephenson locomotive and including a passenger coach among the coal wagons, all packed to bursting with passengers.

With the spread of literacy and the progressive development of publishing and printing, the art of illustration came to flourish at every level from the crudest woodcut to visually subtle mezzotints and aquatints. The print-sellers of the eighteenth century catered for every section of the people, from fairground purchasers of chapbooks illustrated by woodcuts to prosperous farmers and inn-keepers buying the coloured engravings published by Carington Bowles and other old-established City firms. Connoisseurs collected portfolios of expensive repro-ductions of paintings in line and mezzotint. In subject-matter the prints not only embraced anything from caricature and literary illustrations to portraits and historical paintings, but also entered a broad field ranging from straightforward technical illustration and factual record to imaginative compositions of great subtlety, a development of special significance in English art. For, like the docu-mentary film of the 1930s, many of them were inspired by an enthusiasm for science, technology and industry in the broadest sense. Just as the documentary film prepared the way for a distinctly British style of feature film in the Second World War, so the equivalent drawings and prints of the eighteenth century developed by clearly defined stages into the great English schools of art of the romantic era. Both involved 'the creative treatment of actuality', in John Grierson's vivid phrase.[13]

ENGINEERING DRAWINGS AS WORKS OF ART

In its development from the sixteenth to the mid-nineteenth century technical illustration passed, broadly speaking, through the same sequence of styles as the other graphic arts. The illustrations of Georg Agricola's *De Re Metallica* of 1556, with their mountain scenery and busy miners, are in the best manner of the German woodcutters. Although they often combine realistic and diagrammatic present-ation in the same design, both elements are so imaginatively fused that their inconsistency is not obtrusive. Agricola also introduced many modern conventions. On occasions he cut away the ground to show parts of engines otherwise invisible. Sometimes he placed an array of the parts in the foreground, 'exploded', or shown individually.[14]

On the other hand, the Italian technical illustrations of the sixteenth and seven-teenth centuries might well serve to exemplify the principles of mannerist design. In many of them, landscape or architectural backgrounds set off visual descriptions of intricate machines, themselves exercises in perspective, and often seen from a viewpoint higher than the background against which they stand out in relief. Pictures with such double or even triple stances enabled the artist to combine in one plane landscapes, cities and architectural effects stretching back to the horizon,

72

with a detailed appreciation of a machine or piece of engineering seen from a position chosen to give equal emphasis to all the details. The workers, engineers or admiring visitors, rarely absent from these illustrations, have the exaggerated muscles and heroic poses of the saints and heroes in contemporary paintings. Like them, they can trace their ancestory to the Sistine ceiling.

English technical drawings of the late seventeenth and early eighteenth centuries often show marked traces of this tradition, though the ambiguity of perspective is usually more subdued. Indeed, at this period the rules governing technical illustration are very similar to those governing topographical prospects in general, by which, 'the views . . . are formed on a curious union of distinct systems of perspective, having, it may be, three different horizons to one picture. Of the main object, usually a grand Elizabethan or Jacobean mansion standing amidst avenues and gardens laid out in the quaint geometrical style of the time, we have perhaps a strictly bird's-eye view; but the winged observer drops to a lower level to survey the distant landscape; while living objects in the foreground are seen as by a spectator on foot. . .'

'Notwithstanding the inconsistency of their arrangement, these representations convey a curious sense of reality. They are carefully, in many cases vigorously, engraved; and the whole scene being represented in full sunshine, the several objects are made to stand out solidly from the earth; and a certain unity is effected which prevents an uneducated eye from perceiving the incongruity of the drawing. They are full of matter; enlivened with countless figures and objects which, small as they are, tell their historic tale of the habits and manners of the time.'[15]

Topographers and technical illustrators alike adopted a formula designed to convey a clear picture of the main features of the subject, together with a generalized impression of its setting. They combined map-like projections with landscape vistas and picturesque details in the foreground. A typical example of a technical illustration of this type is the first known engraving of a Newcomen engine done in 1717 by Henry Beighton of *The Ladies Magazine* (Fig 6) whose enigma on the steam engine has already been quoted. Not only is the landscape seen from one viewpoint and the engine from another, but there is an ambiguity of style as well, the engine being partly realistic, partly diagrammatic. The side walls of the engine house have been removed to reveal the mechanism within. The engine-man sits in the shadow of the wall supporting the beam. An elegantly dressed gentleman watches the operation of the pump-rods outside. Flames play beneath the boiler and smoke rises from the chimney.

Although specialization in scientific and technical drawing or in topography tended to become the rule as the eighteenth century advanced, many designers and engravers remained equally proficient in either discipline. At the beginning of the eighteenth century, for example, Bernard Lens the Younger (1682–1740), the son of a Flemish engraver and draughtsman, engraved portraits and historical subjects after Antoine Coypel (1661–1772), Rubens, and other masters, while at the same time publishing engraved views of Bath and Bristol in 1718–19. Among his works in the Print Room of the British Museum are wash drawings of the waterworks and mill at the New River Head in Islington, and a proof of an engraving after him by John Sturt (1658–1730), of 'A Prospect and Section' of Rudyard's Eddystone Lighthouse, built of wood and first illuminated on 28 July 1708. Though the intention is technical, the engraving has highly decorated borders of mermen and the four winds of heaven, borrowed from contemporary cartographers. Indeed, the lighthouse is handled less as a diagram than as a map of a piece of architecture.

Sturt is best known as an engraver and letterer responsible for a Book of Common Prayer published in 1717, with pages engraved from silver plates, each with an historical vignette at the top. Similarly, Sutton Nicholls (*fl.* 1725), an architectural draughtsman and medallist, engraved the Newcomen engine at the York Buildings in 1725.

There is a primness about some of the early eighteenth-century technical illustrations, particularly Beighton's Newcomen engine, that is characteristic of its period and yet foreshadows a new style of technical illustration, found particularly in the plates of the semi-popular scientific dictionaries and encyclopaedias that were issued in increasing bulk throughout the eighteenth century in England as well as in France.[16] Here realistic and diagrammatic styles are no longer compounded but exhibited side by side. One half of such an illustration may contain a general view of a tilt-hammer with men at work, while the operative parts of the machinery and the tools used may be shown separately, just as, in many contemporary botanical illustrations, a general view of the plant is shown separately from the detail of stamen and petals. The artist gained freedom to deal with the work process or the workshop as a whole by concentrating the technical detail in accompanying drawings which are often diagrammatic. Sometimes the general account of a process was separated altogether from the technical detail, which might be relegated to a separate page. For example, when Jean Morand commissioned William Beilby to make drawings of the Newcastle wagonways for the first volume of his *L'Art d'exploiter les Mines de Charbon de Terre* (1768–79),

74

the general view of a coal wagon was given a page to itself (Fig. 23), supported by two further pages of technical detail of the permanent way. William Beilby was one of four Newcastle engravers, all brothers, Richard, William, Thomas, and Ralph, of whom the last was the master of Thomas Bewick (1753–1828). They undertook miscellaneous engraving of all kinds, not only preparing plates for printing invoices, billheads, trade cards and even bank notes, but also cutting seals, etching sword blades, and engraving door plates, coffin plates, clock faces and the like.[17] They were provincial craftsmen, which accounts for the old-fashioned style and mixed perspective of William Beilby's engraving of the wagon.

By the second half of the eighteenth century, under the stimulus of the rapid developments in technology, most of Beilby's contemporaries had adopted a freer style of technical illustration combining scientific lucidity with outstanding aesthetic qualities and appealing not merely to technicians but to the educated generally. This freer style appeared also in the later eighteenth century in the drawings by engineers of steam engines and other large machines. Its growth can be traced in the original drawings of John Smeaton (1724–92) preserved in six large volumes in the library of the Royal Society and entitled *Designs of the late John Smeaton F.R.S. made on Various Occasions in the course of his employment as a civil Engineer from the year* 1754–1790. One or two drawings dating from the 1740s are in the stilted manner of Henry Beighton, but Smeaton rapidly freed himself from that convention. From about 1765 onwards many of his drawings are marvels of execution and perfect examples of free design.

According to the engineer John Farey, Jun. (1790–1851), Smeaton was a man 'of laborious habits' who made all his drawings himself. When he became more established he employed a draughtsman. Even so, he continued to do the outline of all his drawings to scale. These were then fair copied by the draughtsmen, who included William Jessop (1745–1814), himself a distinguished railway and canal engineer, and Henry Eastham. One of Smeaton's daughters often 'assisted in the shadows and finishing in Indian ink [wash] which was very well executed.'[18]

Much of the work of James Watt and his assistants from the last quarter of the century, now preserved in the Birmingham Reference Library, shows the same fluency, as do the drawings prepared by William Jones in 1798 for a M.S. Report on mills by Thomas Telford (1757–1834) in the Library of the Institution of Civil Engineers. A typical example of the style is a wash drawing by Joseph Clement (1799–1844) of a rotative engine by Fenton & Co. of Leeds (Fig. 8). It was engraved in 1827 by George Gladwin for *The Steam Engine* by Thomas Tredgold (1788–1829).

This style of drawing continued to be employed in engineering works until the middle of the nineteenth century. The Goodrich Collection in the Science Museum contains many splendid examples from the first quarter of the century, while Messrs Hick, Hargreaves & Co. Ltd, of Bolton, still preserve a fine series of drawings of locomotives made by their founder, Benjamin Hick, in the 1830s and '40s. Such works influenced the illustrators of books of popular science and technology, as witness the large coloured engravings of a locomotive and a stationary engine by John Emslie (1813–75) in James Reynolds' *Diagrams of the Steam Engine*, published in 1848 (Plate II).

From the engine books and other records in Messrs Hick, Hargreaves' archives, it is plain that this elaborate finish was not used merely in the large drawings that might be shown to prospective customers, but also in the ordinary working drawings and records made for the engineers' own use. How intimately it was associated with the engineer's pride in his craftsmanship is shown by a sketchbook kept by John Nuttall, a smith born in 1818 who worked for various Lancashire engineering firms and who ended up in the 1860s as works manager for James Nasmyth. His book, entitled *Sketch Book Old Things from 1831 to 1850*, contains drawings of locomotive wheels, driving gear and valve mechanisms, with brief notes. One of these, accompanying a fine drawing of the smith's work required for a gab motion, runs: 'Making this kind of work I was in my glore.'[19]

The peculiar fascination of the large engineering drawings of the late eighteenth and early nineteenth centuries is that, unlike modern blueprints, they are not reduced to a formal system of lines and measurements. The objects illustrated are carefully shaded to give the impression of solid bodies. Yet they are isolated from their normal setting and shown, partly in their natural appearance, partly in section, as required by the need for elucidation. This was possible because the machines illustrated were still sufficiently simple to enable their construction to be explained with a measure of realism. Unfortunately, reproduction cannot convey a just impression of their aesthetic appeal, dependent for its effect both on their large scale and, often, on their strictly functional yet harmonious colouring—blue for wrought-iron, grey for cast-iron, yellow for brass, and so on. Although these old engines and machines appear before us as solid bodies in space, clean-cut and precise, the artist often could not resist the temptation to endow them with life by adding flames burning lustily beneath the boiler.

That such drawings, the purest expression of the rational element in the outlook of the time, are relieved by flashes of sentiment underlines the fact that the unity of thought and feeling was not yet broken. The process of specialization, of which the scientific and technical illustrations represent one side, still served to enrich and deepen a romantic outlook in which science and poetry were partners. This is shown even more dramatically by the sumptuous pictures in R. J. Thornton's *New Illustration of the Sexual System of Carolus von Linnaeus*, published in 1799–1807 and better known as *The Temple of Flora*. In his dedication, Thornton claimed that 'the Science of Botany, advanced as it is . . . by the glowing imagination of modern Poets . . . seemed, likewise, to have a claim to enlist the fine arts into her service'. Many of the best designers and engravers of the period collaborated in the production of the plates, in which huge plants, minutely detailed, appear with the precision of nightmare images before dreamy landscape background. Scientifically, this work represents one of the first attempts to relate plants to the environment peculiar to each.

TOPOGRAPHY

The topographical artist is an explorer who makes a visual record of his discoveries. When Erhart Reuwich, a Utrecht artist, accompanied Berhnard von Breydenbach, Canon of Mainz, to the Holy Land in 1483, he illustrated the latter's *Peregrinationes in Terram Sanctam* with vivid woodcuts recording the actual appearance of the cities they visited and their inhabitants. In doing so, he started one of the most fascinating chapters in the history of graphic illustration.[20]

In England the demand for topographical views developed step by step with the growing popularity of typographical literature, already mentioned in Chapter 2. At first the majority of topographical prints comprised architectural 'prospects' recording the appearance of both cities and gentlemen's country seats. But as the great feats of road- and canal-building broke down the isolation of rural Britain, bridges, aqueducts and other great engineering works came to occupy a progressively more important place in the range of subject-matter. And even early eighteenth-century topographical prints may be of interest as sources of industrial history. For example, in the vast series of views and prospects of cities produced between 1720 and 1753 by the brothers Samuel and Nathaniel Buck (1696–1779?), that of 'The South East Prospect of the City of Bath' (Fig. 3), engraved in 1734, includes the earliest known representation of an English railway other then the diagrams in Desaguliers' *Course of Experimental Philosophy*, published in the same year. The railway is shown leading to a wharf with a crane on the banks of the Avon. It brought stone blocks down the valley from Ralph Allen's quarries on Combe Down for transhipment across the river to John Wood's Bath. Daniel Defoe considered it almost the only thing worth looking at in the district. It is featured in every guide to the city, and is the subject of constant comment in the diaries and travel books of the day.[21] A local poetess, Mary Chandler (1687–1745), even worked it into her *Description of Bath*:[22]

> View the brown *Shadows* of yon pathless *Woods;*
> And craggy *Hills*, irregular and rude!
> Where Nature sports romantic; Hence is seen
> The *New Made Road*, and wonderful *Machine*,
> Self-moving downward from the Mountain's height,
> A *Rock* its Burden of a Mountain's Weight.

Another picture of Ralph Allen's railway appeared in 1752, engraved on copper in 1750 by Anthony Walker (1726–65), who worked for Boydell and designed vignettes and frontispieces for the book trade. In the background stands Ralph Allen's great mansion, Prior Park. In the foreground, running down the hill, is the railway with flat trucks loaded with blocks of stone, watched by elegant ladies and gentlemen who have come out to inspect so marvellous an engine (Fig. 4).

Walker's engraving is a good example of the type of topographical prospect with multiple perspective. The style lingered on till almost the end of the century. As we have seen, there are traces of it in Beilby's engraving of the coal wagon, and also in 'A South Prospect or Perspective View of Stour Port' (Fig. 22), engraved by Peter Mazell (*fl.* 1770–1800) after James Sherriff in 1776. In the latter a tree in the foreground serves to plant the observer solidly on the earth, although the main works at the terminal of Brindley's Stafford and Worcestershire Canal are spread out before him in bird's-eye perspective.

In 1752 John Boydell (1719–1804) devoted one of his engravings of the Thames to a view of the Chelsea waterworks and its pump driven by a Newcomen engine (Fig. 5). The son of a Derbyshire surveyor, Boydell walked to London. Apprenticed to William Henry Toms, the engraver (d. *c.* 1750), he became a prolific and skilled engraver of landscape and topography. In 1767 Boydell and his nephew, Josiah Boydell (1750–1817), started a publishing business, issuing topographical, portrait, and old master engravings on an enormous scale. Their most notable work was *The Shakespear Gallery*, to which thirty-three of the most celebrated artists of the day and two sculptors contributed designs. They also published the Coalbrookdale line engravings after George Robertson (1742–88) considered in Chapter 5

III DUNDAS AQUEDUCT (1805) after J C Nattes

below (Figs. 14, 15, 26) and the mezzotints after Joseph Wright (Figs. 31, 32, 33) discussed above. Altogether, the Boydells are known to have issued nearly 4,500 plates. They virtually created the English school of line engraving. The French Revolution destroyed their export trade and, like Valentine Green, they were almost ruined. They were able to survive only by obtaining leave to dispose of their property by a lottery. John Boydell was elected Lord Mayor of London in 1791, and served the city with great distinction.

That the artificial formula for 'prospects' was abandoned and replaced by straightforward views based on direct observation from a single viewpoint was mainly due to the influence of Paul Sandby[23] who, as we have already seen, introduced aquatint to England in 1776. Sandby was the leading topographical artist of the second half of the eighteenth century. Starting his career as a draughtsman attached to the military survey that opened up communication in the Scottish Highlands after the suppression of the Jacobite Rebellion in 1745–6, he combined the precision of the trained surveyor with a true feeling for landscape. The luminous quality of his drawings and their delicate colouring reveal also the influence of Canaletto (1697–1768), who worked in England from 1746 to 1753, and of Samuel Scott (c. 1700–75), whose serene and confident paintings along the banks of the Thames were among the first to reveal the changing architectural face of London.

When Paul Sandby left Scotland in 1751 he settled for a time with his brother, Thomas (1721–98), who had recently been appointed Deputy Ranger of Windsor Great Park, and who was also a distinguished draughtsman. But Paul was the more prolific of the two, and his influence on contemporary styles in the '70s and '80s was strong. His early aquatints emphasize the unity of his compositions in which buildings, landscapes and accessory figures are harmoniously combined. From the earlier tradition he took the bright sunlight effect and the crisp detail. With Paul Sandby, documentary recording of the landscape entered its classical phase, comparable to the clear-cut engineering drawings of the same period.

The demand for drawings from the new viewpoint was stimulated by Wedgwood and Bentley, who required no less than 1,282 views of country mansions and gardens for the table service the Empress Catherine of Russia commissioned them to make in 1773, the year she purchased 'An Iron Forge, viewed from without' from Joseph Wright. Finally, the great manufacturers themselves were inspired to emulate the gentry by designing their factories in the style of country houses. One such was the Soho Manufactory of Boulton and Watt. In an aquatint by Francis Eginton in Shaw's *History . . . of Staffordshire* (1798–1801),[24] the buildings are shown standing in what appears to be a splendid park with cattle grazing on the banks of an ornamental lake which is, in fact, the mill pool in disguise. The industrial reference is played down almost to insignificance.

An exact parallel is the description of the same place by James Bisset (1760–1832) in his *A Poetic Survey round Birmingham*, published in Birmingham in 1800:

> On Yonder gentle slope, which shrubs adorn,
> Where grew, of late, 'rank weeds', gorse, ling, and thorn,
> Now pendant woods, and shady groves are seen,
> And nature there assumes a nobler mien.
> There verdant lawns, cool grots, and peaceful bow'rs,
> Luxuriant, now, are strew'd with sweetest flow'rs,
> Reflected by the lake, which spreads below,
> All Nature smiles around—there stands Soho!
> Soho!—Where *Genius* and the *Arts* preside,
> *Europa's* wonder and *Britannia's* pride . . .[25]

Equally, the artists of the day often introduced into their works of topography, architecture, and travel specimens of the great industrial and engineering monuments springing up all round them. Those who dedicated themselves to recording the ruins and ancient monuments of the past on occasions turned aside to extol the great undertakings of their own day that 'rivalled the noblest works of the Romans, when masters of the world, and the legendary tales even of Semiramis herself'. How literally Arthur Young's sentiment expresses the attitude of the artists becomes apparent when their works and those of the designers and engravers of the industrial prints are examined as a whole.

Samuel Scott's painting of the building of Westminster Bridge in 1748–9 is one of the first of a long series of pictures showing the great bridges of the eighteenth century in course of construction or completed. On a minor scale, Gideon Yates (*fl.* 1798–1837) produced an apparently inexhaustible flow of watercolours and a few canvases of bridges, starting with Rennie's aqueduct over the River Lune, which he must have executed in about 1798 (Fig. 37). Though full of charm, this sepia wash drawing is in the old-fashioned eighteenth-century style of artists like William Beilby and James Sheriff, with its mixed perspectives and the clumsy but engaging division of the picture into two by the central bastion of the aqueduct, the whole anchored firmly to the ground by the scraggy tree on the right. When Yates came to London, he seems to have confined himself almost exclusively to studies of the Thames bridges, developing for the purpose a cheerful, bustling, bright-coloured style in the fashionable idiom of the day.

John Claude Nattes, (c.1765–1822) found nothing incongruous in incorporating, in his brilliant folio of coloured aquatints of Bath, published in 1806, the Dundas Aqueduct built by Rennie to carry the Kennet and Avon Canal over the Avon valley near Limpley Stoke (Plate III). Edward Pugh (d. 1813) was responsible for the superb illustrations for *Cambria Depicta*, published posthumously in 1816, took the early railway viaduct at Risca in his stride (Fig. 39).

Of the many artists who painted Italian landscapes and monuments as well as industrial subjects, George Robertson (1742–88) made six striking paintings of Coalbrookdale which were engraved in line and are considered in the next chapter. The ruins of Persepolis, Babylon and other ancient sites in the Near East were drawn by Sir Robert Ker Porter (1777–1842), who astonished the public in 1800 by exhibiting a picture 120 feet long of the storming of Seringapatam. In 1809 he published *Travelling Sketches in Russia and Sweden*, which included a view of the Dannemora Iron Mine (Fig. 52). Thomas Allom (1804–72), a prolific topographical artist who worked extensively in Britain, Europe and the Near East, was the author of countless industrial illustrations in the 1830s and '40s. Of three families who distinguished themselves as illustrators or publishers of graceful volumes on the scenery, monuments and customs of the East, Daniel and William Orme (1766–1802; *fl.* 1797–1819) also executed a view of Brindley's aqueduct over the Mersey at Barton. William Daniell (1769–1837) who, with his brother, Samuel (1775–1811) and his uncle, Thomas Daniell (1749–1840), published many works on the Far East, also did a series of aquatints for *A Voyage Round Great Britain*, issued in eight volumes between 1814 and 1825. This great work contains many studies of harbours and other feats of engineering by Smeaton, Rennie, and Telford. It included, too, one of the earliest views of a steamship—Henry Bell's *Comet*, launched on the Clyde in 1811, and sketched by William Daniell in 1813 (Fig. 48). The brothers Daniell and Robert Havell (*fl.* early *c.* 19) aquatinted *The Costume of Yorkshire* (1813–14) (Figs. 44 and 62) for George Walker (1781–1856), and confirm, at the highest creative levels, the kinship between topography and scientific illustration. For the Havells were also the 'engravers, printers, and colourers' of the 435 matchless plates of Audubon's *Birds of America* published in 1827–30.

The same kind of combination of artistic, scientific, industrial, and even antiquarian interests is found in the exquisitely designed penny and halfpenny tokens that were issued in large numbers between 1786 and 1797, and again between 1810 and 1812 (Fig. 117).[26] With the exception of a few small issues minted in

London and one in Sheffield, all these coins were made in Birmingham, by Matthew Boulton and about fifteen smaller manufacturers, for industrial employers and tradesmen in all parts of the country, who issued them to their workmen and customers. They provide particularly revealing illustrations of middle-class taste in the provinces during the last decade of the eighteenth century. The Anglesea Copper Company, which started the fashion, struck two hundred and fifty tons of pennies and fifty tons of halfpence, or say nine million pennies and three-and-a-half million halfpennies. They chose the Ossianic Druid's head for their device. John Wilkinson of the Broseley Forge had his own portrait stamped in place of the King's head, and on the reverse either Vulcan or a view of one of his tilt-forges, so echoing the old conflict between classical and contemporary imagery. Ironworks, brassworks, woollens factories, mills, glasshouses, collieries, canals and iron bridges are all illustrated on tokens. Gothic churches, castles and ruins appear no less frequently. Sometimes the two interests are catered for, one on each side of the same coin. Portraits of Sir Isaac Newton, Adam Smith and Joseph Priestley, with a view of his laboratory equipment on the reverse, reflect an interest in science for which the tokens issued by the exhibitors of animals, shells, ethnological specimens and other 'natural and artificial curiosities' provide further evidence. In addition to the subjects that recur in topographical and scientific prints, the interest in politics expressed in contemporary caricatures is also reflected on some of the provincial coins, but on the whole with a greater bias towards the left. The faith of the English middle-class intellectuals in the perfectibility of human affairs through science and political reform was not yet clouded by doubt.

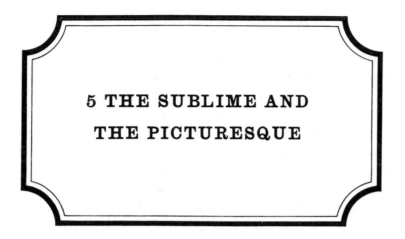

5 THE SUBLIME AND THE PICTURESQUE

Whatever is in any sort terrible, or is conversant about terrible objects, or operates in a manner analogous to terror, is a source of the sublime.[1]   EDMUND BURKE

A piece of Palladian architecture may be elegant to the last degree . . . Should we wish to give it picturesque beauty . . . we must beat down one half of it, deface the other, and throw the mutilated members around in heaps. In short, from a smooth *building we must turn it into a* rough *ruin.*[2]

WILLIAM GILPIN

THE DOMINANT element in the topographical drawing of the classical phase, represented by the work of Paul Sandby and his followers in the 1770s and '80s, is the factual record, lucid and reassuring. The artist's confident sense of discovery or of revelation is reflected in the clear, bright harmony of his designs. In the sublime and picturesque phases the emphasis shifts from discovery to contemplation, and to the poetic recording of the artist's emotions in face of the scene. Coal-pits find themselves sited on remote, desolate heaths. Quarries lie cavernous in the mountains. Mills are perched precariously on the steep banks of tumbling streams. Ironworks are silhouetted against the flare the molten metal casts on the night sky. These things sometimes evoke a menacing sense of power run to seed or out of control. They take on a cyclopean air. In the face of such manifestations of industry some artists turned their backs on the contemporary scene altogether and looked for comfort to an arcadian past or went into a kind of melancholy retreat.

These two divergent attitudes were emphasized by the aesthetic pronouncements

83

of Edmund Burke (1727–97) and of Sir Uvedale Price (1747–1829). Burke's *A Philosophical Enquiry into the Origin of our Ideas of the Sublime and Beautiful* first appeared in 1757. It was followed by a second, fuller edition in 1759, and there were twelve more editions before Burke's death. Price's *An Essay on the Picturesque* first appeared in 1794, followed also by a second, fuller edition in 1796. It was an attempt to formulate with precision theories of the picturesque promulgated by that indefatigable artist and traveller, the Rev. William Gilpin (1724–1804). His tours to various parts of Britain, illustrated by the author in aquatint, were published from 1781, a number of volumes being issued posthumously by the author's trustees.

Burke considers the sublime to be productive of the strongest emotion the mind is capable of feeling. It is associated with the infinitely great, and with gloom and obscurity. 'In nature dark, confused, uncertain images have a greater power on the fancy to form the grander passions than those have which are more clear and determinate.' Vacuity, darkness, solitude and silence evoke the sublime, as do glaring brightness, the sudden alternation of light and dark, the noise of vast cataracts, raging storms, thunder or artillery, and bitter tastes and 'intolerable stenches'. The poet of the sublime is, above all, Milton. 'The passions which belong to self-preservation'—Burke says elsewhere—'turn on pain and danger; they are simply painful when their causes immediately effect us; they are delightful when we have an idea of pain and danger, without being actually in such circumstances . . . What ever excites this delight, I call *sublime*.'

The sense of beauty, Burke considers, is inferior to the sublime. It is aroused by things that are small and smooth, that have a variety in their parts which, however, must not be angular, but must melt into each other, that are delicate, that have clear and bright colours, but not strong and glaring ones. Beauty is identified with the tenderness of love.

Many of the works considered here would be dismissed by Burke as outside the range of any pleasurable ideas at all. At the most they would arouse 'the first and simplest emotion . . . in the human mind', namely curiosity, 'the most superficial of all the affections'. The view that illustration and explanation, or clarity and lucidity, have aesthetic attributes in their own right would be incomprehensible to Burke and to most of his contemporaries.

However persuasively advanced by Burke, the sublime and the beautiful, even if accompanied by things evoking the inferior sense of curiosity, could not for long be regarded as sufficient to account for the whole range of aesthetic experience. So it is not suprising that Gilpin and Price found it necessary to add another aesthetic dimension—the picturesque, the forerunner of romanticism.[3]

Gilpin is imprecise and uses the word 'picturesque' in many ways and with various meanings, far beyond the range of his own elementary definition that it denotes 'such objects, as are proper subjects for painting'.[4] Nevertheless, it is possible from his works to piece together a broad account of what he believed. If Burke's 'beautiful' is neat and smooth, Gilpin's 'picturesque' is rough and rugged. Symmetry, balance, four-squareness are to be avoided. His advice to gardeners is to 'turn the lawn into a piece of broken ground: plant rugged oaks instead of flowering shrubs: break the edges of the walk: give it the rudeness of a road: mark it with wheel-tracks; and scatter around a few stones, and brushwood; in a word . . . make it *rough*; and you make it also *picturesque*.'[5]

When people are introduced into a landscape they have to be handled with caution. 'In a moral view'—writes Gilpin—'the industrious mechanic is a more pleasing object, than the loitering peasant. But in a picturesque light, it is otherwise. The arts of industry are rejected; and even idleness . . . adds dignity to a character. Thus the lazy cowherd resting on his pole; or the peasant lolling on a rock, may be allowed in the grandest scene . . .' as may 'figures in long, folding draperies; gypsies, banditti; and soldiers . . .' always provided that the last are in uniforms appropriately tattered.[6] Patriarchal wrinkles and a shabby beard are to be preferred to the 'sweet, dimpling charms' of youth. For the Arab steed he would substitute 'the worn-out cart-horse, the cow, the goat, or the ass.'[7]

According to Price, the picturesque scene should exclude not only the ploughed field and agricultural work but 'in general the works of man'. However, 'deformities' which he defines as 'something that did not originally belong to the subject in which it exists', such as 'the side of a smooth green hill torn by floods', quarries, gravel-pits, and 'large heaps of mould or stones', become converted to the picturesque by the softening of time and weather.[8]

For stage properties, Price admits not only castles and palaces but hovels, cottages, mills, and the ragged insides of old barns and stables. The extreme intricacy of the wheels and woodwork of a watermill, combined with moss, weather stains, and plants growing out of the joints in the walls, together give such a building great charm for a painter, provided only that it be old and battered.[9]

Theories such as these allowed the artist and his patrons to escape the more baleful aspects of industry by pretending it was already worn out. The rules of the picturesque allowed the intrusion of steam engines or mills or mines only if they were given an air of decrepitude or made to appear ancient and ruinous, and so harmless. For example, John Hassell (*fl.* 1789–1825), a topographical artist with a considerable interest in quarries, lime kilns and coal works, perhaps justified their frequent intrusion into his pictures as picturesque 'deformities' in Price's sense, and there is a splendid example of a pit-head by Paul Sandby (1725–1809) in the National Museum of Wales in Cardiff (Fig. 9).

Julius Caesar Ibbetson (1759–1817),[10] a charming and picturesque artist whose style shows affinities to that of Thomas Rowlandson (1756–1827), often handles industrial themes, for example 'The Coal Staithes at Landore', now in the Werner Collection, which was painted in 1792 and shows an early bullock-drawn railway, and 'Cyfarthfa Ironworks' (Fig. 16). In 1804 Stadler made an aquatint after a painting by John Augustus Atkinson (1775–*c*. 1833) of the Tanfield Arch over the Beckley Burn. Built by Ralph Wood in 1725, with a span of over 100 feet, and the first great railway viaduct in the world, it was disused by 1800, giving Atkinson the chance of according it the status of a classical monument (Fig. 24). In spite of a battery of boilers and a Watt engine, Peter le Cave (*fl.* 1780–1810) managed to give the Goscote Iron Foundry near Walsall an appearance of medieval decay (Fig. 7).

Gothic architecture, says Price, is generally considered as more picturesque, though less beautiful than Grecian, on the principle that a ruin is more picturesque than a new edifice.[11] From ideas such as these sprang the Gothic revival, the Victorian love of ruins, which imbued not only architects and landscape gardeners but even, on occasion, the engineers. Isambard Kingdom Brunel (1806–59), who laid out the Great Western Railway, decided to leave one of his tunnel mouths uncompleted, since, in its unfinished state, it greatly resembled a ruinous medieval gateway. To increase its picturesque effect he had ivy trained over it.[12]

COALBROOKDALE AND THE SUBLIME

The discovery of coal and ironstone in juxtaposition near Coalbrookdale in Shropshire made this area one of the growing points of the industrial revolution. It was here that Abraham Darby solved the problem of smelting iron ore with coke instead of charcoal. The products of his ironworks were shipped down the Severn by barge to Bristol and thence all over Britain and progressively outwards to Europe and the rest of the world.

As an industrial centre, Coalbrookdale also exercised an almost irresistible attraction over the artists of the English school of landscape drawing from its first beginnings to its culmination. This was largely due to the unique circumstance that the most modern and impressive industrial enterprise of the period was situated in an exceptionally romantic landscape. It thus became, as it were, the test place for studying the new relationship between men and nature created by large-scale industry.

The earliest views of Coalbrookdale, published in 1758, a year after the first edition of Burke on the Sublime, were a pair of engravings in line by Francis Vivares (1709–80) after Thomas Smith of Derby (d. 1767) and George Perry. They are titled 'A View of the Upper Works at Coalbrook Dale in the County of Salop' (Fig. 2) and 'The South West Prospect of Coalbrook Dale and the adjacent Country'. Smith earned the reputation of being one of the first English painters of English landscape, particularly in the Peak, the Yorkshire Dales and the Bristol Avon. He was the father of the celebrated engraver John Raphael Smith (1752–1812). Perry was an engineer.

Though in the 'View of the Upper Works' the factories at the bottom of the dale, where it joins the Severn, are deeply shaded, this serves mainly to set off the buildings and prim gardens on the distant hillside, which are sunlit in the early topographical manner. The smoke rising from the coke ovens on the river bank, not yet used to create an atmosphere of sublime obscurity, has the same cotton-wool-like aspect as the clumps of trees on the opposite slope. The dale, with the wagon carrying a huge casting down the winding road in the foreground, suggests the kind of hive of human industry in a smiling landscape the poets of the period loved to describe in heroic couplets. At this stage Coalbrookdale seemed beautiful rather than sublime.

Towards the end of the eighteenth century traffic from Coalbrookdale south across the Severn had become too great for easy handling by ferry. The Darbys decided to erect a single-span bridge and to build it out of iron. Designed by Thomas Farnolls Pritchard, a Shrewsbury architect, and cast at Abraham Darby's Madeley Iron Works, it was opened in 1779 and quickly became one of the wonders of the world. What appears to be the earliest view of it is a simple, unambitious water-colour drawing (Fig. 25). The bridge spans the paper symmetrically between masonry bastions on each side, and reveals a view of the river with a sailing barge approaching round a bend in the distance. From the tight, precise style of the drawing of the bridge, in sharp contrast to the river landscape, it looks as if one of the engineers may have been the artist. From it was evidently derived the crude woodcut in the British Museum Print Room, printed by J. Edmunds of Madeley, with a long caption which begins: 'This amazing Structure was cast at Coalbrook-Dale in the Year 1778, and erected in the Years 1779 & 1780.' It ends: 'The Parishes of Madeley and Benthal are the Atlasses that bear the enormous Load, one foot being placed in the first, the other in the last mention'd Parish; where it now stands an indisputable proof of the abilities of our Mechanics and Workmen.' The watercolour shows, correctly, an ornamental cast-iron rosette supporting a finial in the centre of the span. In the woodcut is substituted an imaginary plaque bearing the intertwined initials A.D., no doubt a piece of gratuitous flattery for Abraham Darby.

On 4 July 1782 the Coalbrookdale Company dedicated to George III a line engraving of the bridge by William Ellis (1747–1810) after Michael Angelo Rooker (1743–1801), Paul Sandby's pupil. Meticulously detailed and brightly lit, the bridge occupies the whole width of the design. The arch is exactly in the centre, revealing a glimpse of neat factory buildings and shipping in the middle distance. Wooded slopes close in from either side, like the wings in a stage set at the Haymarket Theatre, of which Rooker was the principal scene painter. As a commissioned work, it was no doubt designed to create as favourable an impression as possible, and to gloss over the less attractive elements of industrial Coalbrookdale. Such propagandist motives were to play an increasingly important part in the relation between art and industry.

As late as 1823 Matthew Dubourg (*fl.* 1786–1825) issued what was perhaps another commissioned work of the bridge, an aquatint for J. Taylor's Architectural Library which combines a romantic view of the bridge with details set down in the best manner of an engineering draughtsman. Dubourg was a hack artist and engraver of considerable skill who seemed able to turn his hand to anything. He exhibited miniatures at the Royal Academy in 1786, 1797 and 1808, and engraved landscapes after Claude. He illustrated innumerable volumes of classical archaeology and Gothic architecture, but found time to intersperse these works with others more closely related to engineering, such as an aquatint of the embankment at Port Madoc in 1810 (Fig. 38), another of Captain Sam Brown's Suspension Bridge near Berwick on Tweed (1823), the illustrations for T. G. Cummings' *Description of the Iron Bridges of Suspension now erecting over the Strait of Menai . . . and over the River Conway* (1824) and, according to Bénézit, a view of the Iron Pier at Brighton in the same year.

In contrast to the deliberately artificial accounts of artists like Rooker and Dubourg, the true impression Coalbrookdale made on a visitor is summed up in an account written by Arthur Young during a tour of Shropshire in the summer of 1776, eighteen years after the publication of Thomas Smith's engravings, and four years before Rooker's tidy, benign view. The Iron Bridge was not yet built and he had to cross the Severn by ferry to view 'the furnaces, forges, &c. with the vast bellows that give those roaring blasts, which make the whole edifice horribly sublime'. He expressed the discord between the sylvan and the industrial landscape in terms of Burke's opposition of beauty to the sublime:

'Coalbrook Dale itself'—he wrote—'is a very romantic spot, it is a winding glen between two immense hills which break into various forms, and all thickly covered with wood, forming the most beautiful sheets of hanging wood. Indeed too beautiful to be much in unison with that variety of horrors art has spread at the bottom: the noise of the forges, mills, &c. with all their vast machinery, the flames bursting from the furnaces with the burning of the coal and the smoak of the lime kilns, are altogether sublime, and would unite well with craggy and bare rocks, like St. Vincent's at Bristol.'[13]

Young's feelings are powerfully reinforced by a magnificent series of six engravings in line of the Severn near Madeley after oil paintings (which have now disappeared) by George Robertson (1724–88),[14] published by the Boydells on 1 February 1788. Here, indeed, the river enters the emotional climate of Burke and of Salvator Rosa, whose work it is likely Robertson had studied, during his youth, when he spent some time in Italy with William Beckford of Somerley, a cousin of Beckford of Fonthill and, like him, a wealthy West Indian planter. After their Italian tour they both visited Jamaica in about 1770, where Robertson painted a number of views, of which six were engraved and published by the Boydells, also in 1778. He returned to England and settled down as a landscape painter and drawing master, becoming associated with the movement for recording the medieval monuments of Britain. His own published work included views of London and Windsor Castle.

At Coalbrookdale, Robertson was as conscious as Young had been of the contrast between the romantic beauty of the valley and the sublime horrors 'art had spread at the bottom'. Unlike Rooker, he was not concerned with a cool pictorial account of the bridge in the full light of day. Instead, he seems to have divided his Coalbrookdale series into two groups of three, one devoted to the beauties, the other to the horrors of the Dale.

The principal picture in the first group (Fig. 26) dramatizes the bridge by relating

89

it to the surrounding landscape. Towering slopes covered with 'beautiful sheets of hanging wood' are dominant. The arch itself is moved out of the centre of the composition to the right, in line with the rocky bastion above and the horsemen on the shore below, and is darkly silhouetted against the foliage. Only the masonry of the left abutment is lit by the sun. This, with the bright rock above, the rough masonry on the right bank, the dark foreground, the river and the shaded slopes, produced a composition revealing the romantic beauty of the spot.

To reveal the horrors of the Dale, Robertson takes us, first, a short way down river to John Wilkinson's famous cannon foundry and boring mill at Broseley (Fig. 14). There the once green slopes are withered by the fumes that rise from the furnaces and engine-house, blotting out the sky. The valley echoes with those roaring blasts from the great bellows that seemed so horribly sublime to Arthur Young. In a view of a smelting-house at night (Fig. 15) a few figures, bent to their task, make the gloomy hall appear even vaster than it is. It is only partly lit by the glare of the molten metal that is pouring from the furnace in the background into grooves of sand on the floor. A cyclopic crane rears up its mighty arm in the centre of the design. And, to make the whole infernal scene appear by contrast even more sublime, the observer catches a glimpse of a serene landscape outside and a silver moon, as in the pictures of Joseph Wright. The third of the 'horror' pictures shows the mouth of a coal-pit, with its huge horse-driven wheel, placed on the very edge of a wood that is drawn in the romantic style of Rosa. These three pictures and the engravings after them were precursors of an apocalyptic view of industry which thenceforward made its appearance frequently, often in unlikely contexts. It culminated in John Martin's illustrations to the Bible and *Paradise Lost* in which he expressed, in a disguised way, emotions aroused in him by the contemporary industrial scene.

The full titles of the whole series, with their engravers, are:

Title	*Engraver*
A VIEW OF THE IRON BRIDGE, TAKEN FROM THE MADELEY SIDE OF THE RIVER SEVERN, NEAR COALBROOK DALE, IN THE COUNTY OF SALOP	James Fittler (1758–1835)
A VIEW OF LINCOLN HILL, WITH THE IRON BRIDGE IN THE DISTANCE, TAKEN FROM THE SIDE OF THE RIVER SEVERN	James Fittler
A VIEW OF THE IRON BRIDGE, IN COALBROOK DALE, SHROPSHIRE. TAKEN FROM THE BOTTOM OF LINCOLN HILL	Francis Chesham (1749–1806)

90

Title	*Engraver*
A VIEW OF THE MOUTH OF A COAL PIT NEAR BROSELEY, IN SHROPSHIRE	Francis Chesham
AN IRON WORK, FOR CASTING OF CANNON: AND A BOREING [*sic*] MILL, TAKEN FROM THE MADELEY SIDE OF THE RIVER SEVERN, SHROPSHIRE	Wilson Lowry, F.R.S. (1762–1824)
THE INSIDE OF A SMELTING HOUSE, AT BROSELEY, SHROPSHIRE	Wilson Lowry

Fittler and Chesham were miscellaneous engravers who appeared able to turn their hand to anything. Lowry was a much more distinguished man who specialized in mechanical and architectural subjects. A scientist as well as an artist, he devised drawing instruments, played a considerable part in the invention of the steel engraving and was elected F.R.S. in 1812. For twenty years his principal occupation was the preparation of the plates for Rees' Cyclopaedia. He also contributed to George Crabb's *Universal Technological Dictionary*, *The Philosophical Magazine*, and similar publications. He engraved the plates in James Murphy's *Plans of the Church of Batalha* and Peter Nicholson's *Architectural Dictionary*.

Some three years before the publication of the Robertson engravings, Erasmus Darwin's friend, Anna Seward (1747–1809), the 'Swan of Lichfield', had also turned her attention to Coalbrookdale in a vivid poem on the subject, written in about 1785:

> Scene of superfluous grace, and wasted bloom,
> O, violated COLEBROOK! in an hour,
> To beauty unpropitious and to song,
> The Genius of thy shades, by Plutus brib'd
> Amid thy grassy lanes, thy woodwild glens,
> Thy knolls and bubbling wells, thy rocks, and streams,
> Slumbers!—while tribes fuliginous invade
> The soft, romantic, consecrated scenes;
> Haunt of the wood-nymph, who with airy step,
> In times long vanish'd, through thy pathless groves
> Rang'd;—while the pearly-wristed Naiads lean'd,
> Braiding their light locks o'er thy crystal flood,
> Shadowy and smooth . . .
>   —Now we view
> Their fresh, their fragrant, and their silent reign
> Usurpt by Cyclops;—hear, in mingled tones,
> Shout their throng'd barge, their pondr'rous engines clang
> Through thy coy dales; while red the countless fires,
> With umber'd flames, bicker on all thy hills,

91

> Dark'ning the Summer's sun with columns large
> Of thick, sulphureous smoke, which spread, like palls,
> That screen the dead, upon the sylvan robe
> Of thy aspiring rocks; pollute thy gales,
> And stain thy glassy waters.—See, in troops,
> The dusk artificers, with brazen throats,
> Swarm on thy cliffs, and clamour in thy glens,
> Steepy and wild, ill suited to such guests.[15]

To Anna Seward the industries spread out at the bottom of the Coalbrook Dale were, clearly, the violation of pastoral beauty. Yet a long section of her poem, which contains yet another metrical description of the working of the steam engine, is devoted to a glowing account of Birmingham, 'the growing London of the Mercian realm' and the thriving centre of science and industry. 'While neighbouring cities waste the fleeting hours, careless of art and knowledge, and the smile of every Muse', Birmingham expands from month to month. The 'hedges, thickets, trees, upturn'd, disrooted' are changed into 'mortar'd piles, the streets elongated, and the statelier square'. Anna Seward welcomes this expansion, but laments that Birmingham does not draw 'her rattling stores, massy and dun', from regions other than 'sylvan Colebrook's winding vales'. Other cities have been less destructive of beauty. 'See'—she cries—

> Grim WOLVERHAMPTON lights her smouldering fires,
> And SHEFFIELD, smoke-involv'd; dim where she stands
> Circled by lofty mountains, which condense
> Her dark and spiral wreaths to drizzling rains,
> Frequent and sullied; as the neighbouring hills
> Ope their deep veins, and feed her cavern'd flames;
> While, to her dusky sister, Ketley yields,
> From her long-desolate, and livid breast,
> The ponderous metal. No aerial forms
> On Sheffield's arid moor, or Ketley's heath,
> E'er wove the floral crowns, or smiling stretch'd
> The shelly scepter . . .[16]

Chiding the genius of the place for allowing himself to be bribed by Plutus, Anna Seward takes the side of the nymphs and naiads driven from Coalbrookdale by Cyclops and laments the transformation of 'the destined rival of Tempean vales' into 'a gloomy Erebus'. Yet the engines and forges installed in the Dale served also to rouse in Anna Seward a sense of vastness and power. The gloomy halls and smoking furnaces produced that state which Burke praised in Milton's description of Death where 'all is dark, uncertain, confused, terrible, and sublime to the last degree'. Even the sulphurous fumes of which Anna Seward complained could be supposed to contribute to the sublimity of the scene. Does not Burke enumerate among the cause of that emotion excessive bitters and intolerable stenches? Anna Seward's attitude is essentially ambivalent. It is compounded of both horror and exhilaration. Her view of industrial development is essentially different from that expressed half a century later by, among other writers, Charles Dickens and Emile Zola.

IMAGES OF INDUSTRY

Though Coalbrookdale exercised a peculiar fascination over all who approached, other great industrial enterprises also had their attractions. For example, the iron bridge over the Wear at Sunderland, completed in 1796, commanded nearly as much attention as the one at Coalbrookdale. There is an uncoloured aquatint by J. Raffield after Robert Clarke showing the bridge under construction, with the title, 'East View of the Cast Iron Bridge over the River Wear . . . previous to the Centre being taken down' (Fig. 34). Clarke's drawing, with its old-fashioned sunlight effect and its meticulous detail which a more up-to-date artist would probably have avoided by 1796, is a naïve expression of local pride by a provincial draughtsman or, perhaps, engineer. Two years later Clarke and Raffield dedicated a companion print of the completed bridge to the Society for the Encouragement of Arts, Manufactures and Commerce. In this the sunlit masonry is contrasted with a dark, storm-swept sky. As late as 1816 Robert Surtees (1779–1834) was inspired to include a dramatized version of the Sunderland Bridge in his otherwise antiquarian *History and Antiquities . . . of Durham*, engraved by George Cooke (1781–1834) after a drawing by Edward Blore (1789–1879). Cooke later issued a volume of engravings of the building of the new London Bridge.

The opening of the Sunderland Bridge inspired great quantities of commemorative lustre bowls, jugs and mugs decorated by a transfer of the bridge. This agreeable fashion seems to have started with a mug showing the Iron Bridge at Coalbrookdale on one side and Buildwas Abbey on the other. Coalbrookdale and its bridge also occasionally appear as delicate hand-drawn designs on porcelain, perhaps by William Billingsley. The custom of celebrating important industrial enterprises by the issue of souvenirs of this kind extended well into the railway age, and, indeed, has not completely petered out even today.

Besides the bridges at Coalbrookdale and Sunderland, other great works called into existence by the revolution in transport inspired the artists of the period. The aqueduct at Barton (Fig. 20), carrying the Bridgewater Canal over the River Irwell, was an inspiration to innumerable artists and engravers. The great Marple Aqueduct carrying the Peak Forest Canal over the River Goyt in Cheshire, opened in 1794 (Fig. 36), inspired an aquatint engraved in 1803 by Francis Jukes (1746–1812), after a drawing by the Liverpool artist, Joseph Parry (1744–1826). It shows a pleasure barge, drawn by two horses and crowded with passengers, and is a reminder that at this time many canals maintained regular and profitable passenger services. Telford's massive aqueduct at Chirk, near Llangollen, is a subject selected by many artists, including Cotman. A beautiful watercolour drawing by him, in the Victoria and Albert Museum, demonstrates how profoundly his classical sense of design was stirred by the massive simplicity of that great engineering work.[17]

Among industrial operations, the workings of the copper-mines in the Parys Mountain on Anglesey, opened in 1768, seem to have had a profound effect on all the artists who visisted them. A typical example is a picturesque watercolour by Ibbetson, made in the late seventeen-eighties or early seventeen-nineties, and now in the National Museum of Wales (Fig. 12). François Louis Thomas Francia (1772–1839) made an altogether more dramatic, sublime study of the same scene (Plate IV). The latter plainly influenced a view of the Dannemora Iron Mine in Sweden, aquatinted by Joseph Constantine Stadler (*fl.*1780–1812) after a drawing by Sir Robert Ker Porter (1777–1842) for the latter's *Travelling Sketches in Russia and Sweden*, published in 1809 (Fig. 52). That the resemblance is not fortuitous is suggested by the fact that both Francia and Porter belonged to a society of young painters, founded in 1799 and known as the Brothers. Francia was the secretary, and the membership included also Thomas Girtin (1775–1802). Either Ibbetson's picture or that of Francia might serve to illustrate a passage from Wordsworth's 'An Evening Walk', composed in 1787–9.

> I love to mark the quarry's moving trains,
> Dwarf panniered steeds, and men, and numerous wains:
> Now busy all the enormous hive within,
> While Echo dallies with the various din!
> Some (hear you not their chisel's clinking sound?)
> Toil, small as pigmies, in the gulf profound;
> Some, dim between th'aereal cliffs descry'd,
> O'erwalk the viewless plank from side to side;
> Rocks that ceaseless ring
> Glad from their airy baskets hang and sing.[18]

No less dramatic are the illustrations of the tin- and copper-mines of Cornwall,

IV THE PARYS MINE IN ANGLESEA *F. L. T. Francia*

or the slate quarries of North Wales. Joseph Farington (1747–1821) published an engraving of the Curlaze Tin Mine in 1813. I. Tonkin of Penzance made a drawing of the Botallack Mine, near St Just, in 1822 (Fig. 13). Lithographed by George Scharf (1788–1860), a pioneer of the process who specialized in works of geological interest, it shows a dramatic view of one of the outposts of industry's assault on nature. Dwarfed by the rocks, the engines and surface works are perched precariously on the very edge of the ocean under which the mine galleries probed their cautious way. W. Crane of Chester opened his *Picturesque Scenery in North Wales* (1842) by a dramatic lithograph of the great Penrhyn slate quarries (Fig. 11).

Coal-mines represent another, constantly illustrated aspect of the early industrial scene. Paul Sandby's view of a horse-gin for winding coal (Fig. 9) has already been mentioned. A large oil painting by an unknown artist, now at the Walker Art Gallery at Liverpool, strikingly illustrates steam pumping and lifting gear at the top of a shaft of a coal-mine (Fig. 10). In contrast to the image of the busy hive the open workings for tin and copper suggested to Wordsworth, the mood evoked by many early views of coal-mines is often one of haunting loneliness. They echo the description of the coal-pits of Cannock Chase, 'situated on the extremity of an old forest, inhabited by large quantities of red deer', and remembered by Thomas Holcroft (1745–1809), the radical dramatist, when he dictated his childhood recollections on his death-bed. Holcroft was recalling his life in the 1750s, when he was not yet 9 years old and followed his father on his ceaseless travels through the North of England as a hardwareman, a collector and vendor of rags and a dealer in buckles, buttons, pewter spoons and pottery:

Towards Lichfield, on the right, lay Cannock heath and town; and adjoining to this heath, on the left, there were coal-pits situated in a remarkably heavy clay country . . . Desirous of employing his asses, yet averse to go himself (I know not for what reason) my father frequently sent me to these coal-pits to get a single ass loaded, and to drive him over the heath to Rugeley, there to find a customer for my coals. The article was so cheap, and so near, that the profits could be but very small, yet they were something. Had the weather been fine when I was sent on these errands, the task would not have been so difficult, nor the wonder so great; but at the time I was unfortunately sent there, I have a perfect recollection of deep ruts, of cattle, both asses and horses, unable to drag their legs through the clay, and of carts and wagons that were set fast in it . . . When anybody that could assist me happened to be near, I thought myself in luck; but if I was obliged to run from coal-pit to coal-pit, to request the man who turned the wheel to come and help me, the chance of compliance was little. I often got nothing but a surly curse and a denial; so till some unlooked-for accident brought me relief, there my loaded ass, sometimes heaving a groan at what he suffered, was obliged to stay.

The most remarkable instance of this kind of distress may perhaps deserve recounting.

One day, my ass had passed safely through the clay ruts and deep roads, and under my guidance had begun to ascend a hill we had to cross on Cannock heath on our way to Rugeley. The wind was very high; though while we were on low ground, I had never suspected its real force. But my apprehension began to increase with our ascent, and when on the summit of the hill . . . it blew gust after gust, too powerful for the loaded animal to resist, and down it came. Through life I have always had a strong sense of the grief and utter despair I then felt . . .[19]

PHILIP JAMES DE LOUTHERBOURG[20]

One painter, of Alsatian descent, who settled in England in 1771, was greatly to influence the rising generation of young artists at the end of the eighteenth century. This was Philip James de Loutherbourg (1740–1812). Born in Strasbourg, he was the son of a miniature painter who migrated to Paris when he was still a boy. His first teacher was Francesco Casanova (1727–1802), whose battle scenes, hunting pictures, sea pieces and landscapes were much admired in France. At first de Loutherbourg followed the style and themes of his master, sometimes painting also in the style of Nicholas Berchem (1620–83). He was made a member of the Paris Academy and court painter three years before he came to settle in London in 1771 with a letter of introduction to Garrick. Between 1773 and 1785 he not only designed stage sets for Garrick and Richard Brinsley Sheridan but made important contributions to the art of stage design and stage mechanics. His first identified work on the stage is the simulation of a burning palace in Garrick's *A Christmas Tale* which opened at Drury Lane just after Christmas 1773. Thereafter he became famous for ingenious effects suggestive of fire, sun and moonlight and volcanic eruptions. He appears to have been the first to introduce a landscape 'act-drop' or curtain, in January 1779, for *The Wonders of Derbyshire*, deriving his designs from sketches he had made from nature in that county, and the first to use flies and other devices to give artificial perspective. He also introduced 'the picturesque of sound'—thunder, guns, the rushing, lapping sound of waves, the patter of hail and rain and the whistling of winds. His designs for Sheridan's *The Critic*, first produced on 9 October 1779, evoked universal praise, particularly the elaborate presentation of the destruction of the Armada at the end. 'Scene changes to the sea' —Sheridan's stage instruction runs—'the fleets engage—the musick plays "Britons strike home"—Spanish fleet destroyed by fire-ships, &c.—English fleet advances—musick plays "Rule Britannia".—The procession of all the English rivers and their tributaries with their emblems, etc. begins with Handel's water musick . . .'[21]

De Loutherbourg's last production at Drury Lane was O'Keefe's *Omai; or*

Obesa Queen of the Sandwich Islands, a musical spectacle presented on 20 December 1785, set in the South Pacific and culminating with the apotheosis of Captain Cook. De Loutherbourg based his scenes on a series of drawings made by John Webber (1752–93) on Captain Cook's last voyage.

The same sense of movement, dramatic grouping and emotional atmosphere achieved by de Loutherbourg in his stage sets also distinguished the pictures he painted during this period, many of which were reproduced in aquatint. His success, evident from his election as A.R.A. in 1780 and R.A. in the following year, is not surprising. For he had acquired a mastery of dramatic presentation during his Continental baroque training, thoroughly opposed to the classical serenity of the still dominant school of English landscape, and exactly what was needed by the rising generation of artists seeking a more dynamic, emotional style of expression. For de Loutherbourg could move with ease from the sublime to the picturesque, and he seems to have been sensitive to the influences that inspired Gilpin to apply the scheme of the 'ideal day' that Milton used in *L'Allegro* and *Il Penseroso* to the study of colour in the changing light at different times of the day.

Gilpin's effect on the development of romantic painting can scarcely be exaggerated, and he expounded his ideas in several passages of his poem, *On Landscape Painting*, published in 1792. The following is an example:

> With studious eye examine next the arch
> Etherial; mark each floating cloud; its form
> Its varied colour; and what mass of shade
> It gives the scene below, pregnant with change
> Perpetual, from the morning's purple dawn,
> Till the last glimm'ring ray of russet eve.
> Mark how the sun-beam, steep'd in morning-dew,
> Beneath each jutting promontory flings
> A darker shade; while brighten'd with the ray
> Of sultry moon, not yet entirely quench'd,
> The evening-shadow less opaquely falls.[22]

In effect Gilpin anticipated the romantic theory of colour that Baudelaire later expressed with such incomparable magnificence in the third section of his essay on the Salon of 1846 in *Curiosités Esthétiques*:

'Cette grande symphonie du jour, qui est l'éternelle variation de la symphonie d'hier, cette succession de mélodies, ou la variété sort toujours de l'infini, cet hymne compliqué s'appelle la couleur'.[23]

That symphony de Loutherbourg had already attempted to reproduce as early as

97

February 1781, in an exhibition of moving pictures with sound effects, an idea on which he had been working for some twenty years. It was, in effect, a dramatic extension of the children's peepshow to adult entertainment. 'By adding progressive motion to accurate resemblance', he wrote in advertising the show, which he called the 'Eidophusikon', he hoped that a series of incidents might be produced which should display in a most lively manner those captivating scenes which inexhaustible Nature presents to our view at different periods and in different parts of the globe.[24]

Many years later, in 1823, the Eidophusikon was described enthusiastically and in detail by 'Ephraim Hardcastle', the pseudonym of W. H. Pyne, the figure painter.[25] The width of the opening to the stage was only 6 feet and its depth 8 feet. Yet, according to Pyne, 'such was the painter's knowledge of effect and scientific arrangement, and the scenes, which he described, were so completely illusive, that the space appeared to recede for many miles . . .'

The scenes were lighted from above by powerful 'Argands', oil lamps with an annular wick and glass chimney of the type still familiar. No doubt de Loutherbourg had run across them in Europe, for they were scarcely known in England till Boulton and Watt took them up three years later, in 1784. He mounted slips of coloured glass in front of the lamps. By manipulating these, singly and in combination, he was able to produce effects of 'cheerfulness sublimity or awfulness'. (As we have seen, eight years later, in *Loves of the Plants*, Erasmus Darwin suggested Argands might be used to produce 'luminous music', by making the keys of a harpsichord actuate coloured glasses in front of the light.)

De Loutherbourg endowed his scenes with movement and life by all kinds of ingenious mechanical and optical effects, including clouds painted in semi-transparent colours on linen strips, mounted on stretchers, and moved slowly upwards and diagonally, illuminated from behind.

The first performance of the Eidophusikon took place on 26 February 1781, with a scene entitled 'Aurora: or the Effects of the Dawn, with a View of London from Greenwich Park'. The whole city of London was displayed, from Chelsea to Poplar, with, beyond, the hills of Hampstead, Highgate and Harrow. In the middle distance lay the port of London, crowded with shipping, 'each mass of which being cut out in pasteboard'.

The heathy appearance of the foreground was constructed of cork, broken into the rugged and picturesque forms of a sand-pit, covered with minute mosses and lichens, producing a captivating effect, amounting indeed to reality.

When the curtain rose, the whole scene was seen to be enveloped in that mysterious light which is the precursor of day-break, so true to nature, that the imagination of the spectator sniffed the sweet breath of morn. A faint light appeared along the horizon; the scene assumed a vapourish tint of grey; presently a gleam of saffron, changing to the pure varieties that tinge the fleecy clouds that pass away in morning mist; the picture brightened by degrees; the sun appeared, gilding the tops of the trees and the projections of the lofty buildings, and burnishing the vanes on the cupolas; when the whole scene burst upon the eyes in the gorgeous splendour of a beauteous day.

There followed scenes of 'Noon', 'Sunset' and 'Moonlight', representing various romantic spots in the Mediterranean and separated by interludes during which Mrs Arne sang songs composed by Michael Arne, John Christian Bach and Dr Burney. The performance ended with 'The Conclusive Scene, a Storm at Sea, and Shipwreck'. Later seasons included English pastoral scenes, 'The Cataract of Niagara', 'The Relief of Gibraltar' and, most significant for the further development of romanticism, 'Satan arraying his Troops on the Bank of the Fiery Lake, with the raising of the Palace of Pandemonium'. In the last, legions of shrieking demons arose at the summons of their master, while a volcano began to erupt liquid fire to the accompaniment of thunder and lightning.

Eventually, de Loutherbourg sold the Eidophusikon, and it was burned down early in the next century. It led to that most popular of all entertainments, the Panorama, and is one of the direct ancestors of the cinema.[26]

Both in the Eidophusikon and in his paintings de Loutherbourg's sense of dramatic effect was not confined to the sublime in nature, but extended to his treatment of human beings and their works as well. His landscapes are really genre scenes with landscape backgrounds, for the mood of the whole is generally determined by some form of human activity. Hence the dramatic appeal of the new industries had a special fascination for him. His published industrial subjects include 'A View of a Blacklead Mine in Cumberland' (1787) and 'The Slate Mine' (1800). Inevitably he came to look at Coalbrookdale. At about the end of the eighteenth century he did a drawing of the Iron Works at Madeley, no doubt at the same time as a series of small Welsh industrial studies which have found their way to the British Museum with the Turner Bequest. The Madeley drawing was aquatinted by William Pickett (*fl.* 1792–1820) and coloured by John Clark, for inclusion in de Loutherbourg's *The Romantic and Picturesque Scenery of England and Wales*, published in 1805 and reissued in 1824 (Plate V). Pickett was a miscellaneous artist of no particular distinction, but it is unusual to record the name of the tinter or colourer of aquatints, and it is tempting to identify Clark with John Heaviside

Clark, known as Waterloo Clark for the drawings he made on the field of battle, and author of the illustrations for *A Practical Illustration of Gilpin's Day*, published in 1824.

De Loutherbourg was also fortunate not only in his English engravers but in finding those who had been trained, as he had been, in the Continental baroque tradition, and who could translate his intentions faithfully into aquatint. One of these was Maria Catharine Prestel (1747–94), who aquatinted the 'View of a Blacklead Mine'. The wife and pupil of Johann Amadeus Prestel (1739–1808), an accomplished engraver of Nuremberg, she left her husband in 1786 and settled in London, where she produced many engravings, including studies after Gainsborough, Hobbema, Wouverman and Casanova, and the aquatints for J. G. Wood's *Six Views in the Neighbourhood of Llangollen and Bala*, published in 1793. Another German *emigré* who reproduced de Loutherbourg's pictures, including 'The Slate Mine', was Joseph Stadler, one of the best aquatinters in London, where he worked from 1780 to 1812.

The aquatint of the Madeley Iron Works itself might well have been a study for an effect for the Eidophusikon. The chimneys from the blast furnaces, pouring out an evil reddish smoke into the falling light, are silhouetted against the red-yellow glare of the molten metal beyond, reflected in the still waters of the furnace pool. A man on a horse in the foreground is pulling a sledge along a track between piles of castings. Such artists as J. C. Ibbetson, W. H. Pyne and Samuel Prout (1784–1852) were greatly influenced by de Loutherbourg's method of building up his views round groups of figures following some characteristic occupation. Indeed, such groups of figures, some based on engravings of peasants and soldiers by de Loutherbourg himself, studies of cattle and other animals, snatches of landscape and architectural drawing, fill many pages of drawing books issued in profusion by early nineteenth-century drawing masters for the instruction of amateurs. Typical among these are *Rudiments of Landscape* (Prout, 1813), *Easy Lessons in Landscape Drawing*, (Prout, 1819), the delightful *Microcosm or, a Picturesque Delineation of the Arts, Agriculture, Manufactures, &c. of Great Britain* (Pyne, 1808), or the frankly titled *Etchings of Rustic Figures, for the Embelishment of* [other people's] *Landscape* (Pyne, 1815).

ROMANTICISM

The topographers of the late eighteenth century not only enriched the expressive range of the English landscape draughtsmen and engravers, but helped to clear the path for the mature romantic vision, expressing the spontaneous overflow of powerful feelings which take its origin from emotion recollected in tranquillity, and which Wordsworth considered to be the essence of poetry. For Wordsworth, in the final stage of the poetic process, 'the emotion is contemplated till, by a species of re-action, the tranquillity gradually disappears, and an emotion, kindred to that which before the subject of contemplation, is gradually produced, and does itself actually exist in the mind'.

The term 'romantic' is often used by historians of literature or art to identify some single and particular quality. Yet all attempts to give the term a single definition fail, for it covers many of the activities of an age of enormous and variegated range of achievement. Klingender's use of the term appears to derive, at least in part, from Christopher Hussey's view that romanticism can be regarded as coming into existence 'when an art shifts its appeal from the reason to the imagination . . . The romantic movement was an awakening of sensation . . . Thus'—Hussey argues—'the picturesque interregnum between classic and romantic art was necessary in order to enable the imagination to form the habit of feeling through the eyes.'[27] In this sense, romantic painting can be said to derive from a new definition of the picturesque evolved by Richard Payne Knight (1750–1824) in 1805. He held that the term should contain the idea of 'a blending and melting of objects together with a playful and airy lightness, and a sort of loose, sketchy indistinctness'.[28] For Klingender as for Hussey, romanticism contains the germs of what finally came to be termed 'impressionism.'

As with the earlier phases of landscape and topographical painting, the final transition from the picturesque and the sublime to the romantic can be illustrated by works inspired by the valley of the Severn and Coalbrookdale. For example, in the summer of 1802 John Sell Cotman (1782–1842) and Paul Sandby Munn (1773–1845), Paul Sandby's godson, set out on a tour of North Wales by way of Madeley and Coalbrookdale. It was on this trip that Cotman made the drawing, already mentioned, of Telford's Chirk aqueduct. Their steps have been traced by S. D. Kitson in his *Life of John Sell Cotman* (1937) by means of the sketches they made on the spot or the more elaborate drawings they carried out after their return. Included among them are a drawing by Munn of the iron bridge, and sketches by both artists of 'Bedlam Furnace', near Madeley, and of a 'Coal Shaft' on Lincoln Hill, overlooking the Dale. While Paul Sandby Munn's careful pencil drawing of the coal-pit in Mr Kitson's collection is still largely under the influence of his god-father, Cotman's two drawings show a fresh approach, differing alike from Sandby's cool, tranquil attitude to nature and from de Loutherbourg's baroque, theatrical method of composition. They are vivid impressions, built up of contrasted masses of light and shade, with a minimum of detail. Of the coloured sketch of the 'Coal Shaft' now in the Leeds Art Gallery, and probably identical with the drawing Cotman exhibited at Norwich in 1808, Kitson writes: 'The great wheel at the head of the shaft is thrown into relief by a white cloud behind it. The distance is dark and the foreground is littered with the waste implements of industry.' In the other drawing (Plate VI), 'a powerful vision of a stretch of blackened country-side',[29] the outline of the chimneys and the furnaces seem hung in the air, silhouetted against the searing white light of molten metal. A wisp of brown smoke drifts upwards across the low pale blue clouds and the bright yellow-orange of sunrise. The factory buildings themselves are dark smudges above the still waters of the furnace pond, reflecting dimly the light from both the furnace and the sky. To the right figures can be made out picking their way towards the factory, and two groups of trees on either side are a faint echo of the baroque stage convention. In these two drawings Cotman succeeded, with scarcely a trace of de Loutherbourg's artifice, in evoking the emotion engendered by the original scene. Finally, J. M. W. Turner (1775–1851)[30] made a painting of the lime kiln at Coalbrookdale (Fig. 27). The contrast between Turner's design and that of de Loutherbourg is striking. Both are lit up by the glare. Both show the river and a winding road with men and horses. But in de Loutherbourg's design everything is in movement. The straining horse, its driver and the billowing smoke, all are caught up in the spiral pattern of his composition. While in Turner's painting a profound peace reigns. It is night. The horses caught in the light of the kilns are at rest. The kilns themselves are hidden by a dark bank in the middle distance, but their presence is betrayed by the glow reflected from the foliage of the trees behind them.

But the image of the industrial revolution considered as a beneficent blend of past and present, idyllic contemplation and industrial performance, plenty combined with power, is perhaps best summed up in Turner's watercolour of Newcastle on Tyne (Plate VII) in the Turner Bequest, now in the British Museum Print Room.

Turner's attitude to industrial scenery in such pictures as this is defined in a passage in Ford Madox Brown's diary on 5 July 1856, when he was visiting the site of Cromwell's farm at St Ives: 'The river, with the picturesque old bridge . . . combine, with the church and a large factory shaft, to form a scene such as Turner has so often depicted with satisfaction to himself and others, of old England and new

England combined,'[31] In this respect the attitude both of Turner and of the French Impressionists, who shared his view, was opposed to the conception of art prevalent in Victorian England. 'There is M. Camille Pissarro, who has some very ardent admirers'—wrote P. G. Hamerton in *The Portfolio* in 1891—'and yet who is very foreign to me . . . It seems to me that he admits lines and masses that a stricter taste would alter or avoid, and that he includes objects that a more scrupulous artist would reject . . . [and] . . . has so little objection to ugly objects that in one of his pictures the tower of a distant cathedral is nearly obliterated by a long chimney and the smoke that issues from it, whilst there are other long chimneys close to the cathedral, just as they might present themselves in a photograph. By this needless degree of fidelity, M. Pissarro loses one of the great advantages of painting.'[32]

What were the reasons for this radical change of attitude of some of the great nineteenth-century artists to the real world around them?

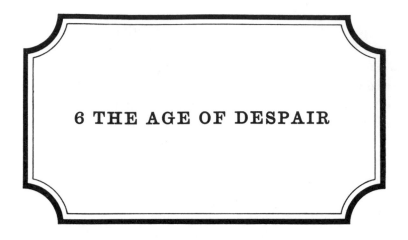

6 THE AGE OF DESPAIR

From Birmingham to Wolverhampton, a distance of thirteen miles, the country was curious and amusing; though not very pleasing to eyes, ears, or taste; for part of it seemed a sort of pandemonium on earth—a region of smoke and fire filling the whole area between earth and heaven; amongst which certain figures of human shape—if shape they had—were seen occasionally to glide from one cauldron of curling-flame to another. The eye could not descry any form or colour indicative of country—of the hues and aspect of nature, or anything human or divine. Although nearly mid-day, in summer, the sun and sky were obscured and discoloured; something like horses, men, women, and children occasionally seemed to move in the midst of the black and yellow smoke and flashes of fire; but were again lost in obscurity. A straggling boy or girl was at times seen in the road, with uncombed, uncut hair, unwashed skin, and naked limbs, which appeared as if smoke-dried, and encased with a compound of that element and soot . . . The surface of the earth is covered and loaded with its own entrails, which afford employment and livelihood for thousands of the human race.[1]

JOHN BRITTON

POETRY AND SCIENCE

'POETRY IS the breath and finer spirit of all knowledge; it is the impassioned expression which is in the countenance of all Science.' With these words, from the Preface to the 1802 edition of *Lyrical Ballads*, Wordsworth reasserted his faith in the innate kinship between poetry and science. But at the same time he noted a distinction which had hitherto been ignored. 'The knowledge both of the Poet and the Man of science is pleasure', but while the pleasure from scientific knowledge 'is a personal and individual acquisition, slow to come to us, and by no habitual and direct sympathy connecting us with our fellow-beings', the poet is under 'the necessity of giving immediate pleasure to a human Being possessed of that information which may be expected from him, not as a lawyer, a physician, a mariner, an astronomer, or a natural philosopher, but as a Man'. The poet 'converses with general nature', the man of science 'with those particular parts of nature which are the objects of his studies.'

Thus Wordsworth, writing in 1802, rejects the aim of 'enlisting the imagination under the banner of science', but, significantly enough, only for the time being, for the passage concludes:

Poetry is the first and last of all knowledge—it is as immortal as the heart of man. If the labours of Men of science should ever create any material revolution, direct or indirect, in our condition, and in the impressions which we habitually receive, the Poet will sleep then no more than at present; he will be ready to follow the steps of the Man of science, not only in those general indirect effects, but he will be at his side, carrying sensation into the midst of the objects of science itself. The remotest discoveries of the Chemist, the Botanist, or the Mineralogist, will be as proper objects of the Poet's art as any upon which it can be employed, if the time should ever come when these things shall be familiar to us, and the relations under which they are contemplated by the followers of these respective sciences shall be manifestly and palpably material to us as enjoying and suffering beings. If the time should ever come when what is now called science, thus familiarized to men, shall be ready to put on, as it were, a form of flesh and blood, the Poet will lend his divine spirit to aid the transfiguration, and will welcome the Being thus produced, as a dear and genuine inmate of the household of man.[2]

The passion with which Wordsworth here speaks of the future reunion between art and science is as remarkable as the pessimism of the twice-repeated 'if the time should ever come', but it is even more remarkable that these words were written in the middle of the greatest material revolution science had yet created in the condition of men.

THE NEW ECONOMY

The first thirty years of the nineteenth century were the critical period of the industrial revolution. The great inventions of the eighteenth century had developed more or less in isolation without transforming the character of the economy as a whole. Now all these changes coalesced, like metals in a crucible forming a new alloy, and the ancient timber economy was at last replaced by the age of coal and iron. In the first three decades of the nineteenth century the main engineering problems of the steam age were solved. In the next twenty years the new powers were triumphantly applied on an ever broader front. The Great Exhibition of 1851—the Crystal Palace—marks the culmination of the whole movement.

Rooted in the earth, the steam engine of the eighteenth century was massive, slow, and ponderous. The steam engine of the nineteenth century was light, swift,

105

and agile. Its birth was marked by the patent which a great engineering genius, Richard Trevithick (1771–1833), took out in 1802 for the 'Construction of Steam-engines; application thereof for driving carriages, and for other purposes'. Trevithick's engine was to transform the whole world. It used high-pressure steam; it was light and portable; it did away with the beam and harnessed the piston directly to its crank by a connecting rod; it could drive light machinery; above all, it could be mounted, with its boiler, on wheels and made to propel itself.[3]

On Monday, 13 February 1804, Trevithick put in motion the first railway locomotive in history on a plateway running from the Penydarren Ironworks near Merthyr Tydfil to the Glamorgan Canal, some ten miles down the valley. Anthony Hill, proprietor of the Plymouth Foundry, bet Samuel Homfray, the Penydarren ironmaster, five hundred guineas that the locomotive could not haul ten tons of iron the whole way. The train set out on February 21. The locomotive ground its way along the line at five miles an hour, hauling not only ten tons of iron but seventy people hanging on to the trucks as well. Hill lost his bet. The locomotive was a great mechanical success, but it was too heavy for the plateway and broke the cast-iron plates. It was soon withdrawn and used to work a hammer, though the railway itself remained in use for many years. It was superseded by the Taff Vale Railway, which followed the same route and was opened in 1841 (Fig. 47).

In 1805 a second locomotive was built to Trevithick's design at Gateshead, and it has been suggested that this may have stimulated George Stephenson (1781–1848) to start making his first locomotive for the Killingworth colliery which started work in 1814. In July 1808 Trevithick exhibited yet another locomotive, 'Catch me who can', on a circular course near Euston Square and wagered it to run twenty-four hours against any horse in the kingdom. The result is not known, but the engine ran for a few weeks till it broke a rail and overturned. This was his last attempt at steam locomotion.[4] His ideas, like those of Savery before him, were in advance of the technical resources of his time, and he did not have the patience to carry his great invention to the point of profitable exploitation. Other men reaped the benefits that were properly his.

Within a month of the Euston demonstration Trevithick started work on what was an almost impossible task, given the resources of his time—boring a tunnel under the Thames. Nevertheless, he succeeded in driving over 1,000 feet of heading out of a total of 1,200 before the work was stopped by an inundation. The directors of the enterprise refused to support Trevithick's plans to dam the water back and make the heading dry, and it was abandoned. Seventeen years later, in 1824, Mark

Isambard Brunel (1769–1849) started work on a second Thames Tunnel. Even with the help of equipment not available to Trevithick, it took nearly twenty years to complete and was not opened until 1843 (Fig. 54).[5] In 1816 Trevithick anticipated the era of the export of British capital goods by embarking with a shipment of Cornish pumping engines for Peru. Ten years of wild adventures as engineer, prospector, soldier of the national liberation movement, and explorer in Peru, Chile and Costa Rica culminated in a hazardous crossing, on foot, of the Isthmus of Nicaragua. In 1827 he returned penniless to his native Cornwall, where he was received in triumph. One of his last and unrealized projects was to design a column to celebrate the passing of the Reform Bill in 1832. One thousand feet high—more than five times the height of the Nelson Column—it was to be 'a gilded conical cast-iron monument', 100 feet in diameter at the base and 12 feet at the top. It would weigh a mere 6,000 tons and its cost, he thought, would be less than £80,000. His roving imagination, his boundless belief in the ability of man's genius to overcome all obstacles and solve all problems, combined with an eduring sense of frustration and pessimism, made him as much part of the age of Byron and Shelley as James Watt's complacent certainty that all was well made him part of the age of reason.

The Railway Age may be said to have started with the opening of the Liverpool and Manchester Railway in 1830, the Steamship Age with the regular trans-atlantic service in 1838 from Bristol to New York, inaugurated by Kingdom Isambard Brunel's s.s. *Great Western*. What Trevithick, John Blenkinsop (1783–1831), Matthew Murray (1756–1826), George Stephenson and some of the other early engineers did for the steam locomotive, William Symington (1763–1831), Robert Fulton (1765–1815) and Henry Bell (1767–1830) did for the marine engine. Bell launched his steamboat *Comet* on the Clyde in 1811 and started a steam ferry service between Glasgow and Greenock in 1821. William Daniell sketched her in 1813 for inclusion in his *Voyage round Great Britain* (Fig. 48).

The design and manufacture of high-pressure engines and boilers for loco-motives and ships and to drive machines of all kinds could only proceed if the design and manufacture of machine-tools kept pace with them. The result was that by 1830 most of the main types of machine-tool still in use to this day had been evolved by a brilliant generation of mechanical engineers. They included Henry Maudslay (1771–1831), Joseph Clement (1779–1844) and Joseph Bramah (1748–1814) of London, James Fox (1789–1859) of Derby, Matthew Murray of Leeds, and Richard Roberts (1789–1864) and Sir Joseph Whitworth (1803–87) of Manchester. James Nasmyth (1808–90), son of Alexander Nasmyth, the Edinburgh

107

painter and engineer, perfected his steam hammer in 1838, so completing the range of technical equipment required for the wholesale mechanization of industry, which could now proceed apace, step by step with the expansion of the engineering trade.[6] How closely the two processes were interlocked is evident from the rate at which power looms were introduced in England. They only became serviceable machines in 1803, and by 1820 there were still only 14,150 of them in England. But by 1829 the number had risen to 55,000. It reached 100,000 in 1833. By that time the capitalist factory-owner had emerged as the dominant figure in the economic life of Britain.[7]

The combined effects of these changes on the size of the population and the physical volume of production is summarized in the following table.

Population and Production in Great Britain 1800–01 to 1850–51

	Population (millions)[8]	Coal (output, million tons)[9]	Pig-iron (output, thousand tons)[10]	Cotton (imports, million lb)[11]
1801	10·6	10	191	56
1831	16·4	29	668	513
1851	21·0	57	2,700	872

THE MARCH OF INTELLECT

In spite of Wordsworth's view that the pleasure from scientific knowledge is something personal, only to be attained slowly and with difficulty, it is probably true that so broad a section of the English middle class has never again been as genuinely interested in science as in the early nineteenth century. The provincial philosophical societies multiplied rapidly, and the best of them became centres where the most important research of the period was undertaken. After the establishment of the Royal Institution in 1806 by that adventurous figure Benjamin Thompson, Count von Rumford (1753–1814), who was acute enough to recognize as early as 1798 that heat is motion, the middle-class enthusiasm for science even invaded the west end of London. People all over Britain followed John Dalton, Sir Humphry Davy and Michael Faraday (1791–1867) as they made their epoch-making advances in atomic theory and electro-chemistry. Thousands of amateur scientists formed an appreciative public for the astronomical discoveries of Sir William Herschel (1738–1822) and of his son, Sir John (1792–1871), or for the restatement of geology by Sir Charles Lyell (1797–1875). By 1830 the ground had been prepared for the two great achievements of nineteenth-century science, the theory of thermodynamics, and that of evolution by natural selection.

With the interest in research came a new enthusiasm for education. The more radical wing of the middle class provided an institution of higher learning for its own needs with the foundation, in 1828, of University College, London, and it supported the Lancastrian system of elementary education. Fearing the spread of radicalism, the Conservatives sponsored parallel enterprises in both these spheres under the guidance of the Church. At the same time Mechanics' Institutions were founded in many cities to cater for manual workers. From 1827 onwards the Societyfor the Diffusion of Useful Knowledge and its indefatigable publisher Charles Knight (1791–1873) issued an ever-growing list of illustrated textbooks, pamphlets and periodicals, covering the whole range of science and culture and including the *Penny Magazine*, the *Penny Cyclopaedia* and the *Library of Entertaining Knowledge*. Despite this enthusiasm for science and education, to which the artists and poets made their full contribution, it is of this period that Shelley (1792–1822) wrote in 1817: 'Methinks, those who now live have survived an age of despair.'

THE AGE OF DESPAIR

There was a palpable change in the mood of British intellectuals after 1798 which, according to Shelley, 'tainted the literature of the age with the hopelessness of the minds from which it flows'. One cause for this change was analysed with great acuteness by Shelley himself in his Preface to *The Revolt of Islam* (1817). 'The French Revolution', he writes:

may be considered as one of those manifestations of a general state of feeling among civilized mankind, produced by a defect of correspondence between the knowledge existing in society, and the improvement or gradual abolition of political institutions. The year 1788 may be assumed as the epoch of one of the most important crises produced by this feeling. The sympathies connected with that event extended to every bosom. The most generous and amiable natures were those which participated the most extensively in these sympathies. But such a degree of unmingled good was expected as it was impossible to realise.[12]

Hence, Shelley points out, the inevitable excesses of the Revolution and the 're-establishment of successive tyrannies in France' caused a revulsion in feeling that was so much the more terrible since what gave rise to it was so wholly unexpected. The despondency thus created was further deepened by the horrors of the twenty years of war that followed.

Wordsworth's ambivalent attitude towards science suggests, however, that the mood of despondency, of which Shelley was so conscious, may also have been fed from another source, less apparent, but perhaps deeper than political dissillusionment. It is worth inquiring, therefore, whether there was not only a defect of correspondence between the knowledge existing in society and the political changes that were taking place—to borrow Shelley's striking phrase—but also a dissonance between the knowledge existing in society and the *economic* changes of the time.

What those changes were, and how they affected the outlook of an amiable and enlightened member of the provincial middle class, is illustrated by the text and plates of *The Costume of Yorkshire*, by George Walker (1781–1856), published at Leeds. First issued in ten parts between August 1813 and June 1814, it was published as a single volume shortly afterwards. Walker was the grandson of a Nonconformist minister who had settled at Leeds in about 1748. His father had worked up a drysalter's business in that city so successfully that he was able to buy a country estate at Killingbeck near Seaford with the proceeds. His fifth son, George, was born at Killingbeck Hall in 1781. After an education at the school of the Rev. Charles Wellbeloved at York he was taken into his father's business. Preferring the study of natural history and the fine arts, he returned to the family estate, where he lived for the rest of his life, first in the Hall and later in Killingbeck Lodge. In that retreat among the Yorkshire moors George Walker led an active and pleasant life as a sportsman, naturalist, amateur painter, and supporter of the arts. His only adventure seems to have been a six-month tour through France, Switzerland and Italy with two friends in 1824. At Leeds he helped to run the 'Northern Society for the Encouragement of the Fine Arts' that held exhibitions of paintings from 1809 to 1824. When not watching birds on Killingbeck Lake or shooting grouse on Roggan Moor, 'he constantly made sketches of the scenery in Yorkshire . . . and so careful was he in the representation of figures in his drawings, that he first sketched a skeleton in the required position, and then put in the drapery.'[13]

The forty aquatints by R. and D. Havell after drawings by Walker give a vivid picture of the workers in the North of England towards the end of the Napoleonic period: colliers, labourers in an alum works, peat-cutters, fishermen and peasants appear alongside Sheffield cutlers, cloth-dressers or croppers with their assistant 'preemer-boys', and cloth-makers, the aristocrats of the woollen workers, carrying their finished cloth on packhorses to the Cloth Hall at Leeds. But there are also illustrations of paupers breaking stones and of a host of miscellaneous country

110

V IRON WORKS, COLEBROOK DALE (*1805*) *after de Loutherbourg*

occupations of the kind Wordsworth loved to romanticize: leech-finders, moor guides, hawkers, horse dealers, cranberry girls and whalebone-scrapers.

The book, taken as a whole, conveys a remarkable impression of the industrial revolution as a process. The most advanced stages of that revolution are represented by the factory children (Fig. 62) and by the coal-miner on his way home from the Middleton Colliery, near Leeds, with one of Blenkinsop's locomotives in the background (Fig. 44). However, users of such modern methods were still in a minority, and the mechanized equipment at Middleton Colliery is offset by pictures of primitive alum and ruddle pits, the source of iron oxide for dyes and paints, the latter a mere hole in the ground surmounted by a hand-winch served by a discharged soldier and a boy. The children at the machines in the cotton or worsted factories are offset by the handicraft workers in the woollen trade, and the majority of occupations seem scarcely to have been touched by mechanization. Nevertheless, it is evident from the ragged clothes and squalid hovels which even the cloth-dressers inhabit that the new forces of production are affecting the lives and conditions of all these people, regardless of whether or not they still cling to their old ways of work. This impression is confirmed by the text. The cloth-dressers, for example, are described in the following terms:

The Cloth-dressers are a numerous body in the West Riding of Yorkshire, many of them natives, and many from Ireland and the West of England. An able workman will earn great wages, and, if industrious and steady, is certain to make his way in the world; but it is to be lamented that comparatively few are found of this description. The majority are idle and dissolute, owing perhaps partly to the labourious nature of their occupation, which too often induces habits of drunkenness, and partly to their working in numbers together, a circumstance always injurious to morale. To the unsteady conduct of the Croppers, by which in times of urgent business much loss and inconvenience were suffered by their employers, and from the great improvements lately made in mechanicks, may be attributed the invention of the gig mills and shearing frames. This machinery effects with certainty and dispatch almost every operation of cloth-dressing, with very trifling manual assistance. The establishment of these mills excited considerable alarm amongst the Croppers, and was the alleged cause of the late unhappy disturbances. By the active vigilance of the magistrates, the prompt execution of some of the ringleaders, and the well-timed lenity shewn to others, tranquillity is now restored, and there no longer appears any disposition to outrage or even dissatisfaction.

MACHINE WRECKING

The 'late unhappy disturbances' are the Luddite riots which had thrown the whole of the manufacturing North into a state of alarm in 1811–12. In Yorkshire, where they had lasted longest and where the arrested leaders had only just been tried when Walker was writing, the workers most concerned were the cloth-dressers he is describing. Although, no doubt, he was sincere in his humanitarianism, he is divorced from the workers in thought and feeling, as from a hostile nation, and adopts the language of a military communiqué in reporting their actions. His point of view is strikingly different from that adopted some thirty-three years earlier by Josiah Wedgwood when confronted by a crowd of 500 workers who told him that 'they had been destroying some engines, & meant to serve them all so through the country'. It is evident from the spirited letters he wrote to Bentley describing the occasion in October 1779 that he regarded the machine-wreckers as deluded, but not as enemies. That he did not fear them is evident, for he not only asked the mob what they were about, but on another occasion allowed a coach carrying three ladies of his acquaintance to proceed into the very centre of the disturbances at Bolton. Later he expressed extreme concern at the news that soldiers had been sent into the district with orders to shoot into the crowd, instead of above their heads. 'This may . . . cause the least bloodshed in the end'—he writes—'but it is dreadful . . . I do not like to have the soldiery familiaris'd to spilling the blood of their countrymen & fellow citizens.'[14]

By the time Walker was writing the climate of opinion had changed radically. He now recognizes that the role of machinery in the newly developing industrial communities is that of a weapon with which to discipline the workers and subject them to the will of the employers. The more skilled the workers who resist the employers' claims to regulate their lives, the more anxious are the latter to speed up the process of mechanization. What, then, is George Walker's view of the conditions that machinery imposed upon the workers? His description of Factory Children (Fig. 62) is as follows:

A great part of the West Riding of Yorkshire abounds with cotton mills, cloth manu-factories, and other large buildings appropriated to trade, which are now usually known under the general, though perhaps vulgar, denomination of Factories. They are essentially requisite for the widely extended commerce of Britain, and furnish employment, food and raiment to thousands of poor industrious individuals. It is much, however, to be lamented that this is too frequently at the expense of health and morale. The little blue dirty group in the Plate are painted in their true colours; but where in their complexions would the painter discover the blooming carnations of youth, or the valetudinarian, in the surround-ing scenery, the pure air necessary for health? Many proprietors of factories have, much to their credit, remedied these evils by a strict attention to the morals, behaviour, and cleanliness of the children, and by adopting the very easy and effectual plan of consuming or burning the smoke.

What child labour involved is revealed also by Robert Owen (1771–1858), writing of the New Lanark mills (Fig. 29) of David Dale (1739–1806):

These children [obtained from workhouses and charities in Edinburgh] were to be fed, clothed, and educated; and these duties Mr Dale performed with the unwearied benevolence which it is well known he possessed . . . The benevolent proprietor spared no expense to give comfort to the poor children. The rooms provided for them were spacious, always clean, and well ventilated; the food was abundant . . . But to defray the expense of these well-devised arrangements, and to support the establishment generally, it was absolutely necessary that the children should be employed within the mills from six o'clock in the morning till seven in the evening, summer and winter; and after these hours their education commenced. The directors of the public charities . . . would not consent to send the children under their care to cotton mills, unless the children were received by the proprietors at the ages of six, seven, and eight. And Mr Dale was under the necessity of accepting them at these ages, or of stopping the manufactory which he had commenced.

It is not to be supposed that children so young could remain, with the intervals of meals only, from six in the morning until seven in the evening, in constant employment, on their feet, within cotton mills, and afterwards acquire much proficiency in education. And so it proved; for many of them became dwarfs in body and mind, and some of them were deformed . . . Thus Mr Dale's arrangements, and his kind solicitude for the comfort and happiness of these children, were rendered in their ultimate effect almost nugatory. They were hired by him and sent to be employed, and without their labour he could not support them . . .[15]

Indeed, without their labour he could not support himself. As Walker confirms so sanctimoniously, the factories and all they imply in terms of human misery 'are essentially requisite for the widely extended Commerce of Britain'. True, he says in the introduction to *The Costume of Yorkshire*, the eye will not be 'dazzled by the splendid colouring of oriental drapery; but it is to be hoped the British heart will be warmed by the reflection that most of the humble individuals here depicted in their simple and sometimes squalid garb, contribute essentially by their honest labours to the glory and prosperity of their country.' (Figs 62–5.)

MALTHUS AND THE POETS

George Walker was an amiable and enlightened dilettante, who spent his life on the open moors with his gun and dogs and sketchbooks. That he could look with such complacency on the evils impinging from all sides on his retreat was largely due to the persuasive powers of the Rev. Thomas Robert Malthus (1766–1834). Adam Smith, expressing the boundless confidence of his age in science, had claimed that, despite the contrast between rich and poor, even the meanest labourer was better provided in 'civilized' society than the mightiest prince in a 'savage' community. Yet the evils of the early factories and the general distress in the last years of the eighteenth century seemed to point to the opposite conclusion. Was this unexpected result due to some cause inherent in nature that Adam Smith had overlooked? Or was the paradox of advancing technique coupled with increasing poverty the result of a temporary maladjustment that might be remedied by political action? Malthus seized upon the moment to publish his *Essay on the Principle of Population* when the rising industrial capitalists needed some new theory of political economy to justify their wholesale adoption of industrial practices incompatible with the humanism of Adam Smith.

The *Essay* was first published in 1798, the year in which Canning launched his attack on Erasmus Darwin. A second greatly enlarged and rewritten edition appeared in 1803. Malthus demonstrated to the satisfaction of the propertied classes that misery and vice would always be the lot of the majority of mankind. However rapidly the power to produce the necessities of life increased, Malthus argued, the population was bound to increase faster still, by a natural law he deduced, like so many later apologists, from a mathematical figment. The wealth of the nation was shown to be conditioned by the poverty of most of its members. The theory of economic liberalism was turned into a defence of capital and of the exploitation it implied: 'A man who is born into a world already possessed', wrote Malthus, 'if he cannot get subsistence from his parents on whom he has a just demand, and if the society do not want his labour, has no claim of *right* to the smallest portion of food, and, in fact, has no business to be where he is. At nature's mighty feast there is no vacant cover for him.'[16]

By making the principle of Malthus the corner-stone of their social and economic theory and the main burden of their message to the working classes, the followers of Jeremy Bentham (1748–1832) vitiated the concept of the adult education movement of the early nineteenth century and withered it at its root. To the 'Scotch Feeloosofers' who tried to persuade him to join the Mechanics' Institution and learn about the blessings of machinery, the unemployed weaver might well have replied, in the words of Cobbett: 'An *Institution* to get the *Combination Law* repealed would, I fancy, be the most advantageous that you could, at this time, establish. The *expansion* of the *mind* is very well; but really, the thing which presses most, at this time, is, the getting of something to *expand the body* a little more: a little more *bread, bacon,* and *beer;* and, when these are secured, a little "expansion of the mind" may do *vary weele.*'[17]

114

The alliance that had grown up in the later eighteenth century between science and art had a common foundation of humanism. When political economy abandoned the humanist standpoint for the defence of property the link between science and art was broken. For the Malthusian perversion of science was as incompatible with the outlook of the artist as with that of the worker. Though ranged in two bitterly hostile camps on most other political issues, the poets protested as with one voice against Malthus. It was not only Shelley who expressed his contempt for the 'population principle' when he spoke of the 'sophisms . . . of Mr Malthus, calculated to lull the oppressors of mankind into a security of everlasting triumph',[18] or Byron, in his new eleventh commandment, ' "Thou shalt not marry", unless *well*.'[19] John Keats wrote, in September 1819: 'They spread a horrid superstition against all innovation and improvement. The present struggle in England of the people is to destroy this superstition. What has rous'd them to do it is their distresses—perhaps on this account the present distresses of this nation are a fortunate thing—tho' so horrid in their experience.'[20] William Blake too, voiced his indignation in *The Four Zoas*;

> Listen to the Words of Wisdom,
> So shall [you] govern over all; Let Moral Duty tune your tongue,
> But be your hearts harder than the nether millstone . . .
> Compell the poor to live upon a Crust of bread, by soft mild arts.
> Smile when they frown, frown when they smile; & when a man looks pale
> With labour & abstinence, say he looks healthy & happy;
> And when his children sicken, let them die; there are enough
> Born, even too many, & our Earth will be overrun
> Without these arts.[21]

One of Malthus' persistent opponents was William Hazlitt. His long and reasoned *Reply to the Essay on Population by the Rev. T. R. Malthus* was published in 1807. The *Edinburgh Review* gave it an unfavourable notice in 1810[22] which, Hazlitt complained, took the title of his essay 'as a pretence for making a formal eulogy' of Malthus' work. In 1823 Hazlitt had a controversy with de Quincey, who had taken up the cudgels for Malthus, and there is a further essay on Malthus in his *Spirit of the Age*, published in 1825.[23] But no less savage than the radical Hazlitt's attack on Malthus was that of the radical-turned-Tory Robert Southey. He wrote a review of the second edition of Malthus' *Essay* while he was staying with Coleridge at Keswick. The copy they read together is full of notes by both poets, and is now in the British Museum. On page 8, for example, Coleridge wrote: 'Quote this Paragraph, as the first sentence of your Review: & observe that this is the sum & substance of 8 pages—& that the whole work is written in the same Ratio, viz. 8 lines of sense & Substance to $8 \times 30 = 240$ lines of verbiage & senseless Repetition . . .' The review was published in 1803 in Arthur Aikin's *Annual Review and History of Literature*.[24]

Southey returned violently to the attack in The *Quarterly Review* for December 1812, calling Malthus' theory 'a technical sophism, and a physical assumption, as false in philosophy as pernicious in morals', and accusing him of placing the blame for man-made evils not on man but on the system of nature.[25]

Many years later, in 1820, Coleridge remarked to Thomas Allsop:

It is not uncommon for 100,000 *operatives* (mark this word, for words *in this sense* are things) to be put out of employment at once in the cotton districts . . . and, thrown upon parochial relief, are dependent upon hard-hearted taskmasters for food. The Malthusian doctrine would indeed afford a certain means of relief, if this were not a two-fold question. If, when you say to a man,—'You have no claim upon me; you have your allotted part to perform in the world, so have I. In a state of nature, indeed, had I food, I should offer you a share from sympathy, from humanity; but in this advanced and artificial state of society, I cannot afford you relief; *you must starve*. You came into the world when it could not sustain you.' What would be this man's answer? He would say,— 'You disclaim all connexion with me: I have no claims upon you? *I can then have no duties towards you,* and this pistol shall put me in possession of your wealth. You may leave a law behind you which shall hang me, but what man who saw assured starvation before him, ever feared hanging.' It is this accursed practice of ever considering *only* what seems *expedient* for the occasion, disjoined from all principle or enlarged systems of action, of never listening to the true and unerring impulses of our better natures, which has led the colder-hearted men to the study of political economy, which has turned our Parliament into a real committee of public safety. In it, is all power vested; and in a few years we shall either be governed by an aristocracy, or, what is still more likely, by a contemptible democratical oligarchy of glib economists, compared to which *the worst form of aristocracy would be a blessing*.[26]

The poets' general case against the destructive forces of industry was summarized most memorably by Wordsworth. In the eighth book of *The Excursion*, written in 1809–13 and published in 1814, the year in which *Costume of Yorkshire* appeared, he gives substance to his lament, published eleven years earlier, that science could not yet be 'a dear and genuine inmate in the household of man':

> I have lived to mark
> A new and unforseen creation rise
> From out the labours of a peaceful Land
> Wielding her potent enginery to frame
> And to produce, with appetite as keen
> As that of war, which rests not night or day,
> Industrious to destroy!

116

The simplicities of country life, 'the foot-path faintly marked, the horse-track wild'

> Have vanished—swallowed up by stately roads
> Easy and bold, that penetrate the gloom
> Of Britain's farthest glens. The Earth has lent
> Her waters, Air her breezes; and the sail
> Of traffic glides with ceaseless intercourse,
> Glistening along the low and woody dale;
> Or, in its progress, on the lofty side
> Of some bare hill, with wonder kenned from far.

There follows a view of a great industrial town that has swallowed up both village and countryside:

> Here a huge town, continuous and compact,
> Hiding the face of earth for leagues—and there,
> Where not a habitation stood before,
> Abodes of men irregularly massed
> Like trees in forests,—spread through the spacious tracts,
> O'er which the smoke of unremitting fires
> Hangs permanent, and plentiful as wreathes
> Of vapour glittering in the morning sun.[27]

But there is a darker side, as Wordsworth explains in a note:

In treating this subject, it was impossible not to recollect, with gratitude, the pleasing picture, which, in his Poem of the Fleece, the excellent and amiable Dyer has given of the influence of manufacturing industry upon the face of this Island. He wrote at a time when machinery was first beginning to be introduced, and his benevolent heart prompted him to augur from it nothing but good. Truth has compelled me to dwell upon the baneful effects arising out of an ill-regulated and excessive application of powers so admirable in themselves.[28]

Consequently the 'Wanderer' turns abruptly from his vision of the morning to paint a wild and lurid picture of what goes on beneath the soothing darkness:

> . . . an unnatural light
> Prepared for never-resting Labour's eyes
> Breaks from a many-windowed fabric huge;
> And at the appointed hour a bell is heard,
> Of harsher import than the curfew-knell
> That spake the Norman Conqueror's stern behest—
> A local summons to unceasing toil!
> Disgorged are now the ministers of day;
> And, as they issue from the illumined pile,
> A fresh band meets them, at the crowded door—
> And in the courts—and where the rumbling stream,

117

> That turns the multitude of dizzy wheels,
> Glares, like a troubled spirit, in its bed
> Among the rocks below. Men, maidens, youths,
> Mother and little children, boys and girls,
> Enter, and each the wonted task resumes
> Within this temple, where is offered up
> To Gain, the master-idol of the realm
> Perpetual sacrifice.[29]

From England, as from Thebes, Tyre, Palmyra and vanished Syracuse, 'the old domestic morals of the land' have fled,

> Ne'er to return! That birthright now is lost.
> Economists will tell you that the State
> Thrives by the forfeiture—unfeeling thought,
> And false as monstrous!

Even 'the short holiday of childhood' has been taken away from the workers. A young boy in industry 'is a slave to whom release comes not, and cannot come'. Behold him:

> His raiment, whitened o'er with cotton-flakes
> Or locks of wool, announces whence he comes.
> Creeping his gait and cowering, his lip pale,
> His respiration quick and audible;
> And scarcely could you fancy that a gleam
> Could break out from those languid eyes, or a blush
> Mantle upon his cheek. Is this the form,
> Is that the countenance, and such the port,
> Of no mean Being? One who should be clothed
> With dignity befitting his proud hope;
> Who, in his very childhood, should appear
> Sublime from present purity and joy!
> The limbs increase; but liberty of mind
> Is gone for ever . . .
> —Can hope look forward to a manhood raised
> On such foundations?[30]

This was the root of the 'age of despair', as Wordsworth saw it: arts, in themselves good, turned into fearful scourges of mankind, and science turned sophistry through attempting to justify the evil. That is the thought the 'Wanderer' sums up in his final discourse in the ninth book of *The Excursion*:

> My thoughts
> Were turned to evils that are new and chosen,
> A bondage lurking under shape of good,—
> Arts, in themselves beneficent and kind,

> But all too fondly followed and too far;—
> To victims, which the merciful can see
> Nor think that they are victims—turned to wrongs,
> By women, who have children of their own,
> Beheld without compassion, yea, with praise!
> I spake of mischief by the wise diffused
> With gladness, thinking that the more it spreads
> The healthier, the securer, we become;
> Delusion which a moment may destroy![31]

With this false philosophy, this vulgarized and prostituted science, the artist and the poet can have no truck. The 'Wanderer' 'cannot share the proud complacency' of those who worship the idol of Gain. The gay confidence and faith that science inspired only yesterday have vanished. But, like Shelley, Wordsworth too did not despair, for he saw the continued growth of true science beneath the perversion forced upon it by a false morality and evil institutions: 'Yet do I exult', he writes in an earlier passage in the eighth book:

> Casting reserve away, exult to see
> An intellectual mastery exercised
> O'er the blind elements; a purpose given,
> A perseverance fed; almost a soul
> Imparted—to brute matter, I rejoice,
> Measuring the force of those gigantic powers
> That, by the thinking mind, have been compelled
> To serve the will of feeble-bodied Man.
> For with the sense of admiration blends
> The animating hope that time may come
> When, strengthened, yet not dazzled, by the might
> Of this dominion over nature gained,
> Men of all lands shall exercise the same
> In due proportion of their country's need;
> Learning, though late, that all true glory rests,
> All praise, all safety, and all happiness,
> Upon the moral law . . .[32]

In *The Excursion* of 1814, therefore, the doubts Wordsworth had expressed in the Preface of 1802 ('if the time should ever come') have been replaced by the 'animating hope' that ultimately humanism will triumph and science be reconciled to art. Meanwhile, however, it is important to realize that in the capitalist setting of the early nineteenth century this ruthless disregard of all 'sentimental' values was for the time being a condition of the progress of science. The principle of competition, the 'struggle for existence' on which Malthus' theory is based, was

119

the overriding pattern which capitalist conditions imposed upon the thought of the time. The Malthusian theory of population was not only, in the words of Frederick Engels, 'the most open declaration of war of the bourgeoisie upon the proletariate',[33] it was also the foundation on which Ricardo completed the classical structure of political economy. Finally, Charles Darwin read Malthus' *Essay* 'for amusement' in October 1838. As de Beer has pointed out, its effect on him was to suggest 'the inexorable pressure exerted by selection in favour of the better adapted and against the less well adapted . . .' 'The view'—states de Beer—'that Darwin was led to the idea of natural selection by the social and economic conditions of Victorian England is devoid of foundation. There is irony in the fact that Malthus' aim was to prove that man was socially unimprovable, while Darwin used one point in his argument to show that all species can improve their adaptations.'[34]

JOHN MARTIN

The mood of despondency which sprang from the unexpected frustration of the hopes placed in science and political reform led to a revival of the eighteenth-century taste for the sublime. Horror assumed a new and startlingly topical meaning when, in 1818, Mary Wollstonecraft Shelley (1797–1851) created the symbol of 'Frankenstein' to express the fear that science might cease to be the slave of man and become instead his master and destroyer. The stresses and contradictions arising from the conflict of classes in a rapidly changing economy were dramatized as a struggle between 'man' and 'nature' or between rival forces in nature. Milton's Satan was readily accepted as the symbol of the new scientific forces in society, because he embodied intelligence, ingenuity and science in the cosmic struggle, and was at the same time a symbol of man's self-destruction and inevitable doom. Similarly, the ruins of the ancient East fascinated the romantics, not merely as memorials of a period when man's power over nature had attained a level which contemporary engineers were only just beginning to surpass, but also as emblems of the ephemeral, self-destroying nature of that power. Joseph Michael Gandy (1771–1843), the favourite perspective artist of Sir John Soane (1753–1837), even made a coloured drawing, now hanging in Sir John Soane's Museum, of what the Rotunda at the Bank of England would look like in ruins, giving it the title 'Architectural Ruins—A Vision'. Other artists and poets vied with each other in creating lurid visions of 'The Last Man'. It is as if science and art, before parting company, had joined in one last, wild, witches' sabbath. The great 'sea-dragons', reconstructed by the palæontologists, and illustrated by the artist-reformer-engineer John Martin (1789–1854),[35] the mysteries of desert and jungle, mines and aqueducts, the Pyramids, the ruins of Palmyra, the Caves of Elephanta, all added their quota to the bric-a-brac out of which the romantics of the Regency created a mirage of the time to come. As John Martin put it in his catalogue for the exhibition of his 'The Fall of Nineveh' in 1827:

The mighty cities of Nineveh and Babylon have passed away. The accounts of their greatness and splendour may have been exaggerated. But, where strict truth is not essential, the mind is content to find delight in the contemplation of the grand and the marvellous. Into the solemn visions of antiquity we look without demanding the clear daylight of truth. Seen through the mist of ages, the *great* becomes *gigantic*, the *wonderful* swells into the *sublime*.[36]

Seen in this mood, even the down-to-earth works of the contemporary engineers seemed dramatic or even sinister. 'It had more the effect of a scene in a pantomime than of anything in real life', Southey wrote of the entrance to the Caledonian Canal which he visited with Thomas Telford, its engineer, in 1819:

A panorama painted from this place would include the highest mountain in Great Britain, and its greatest work of art. That work is one of which the magnitude and importance become apparent, when considered in relation to natural objects. The Pyramids would appear insignificant in such a situation, for in them we should perceive only a vain attempt to vie with greater things. But here we see the powers of nature brought to act upon a great scale, in subservience to the purposes of men; one river created, another (and that a large mountain-stream) shouldered out of its place, and art and order assuming a character of sublimity. [37]

After a description of the great locks of the Caledonian Canal, Southey adds a vivid detail: 'Sometimes a beck is conducted under the canal, and passages called culverts serve as a roadway for men and beasts. We walked through one of these, just lofty enough for a man of my stature to pass through with his hat on. It had a very singular effect to see persons emerging from this dark, long, narrow vault.' It is as if Southey is describing, not his impressions of a great engineering work, but a passage from one of Martin's pictures. For 'the powers of nature brought to act upon a grand scale', as Southey puts it, is exactly what Martin was trying to achieve for more than forty years in the paintings that excited his contemporaries to ecstatic praise each time they were exhibited at the Royal Academy or the British Institution. It was his aim, he says in the Prospectus for *Illustrations of the Bible* (1831–5), to avail himself 'of all the objects afforded by inanimate nature, as well as by the passions and ingenuity of man, by bringing before the eye the vast and

121

magnificent edifices of the ancient world, its forests, wilds, interminable plains, its caverns and rocks and mountains, by freely employing the aid of its powerful and primitive elements of fire and water, which, when agitated by their Almighty Disposer (using the language of the poet) "Between the green sea and the azure vault sets roaring war".'[38]

With his apocalyptic views, it is not surprising that Martin executed a series of paintings illustrative of *Paradise Lost* and some of the more lurid episodes in the Old Testament, in many cases drawing his imagery from industry and overcoming anachronism by sheer intensity of feeling (Figs. 53, 55, 57). Their fame was spread far and wide by mezzotints, issued independently or incorporated in such works as *The Paradise Lost of Milton* (1827) and *Illustrations of the Bible* (1837).

Paradise Lost lent itself naturally to Martin's genius. The identification of Satan with the new powers of industry had already been made explicit in Blake's Milton:

> O Satan, my youngest born, art thou not Prince of the Starry Hosts
> And of the Wheels of Heaven, to turn the Mills day & night? . . .
> Get to thy Labours at the Mills & leave me to my wrath . . .
> Thy work is Eternal Death with Mills & Ovens and Cauldrons.[39]

John Martin was not, therefore, breaking new ground when he created his picture of Milton's hell from a jumble of images, among which must have been insistent the pit disasters he would have heard described again and again in his childhood at Haydon Bridge near Hexham in the Newcastle coalfield. For Martin had more than a merely casual knowledge of industry, and he retained an interest in mines all his life. Even as a boy in Newcastle he had drawn, at the age of 16, a plan for a railroad to carry coal from the pit-mouth to the screens for his brother, William, anti-Newtonian, mystic, prolific inventor and pamphleteer, who paraded the streets of Newcastle wearing a hat made out of a turtle shell bound in brass.[40] In 1835 John Martin submitted a 'Plan for Working and Ventilating Coal Mines' to the Select Committee on Accidents in Mines.

On occasion Martin did not hesitate to substitute Milton's images by others he felt more suited to his time. For example, in Book X of *Paradise Lost*, Milton describes in some detail the bridge built by Satan, Sin and Death from earth over chaos down to Hell—a 'mole immense wrought on over the foaming Deep high-arched, a bridge of length prodigious', 'a ridge of pendent rock over the vexed abyss'. 'With pins of adamant and chains they made all fast, too fast and durable.' But when Martin came to illustrate 'this new wondrous pontifice' he changed it into a kind of causeway within a tunnel (Fig. 55). This was no accidental aberration. At the time Martin was at work on the picture, Mark Isambard Brunel was driving the Thames Tunnel. The public were first admitted to its lime-washed, gas-lit workings on 27 February 1827, the year in which Martin's *Paradise Lost* was published. This is perhaps the reason why Martin substituted a tunnel for Milton's bridge—a view confirmed by the fact that his picture echoes contemporary illustrations of the tunnel. Though the bore was only partly completed in 1827, enough had been finished to give a clear impression of its final form (Fig. 54).

Although Martin's visions of Hell, his illustrations of the Old Testament, and his tortured, storm-wracked landscapes reflect the elements of doubt and terror in the complex mood of romanticism before 1830, they display at the same time a kind of exultation in the ever-increasing power of science. So completely did Martin express the mood of his time that he was widely regarded as the greatest English artist after Turner. Moreover, he was much more than a passive interpreter of sub-conscious feelings and impressions. The grandiose architectural fantasies, which form such a striking feature of many of his pictures, influenced the style of many of the greatest engineering works of his day. This was due not merely to his success as a painter but also to his persistent efforts to translate his visions into masonry and cast-iron. From 1827 onwards he became more and more interested in metropolitan improvements, devising innumerable plans to ensure the supply of pure water to London and the disposal of sewage, to reconstruct the bridges and embankments on both sides of the Thames, to improve the navigation of the river and to reorganize rail communication. Finally, he invited the public he hammered year by year with his visions of cosmic doom to support his *Metropolitan Sewage Manure Company*, which obtained an Act of Parliament in 1846 but which became a total failure only four years later.

Nevertheless, some of his earlier schemes had been treated with great respect. A large voluntary committee, under the chairmanship of Lord Euston and containing forty-four M.P.s, eighteen F.R.S.s, including Wheatstone and Faraday, and six R.A.s, including Turner, Etty and Eastlake, was established in 1836 to support his plan to supply London with water from the River Colne. Alas, he lacked all practical experience. Even though his plans often had sound and imaginative features, their importance today resides mainly in the influence they exerted on the aesthetic ideas of his friends. His architectural style strengthened the link between Oriental archaeology and Victorian engineering already established by the topographical draughtsmen of the previous generation. In 1818 or 1819 he was commissioned to prepare ten etchings of Sezincot House, the home which

Sir Charles Cockerell (1788–1863), a retired Indian official, was building for himself in Gloucestershire in imitation of the mausoleum of Hyder Ali Khan at Laulbaug. Thomas Daniell (1749–1840), uncle of William Daniell and author of *A Voyage Round Great Britain*, who had known Cockerell in India, designed the temples, grottoes, fountains and Buddhas dotted about the grounds of this bizarre but delightful house.[41]

Although Indian and Chinese elements contributed to Martin's architectural vision, the influence of Persian, Egyptian and Hellenistic monuments in the Near East was even greater. He and many of his contemporaries, architects and engineers alike, were strongly influenced by such works as the splendid coloured aquatints after Luigi Mayer (d. 1803), of whom very little appears to be known. He was commissioned to do a series of drawings in the Near East by Sir Robert Ainslie (1730–1812) when the latter was British Ambassador in Constantinople from 1776 to 1792. They were engraved in aquatint by Thomas Milton (1743–1827) and published in three splendid folios, *Views in Egypt* (1801), *Views in the Ottoman Empire* (1803), and *Views in Palestine* (1804). They were issued together in a single volume in 1804, with an extra collective title-page: *Views in Egypt, Palestine and other Parts of the Ottoman Empire.*

A remarkable instance of the interaction between architects and archaeologists, too marked for coincidence, is the correspondence between the view by Thomas Talbot Bury (1811–77) of the Moorish Arch which John Foster (1786–1846) designed to embellish the Liverpool terminus of the Liverpool and Manchester Railway (Fig. 69), and Mayer's view of the Gate of Grand Cairo (Fig. 70). There are further resemblances, nearly as striking (Figs. 71, 72).

Martin probably knew also the works of Louis François Cassas (1756–1827), particularly his *Voyage Pittoresque de la Syrie, de la Phénicie, de la Palestine, et de la Basse Egypte*, published in 1799 in association with the Report of the French Scientific Commission. Some of Cassas's reconstructions of ancient buildings, especially those of the temple court at the foot of the Great Pyramid, share the exaggerated dimensions and resounding detail of Martin's fantasies. But for justification of his celestial and infernal architectures Martin could also appeal directly to the authority of Mulciber himself, architect of Heaven, who had joined Satan's revolt and had been 'headlong sent with his industrious crew, to build in Hell'. There he had designed the great palace of Pandemonium:

> Built like a temple, where pilasters round
> Were set, and Doric pillars overlaid

> With golden architrave; nor did there want
> Cornice or frieze, with bossy sculptures graven:
> The roof was fretted gold. Not Babylon,
> Nor great Alcairo such magnificence
> Equalled in all their glories, to enshrine
> Belus or Sérapis their Gods; or seat
> Their Kings, when Egypt with Asyria strove
> In wealth and luxury. The ascending pile
> Stood fixed her stately height; and straight the doors,
> Opening their brazen folds, discover, wide,
> Within, her ample spaces o'er the smooth
> And level pavement: from the arched roof,
> Pendant by subtle magic, many a row
> Of starry lamps and blazing cressets, fed
> With naphtha and asphaltus, yielded light
> As from a sky.

Under Martin's hand, the Palace of Pandemonium became a great rotunda, prophetically reminiscent of the Albert Hall and illuminated not by cressets fed by naphtha and asphaltus but by coronas of flaring gas lights which Martin no doubt appropriated after a visit to the workings of the Thames Tunnel or borrowed from some cotton mill, where their use made possible the imposition of unlimited overtime, far into the night. Satan himself is enthroned on a great stone seat poised on top of a vast sphere and resembling the seat occupied by Abraham Lincoln in Daniel Chester French's statue in Potomac Park (Fig. 57).

Edge Hill Station (Fig. 67), the terminus of the Liverpool and Manchester Railway, might have been chosen as the site of one of Martin's more spectacular cataclysms. Set in a deep excavation in the solid rock, at one end three tunnel mouths entered the face of the cliff, leading apparently into the bowels of the earth. Two great chimney stacks, one on each side, tower above them, decorated like columns in honour of some long-dead Roman Emperor. At the other end the railway led out under a huge Moorish Arch (inspired, as we have seen, by Luigi Mayer's View of the Grand Gate of Cairo) into a yawning chasm through Olive Mount into a receding and apparently infinite perspective (Fig. 66). Martin's extravagant account of Belshazzar's Feast (Fig. 68), painted in 1821 and many times repeated in mezzotint, bears a striking resemblance to the great railway stations that were soon to spring up in most of the cities of the Western world. For a time Martin's monolithic style competed with the Gothic and the Tudor as inspiration for the design of many a railway station and bridge (Figs. 78, 79).

It is perhaps partly due to Martin's influence that Isambard Kingdom Brunel's proposal for the Clifton Suspension Bridge over the Avon Gorge was preferred to Telford's elaborate structure, supported by two huge Gothic towers built up from the banks of the river far below. Brunel's original design of 1829 shows the four pylons surmounted by reproductions of the sphinx and encased with cast-iron reliefs in the Egyptian style, illustrating the building of the bridge (Fig. 43). Drawings for these were actually submitted by Brunel's friend, the portrait painter John Calcott Horsley (1817–1903). Alas, they were never executed, and Brunel's designs were much simplified and whittled down before the bridge was finally completed in 1864, five years after his death.[42] (Martin and Brunel may well have been friends, for, in 1841, they travelled together on the footplate of a broad-gauge engine which, it is said, Brunel coaxed up to a speed of ninety miles an hour.)[43] Both Brunel and Robert Stephenson used the Egyptian style elsewhere, and with superb effect, the former for his great viaduct at Hanwell, opened in 1838 (Fig. 92), and the latter for his famous Britannia Tubular Bridge, opened in 1850 to carry the Chester and Holyhead Railway across the Menai Strait (Figs. 94, 95).

SATANIC MILLS

If John Martin gave Hell the image of industry (Figs. 52, 53), contemporary illustrators often gave industry the image of Hell. It looks as if they had a special preference for those industrial views which challenged such a comparison. It would have been difficult even for Martin to imagine a more infernal sight than W. Read's aquatint entitled 'Drawing the Retorts at the Great Gas Light Establishment, Brick Lane, London' (Fig. 61), the frontispiece of the 1821 volume of *The Monthly Magazine*. By now the cotton mills themselves have lost their pleasant country-house appearance and their classical proportions. Immense and forbidding, contemporary engravers depict them as fortress prisons, fitted equally for defence against armed assault from without as for the maintenance of a rigid discipline within. All that W. H. Pyne can find to say about the mills in Union Street, Manchester (Fig. 30), is that, in their external appearance, 'we remark little else than their great height.'[44]

It is significant, too, that now for the first time in their long history an artist selected coal-mines as a subject for systematic study. In 1839 Thomas H. Hair, a painter who exhibited at the Royal Academy and British Institution between 1838 and 1849, issued *Sketches of the Coal Mines in Northumberland & Durham*, a volume of etching after his own drawings, now preserved in the School of Mines,

126

VI BEDLAM FURNACE (*1802*) *J S Cotman*

Newcastle upon Tyne (Figs. 45, 106). They were reissued in 1844 in a volume containing additional plates with a text by M. Ross, the printer of the work and the editor of two books on the topography of Durham and Newcastle upon Tyne. Yet another edition, with a text much revised by W. Fordyce, was published in 1860.[45]

Although Hair's drawings are objective records of pit-heads, coal-staiths, railroads and underground workings, the extraordinary primitive-looking installations and their desolate surroundings have an air of forbidding gloom in conformity with the mood of the period. Their effect on a visitor from the south is illustrated in an account of the coalfields contained in *Visits to Remarkable Places* by the Nottingham druggist, William Howitt (1792–1879), another writer interested in both archaeology and industry. '. . . Here and there'—he wrote—

you saw careering over the plain, long trains of coal-waggons, without horses, or attendants, or any apparent cause of motion, but their own mad agency. They seemed, indeed, rather driven or dragged by unseen demons, for they were accompanied by the most comical whistlings and warblings, screamings and chucklings, imaginable. When you came up to one of these mad dragon trains, it was then only that you became aware . . . [that they] . . . were impelled by stationary engines . . . A huge rope running over . . . pulleys or rollers, all in busy motion on their axles, made the odd whistlings and warblings that were heard around . . . Amid all these uncouth sounds and sights, the voice of the cuckoo and the corn-crake came at intervals to assure me that I was still on the actual earth, and in the heart of spring, and not conjured into some land of insane wheels and machinery possessed by riotous spirits.

A paragraph earlier he had noted:

Wherever reared themselves those tall engine-houses, also towered aloft two vapoury columns, one of black smoke, and one near it of white steam. These neighbouring columns, like the ghosts of Ossian, slanted themselves in the wind, and wavered spectre-like in the air, each like some black demon with a pale spirit in his keeping, whom he was compelling to enormous labours; and such noises filled the air, as served to confirm the belief of it. Some of these engines were groaning, some puffing, some making the most unearthly sighings and yawnings, as if the very Gouls and Afrits of the Eastern stories, were set to stupendous labours, and were doing them in despair.[46]

Scott used the same image in his panegyric of James Watt in his introductory epistle to *The Monastery*, first published in 1820. There he speaks of that engineer as 'the man whose genius discovered the means of multiplying our national resources to a degree even perhaps beyond his own stupendous powers of calculation and combination, bringing the treasures of the abyss to the summit of the earth—giving the feeble arm of man the momentum of an Afrite—commanding

127

manufactures to arise, as the rod of the prophet produced water, in the desert, affording the means of dispensing with that time and tide which wait for no man, and of sailing without that wind which denied the commands and threats of Xerxes himself. . .'[47]

In his text to the 1844 edition of Hair's *Sketches*, Ross gives a portrait of the miners themselves. They went to work in checked flannel jacket, waistcoat and trousers, with a bottle slung across the shoulder and a satchel at their side.

At all hours, night and day, groups of men and boys are seen, dressed in this fashion, wending their way to their colliery . . . They descend the pit by means of a basket or 'corfe', or merely by swinging themselves on to a chain, suspended at the extreme end of the cordage, and are let down with inconceivable rapidity, by a steam-engine. Clean and orderly, they coolly precipitate themselves into a black, smoking, and bottomless-looking crater, where you would think it almost impossible human lungs could play, or blood dance through the heart. At nearly the same moment, you see others coming up, as jetty as the object of their search, drenched and tired. I have stood in a dark night, near the mouth of a pit, lighted by a suspended grate, filled with flaring coals, casting an unsteady but fierce reflection on the surrounding swarthy countenances: the pit emitting a smoke as dense as the chimney of a steam-engine; the men, with their sooty and grimed faces, glancing about their sparkling eyes, while the talking motion of their red lips disclosed rows of ivory; the steam-engines clanking and crashing, and the hissing from the huge boilers, making a din, only broken by the loud, mournful, and musical cry of the man stationed at the top of the pit 'shaft', calling down to his companions at the bottom. This, altogether, is a scene as wild and fearful as a painter or poet could wish to see.[48]

Substituting the sentimental for the sublime, it is difficult to believe that 'Pitmen, Playing at Quoits' (Plate I), by the Newcastle genre painter, Henry Perlee Parker (1795–1873), was not composed to illustrate this passage and it is certain that he rendered the pitmen's dress and tools with the greatest fidelity.

Howitt rounds off Ross's description by a vivid passage on the pitmen off duty:

In their dress they often affect to be gaudy, and are fond of clothes of flaring colours. Their holiday waistcoats, called by them posey jackets, are frequently of very curious patterns, displaying flowers of various dyes; and their stockings mostly of blue, purple, pink, or mixed colours. A great part of them have their hair very long, which on work-days is either tied in a queue, or rolled up in curls; but when dressed in their best attire, is commonly spread over their shoulders. Some of them wear two or three narrow ribbons round their hats, placed at equal distances, in which it is customary with them to insert one or more bunches of primroses or other flowers![49]

The sense of awe and terror which the middle-class visitor was likely to experience at a mine was not, however, entirely due to the strangeness of the scene, the wild appearance of the men or the danger of their work. The effect produced

128

was heightened by a growing consciousness that the miners, and indeed the industrial workers generally, were beginning to form a distinct, ever more numerous and more hostile nation. It is in scattered references through the literature of the time that one hears a faint echo of the tremendous struggle the Northumberland and Durham miners were waging in the 1820s and early '30s for the recognition of their union. This, for example, from South Hetton Colliery:

During the excitement of a *stick* [*sic*] in 1832, a pitman named Errington, who had consented to be bound, was found dead on the morning of Sunday 22 April, having been shot in the course of the night. Such was the savage feeling of the pitmen at this time, that the funeral of the murdered man, on passing their doors, was assailed with yells and execrations.

Or this from Waldridge Colliery, where the owners had imported lead-miners to break a strike:

On December 24, 1831, while 20 or 30 of these men were in the pit, above 1000 of the pitmen assembled in a riotous manner at the shaft, stopped the engine, necessarily kept going in order to pump out the water, and then threw large iron tubs, wooden cisterns, corves, and other articles down the shaft, by which those below were placed in the most imminent danger . . .[50]

With the growth of Chartism in the later 1830s and '40s the impression made by industry on the visiting writer from the south tended to be coloured more and more by his attitude to the social and political struggle. It is instructive to compare Dickens' description of Mr Pickwick's visit to Birmingham, which was written in 1836 when Chartism was still a peaceful movement led by moderate leaders, with his lurid account of the Black Country as seen by Little Nell in 1840.[51] This is what Mr Pickwick saw when he roused himself sufficiently to look out of the window of the coach:

The straggling cottages by the road-side, the dingy hue of every object visible, the murky atmosphere, the paths of cinders and brick dust, the deep red glow of the furnace fires in the distance, the volumes of dense smoke issuing heavily forth from high toppling chimneys, blackening and obscuring everything around; the glare of distant lights, the ponderous wagons which toiled along the road, laden with clashing rods of iron, or piled with heavy goods—all betokened their rapid approach to the great working town of Birmingham.
As they rattled through the narrow thoroughfares leading to the heart of the turmoil, the sights and sounds of earnest occupation struck more forcibly on the senses. The streets were thronged with working-people. The hum of labour resounded from every house; lights gleamed from the long casement windows in the attic stories, and the whirl of wheels and noise of machinery shook the trembling walls. The fires, whose lurid sullen

light had been visible for miles, blazed fiercely up in the great works and factories of the town. The din of hammers, the rushing of steam, and the dead heavy clanking of the engines, was the harsh music which arose from every quarter.

Four years later, after the defeat of the first great Charter agitation, when many of the Chartist leaders were still in jail and both sides were rallying their forces for the second round of the struggle, Dickens' own mental agitation expressed itself, not only by his choice of Anna Seward's 'grim Wolverhampton' for the scene where Little Nell and her grandfather were to suffer their final and worst tribulations, but also by an indictment, so charged with emotion as almost to cease to be prose:

A long suburb of red brick houses,—some with patches of garden-ground, where coal-dust and factory smoke darkened the shrinking leaves, and coarse rank flowers; and where the struggling vegetation sickened and sank under the hot breath of kiln and furnace, making them by its presence seem yet more blighting and unwholesome than in the town itself— a long, flat, straggling suburb passed, they came by slow degrees upon a cheerless region, where not a blade of grass was seen to grow; where not a bud put forth its promises in the spring; where nothing green could live but on the surface of the stagnant pools, which here and there lay idly sweltering by the black roadside.

. . . On every side, and as far as the eye could see into the heavy distance, tall chimneys, crowding on each other, and presenting that endless repetition of the same dull, ugly form, which is the horror of oppressive dreams, poured out their plague of smoke, obscured the light, and made foul the melancholy air. On mounds of ashes by the wayside, sheltered only by a few rough boards, or rotten pent-house roofs, strange engines spun and writhed like tortured creatures; clanking their iron chains, shrieking in their rapid whirl from time to time as though in torment unendurable, and making the ground tremble with their agonies. Dismantled houses here and there appeared, tottering to the earth, propped up by fragments of others that had fallen down, unroofed, windowless, blackened, desolate, but yet inhabited. Men, women, children, wan in their looks and ragged in attire, tended the engines, fed their tributary fires, begged upon the road, or scowled half-naked from the doorless houses. Then came more of the wrathful monsters, whose like they almost seemed to be in their wildness and their untamed air, screeching and turning round and round again; and still, before, behind, and to the right and left, was the same interminable perspective of brick towers, never ceasing in their black vomit, blasting all things living or inanimate, shutting out the face of day, and closing in on all these horrors with a dense dark cloud.

But night-time in this dreadful spot!—night, when the smoke changed to fire, when every chimney spirted up its flame; and places, that had been dark vaults all day, now shone red-hot, with figures moving to and fro within their blazing jaws, and calling to one another with hoarse cries—night, when the noise of every strange machine was aggravated by the darkness; when the people near them looked wilder and more savage; when bands of unemployed labourers paraded in the roads, or clustered by torchlight round their leaders, who told them in stern language of their wrongs, and urged them on to frightful cries and threats . . .

130

Then follows the famous description of the Chartists as maddened men, who

armed with sword and firebrand, spurning the tears and prayers of women who would restrain them, rushed forth on errands of terror and destruction, to work no ruin half so surely as their own—night, when carts came rumbling by, filled with rude coffins (for contagous disease and death had been busy with the living crops); . . . —night, when some called for bread, and some for drink to drown their cares; and some with tears, and some with staggering feet, and some with bloodshot eyes, went brooding home—night, which . . . brought with it no peace, nor quiet, nor signs of blessed sleep . . .

There were many illustrations by contemporary artists of the kind of scene Dickens described in this passage. As we have seen, they may have had their origin in George Robertson's tormented vision of industrial Coalbrookdale, as he saw it in 1788, just before his death. To his hand can be attributed also, with some conviction, a smouldering view of Richard Crawshay's ironworks at Nant-y-glo (Plate VIII). Hugging the banks of a sluggish polluted stream, furnaces and chimneys stand out against the red glare of molten iron with a harsh, unnatural vitality. Overhead a full moon shines through a sallow haze. Its yellow light, reflected from the water, picks out in silhouette a lonely figure standing on the bridge across the river. Though Robertson's vision is realistic it has undertones that anticipate the wilder apocalyptic vision of John Martin.

Later examples include Lymington Ironworks, on the Tyne (Fig. 60), engraved in 1832 by James Sands (*fl.* 1811–41) after Thomas Allom (1804–72). Into a book of lithographs designed to instruct students of drawing, Francis Nicholson (1753–1844) inserted without warning 'Explosion and Fire at Shiffnal' (Fig. 58), a study proving Dickens' account of the Black Country not exaggerated. Apart from this unexpected industrial reference, the rest of the illustrations deal with blasted trees, ruins, decaying watermills, dashing torrents, wild mountain landscapes and distant views of cities: in short, all the stock-in-trade of the seeker after the picturesque. However, in a view of Chester, seen through a vignette of trees, the tower of the cathedral is balanced by a factory chimney emitting a plume of black smoke which curls its way towards the centre of the composition.

Another industrial scene from South Wales is 'Rolling Mills, Merthyr Tydfil' (Fig. 17) by Thomas Hornor (*fl.* 1800–44), a surveyor who claimed membership of the Middle Temple. Between 1817 and 1819 he produced at least seven magnificently bound albums of *Views in South Wales* for the local gentry and a number of wealthy clients, including the Duke of Sutherland and the Earl of Jersey. These contained a series of romantic landscapes and topographical studies interspersed

131

with scenes of industry along the Vale of Neath. Some albums contain also views along the Valley of the Taff. The watercolours or wash drawings in each album are almost identical with each other, and Hornor must have prepared up to seven or eight copies of each without at any point losing his freedom of touch. Each is described on the back in a beautiful copper-plate hand.

When he came to Merthyr, Hornor was evidently shaken out of his conventional style by the searing glare of the iron passing to and fro under the rolls, and the interweaving shadows cast by the stanchions of the mill on the white-hot flare outside. Indeed, the shadows are as hard or harder than the finished iron bars themselves, stacked loosely in the foreground, soft and pliable under the night. Such an effect was scarcely to be seen again till the angularities of artists like C. R. W. Nevinson (1889–1946) and Paul Nash (1889–1946), seeking to capture the anguish and destruction of the first World War.

Merthyr, Hornor says on the back of one of the views, abounds with ingenious contrivance and wonderful mechanism,

which contrasting with the rude and sterile mountains realize those apparent contrarieties [sic] of luxury and leafless desolation. At night the view of the town is strikingly singular. Numbers of furnaces and truly volcanic accumulations of blazing cinders illuminate the vale, which combining with the incessant roar of the blasts, the clangour of ponderous hammers, the whirl of wheels, and the scarcely human aspect of the tall gaunt workmen seem to realise without too much aid from fancy many of our early fears.

Partly documentary, partly symbolic, the 'Rolling Mills' leads towards John Martin's works. Of these, perhaps the greatest was painted just before he died in 1854, called first 'The End of the World' and finally 'The Great Day of his Wrath' (Fig. 59). According to his son, Leopold, it was inspired by a journey through the Black Country in the dead of night: 'The glow of the furnaces, the red blaze of light, together with the liquid fire, seemed to his mind truly sublime and awful. He could not imagine anything more terrible even in the regions of everlasting punishment. All he had done or attempted in ideal painting fell far short, very far short, of the fearful sublimity.'[52] With this impression still in his mind, Martin conceived a prophetic composition, based, he said, on extracts from Revelations VI, a text that may be used fittingly to terminate a chapter bearing the title *The Age of Despair*:

And I beheld when he had opened the sixth seal, and, lo, there was a great earthquake; and the sun became black as sackcloth of hair, and the moon became as blood; and the stars of heaven fell unto the earth . . . And the heaven departed as a scroll when it is rolled together; and every mountain and island were moved out of their places. And the kings of the earth, and the great men, and the rich men, and the chief captains, and the mighty men, and every bondman, and every free man, hid themselves in the dens and in the rocks of the mountains; and said to the mountains and rocks, Fall on us, and hide us from the face of him that sitteth on the throne, and from the wrath of the Lamb: For the great day of his wrath is come; and who shall be able to stand?

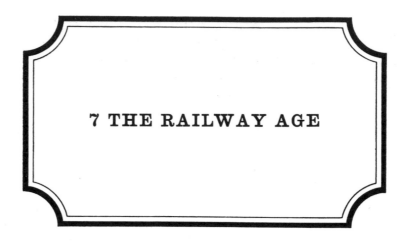

7 THE RAILWAY AGE

If the realities of our own age are not so propitious to the aspirations of the poet, they afford abundant matter for the study, the admiration, and delight of the philosopher. They abound with scientific wonders, they manifest the rapid march of intellect, they exhibit man competing with man, and nation with nation, in glorious rivalry for pre-eminence in art, science, and literature; in conquering prejudice; and advancing the 'end and aim' of creation—human happiness. Of all the promoters of civilisation, the Railway System of communication will be amongst the foremost in its effects, for it cannot fail to produce many and mighty changes in manufactures, in commerce, in trade, and in science . . .[1]

THE REV. EDWARD STANLEY

THE CROWLEYS, Wedgwood, Boulton, Oldknow, and the other pioneers of capitalist organization in the eighteenth century had aspired to be community-builders. Their outlook retained many elements of aristocratic paternalism. Even the hard-headed Arkwrights supported Oldknow long after his great mill at Marple and the community based on it had ceased to be profitable. During the romantic period this philanthropic paternalism culminated in Robert Owen's famous experiment at New Lanark, and in such boldly conceived enterprises as those of William Alexander Madocks (1773–1828). A younger son of a Welsh landowner and barrister, and a Fellow of All Souls, Madocks was radical Whig M.P. for Boston, Lincolnshire, from 1802 to 1820. On his father's death in 1773 he inherited a little money and land and bought a small estate near Dolgelly. Developing a passionate and all-enveloping interest in local economic and social affairs and the problems of regional communication, in 1789 he bought land near Penmorfa on the north side of the River Glasyn running into Cardigan Bay. Its

134

estuary, an expanse of marsh and quicksand, known as Traeth Mawr, 'the great sand', blocked communications to the whole of north-west Wales. Madocks' first act was to build a charming Regency house called Tany-yr-Allt in which, to the astonishment of his neighbours, he installed a water closet. At the same time, he began a reclamation scheme on the north side of Traeth Mawr by throwing an embankment of sand and sods across the mouth of an inlet. It was two miles long and varied in height from eleven to twenty feet. He put most of the reclaimed land down to permanent pasture and built a complete new town, Tremadoc, on part of it, with an Anglican church, a dissenting chapel, public buildings, and a manufactory for carding and fulling the woollen cloth for which the district was famous. He encouraged pig-rearing, laid out a rope-walk, and started the export of paving-stones. Meanwhile, an even more splendid project attracted his interest, the building of a great embankment or Cobb across the mouth of Traeth Mawr itself, designed to reclaim several thousand acres of waterlogged land and to carry the road from London across the estuary to Porthdinllaen, then an important harbour for the Dublin traffic.

Madocks' Traeth Mawr Bill received the Royal Assent in the middle of 1807. It called on him to build the embankment at his own expense. In return, the reclaimed land would be vested in him and his heirs, and he would receive one-fifth of the rent from the marshlands which would be drained. From the beginning the success of the scheme was threatened by the growing preference of the Government for Holyhead instead of Porthdinllaen as the port for Dublin. Nevertheless, Madocks plunged ahead, buoyed up by enthusiasm, but without the help of a professional engineer or even an office on the site. Appointing his estate agent as manager and his butler as clerk of the works, he began to import timber, gunpowder, bricks, glass, paint, and tools from London by the shipload. The Cobb had to withstand both the winter floods of the Glaslyn behind, and the full force of the Irish Sea in front, under gales from the south-west. No bank of sand could survive, so thousands of tons of stone had to be quarried at each end and carried to site by railway wagons running on iron tracks, cast at the Brymbo ironworks, in which Madocks had an interest, and laid on temporary timber piers built out into the Traeth from either bank. The war with France drained the district of labour, which became difficult to engage. Costs mounted. Money became tight, creditors unfriendly. But Madocks struggled imperturbably on, and the Cobb was opened with a flourish on 17 September 1811. It was just short of a mile long, thirty-six feet wide at the top and ninety feet wide at the base.

In the same year Boydell and Colnaghi issued an aquatint, plain, or in sepia and pale blue (Fig. 38), engraved by Matthew Dubourg after a drawing by Madocks' friend, Horace W. Billington (d. 1812). It shows the work as it appeared in the autumn of 1810. From the drawing, it looks as if neither designer nor engraver understood the principle of the railway point.

The original estimate for the Cobb had been £23,500. Its final cost exceeded £60,000. Madocks was almost penniless by the time it was finished. Creditors haunted the works, making inventories, nosing into his business. So it is a miracle that he survived at all when, in February 1812, a spring tide, lashed by a south-westerly gale, breached the Cobb in the centre and washed out about a hundred yards of it. A desperate attempt to make immediate repairs failed. Madocks' creditors in London got wind of the disaster and closed in on him. Although he was not made bankrupt and, as a Member of Parliament, he could not be put into a debtor's prison, Tany-yr-Allt and his personal property were seized and his estate sequestrated. Undeterred, he fought to raise more funds. He never lost the support of the small farmers round the Traeth, who helped him with men and horses. His efforts roused admiration all over the country.

One whose imagination was fired by the works at Traeth Mawr was Shelley and his sixteen-year-old wife, Harriet. They came to Tremadoc from Lynmouth and rented Tany-yr-Allt from one of Madocks' creditors. Though Shelley was at this time working on *Queen Mab*, he threw himself into Madocks' scheme with energy and enthusiasm, lending some of his own money towards the repair of the Cobb, even though he was himself deeply in debt, and helping to raise funds in Wales and London. Addressing a dinner party given to enlist support for Madocks at Beaumaris, the home of Lord Bulkeley, Lord Lieutenant of Wales, Shelley asked: 'How can anyone look upon that work and hesitate to join me when I here publicly pledge myself to spend the last shilling of my fortune, and devote the last breath of my life, to this great, this glorious cause?'[2] Though the Shelleys became disillusioned and left Tremadoc for Ireland in the spring of 1813, Madocks was able to raise enough money to close the gap by the autumn of 1814. He never lost courage or faith. As he said in a letter written just after the repairs were completed,

I . . . employ my mind incessantly in thinking how to compass those important objects necessary to complete the system of improvements in Snowdonia, any one of which wanting, the rest lose half their value. If I can only give them *birth, shape* and *substance* before I die, they will work their own way to posterity . . .[3]

136

Though Madocks' affairs became less tangled when he married a rich widow in 1818, and he regained both Tany-yr-Allt and some of his other property, he was never able to complete the drainage and reclamation of the land behind the embankment. Nevertheless, Tremadoc remains a model of late eighteenth-century town planning; Portmadoc, the other town Madocks founded, grew into a flourishing port for the Welsh slate industry; the Cobb still carries the Ffestiniog Railway and a road over Traeth Mawr. When Madocks died in 1826, on his way back to his beloved Wales from a European tour, he may have had the satisfaction of knowing that, as he had hoped, his schemes would work their way to posterity.

THE NEW MASTERS

The new masters thrown up by the industrial revolution in the first half of the nineteenth century were men of a different stamp from Owen and Madocks. Their origin and point of view are outlined in the words Elizabeth Gaskell put into the mouth of the 'Darkshire' mill-owner, John Thornton, in *North and South*. Thornton has called to have tea with the Hale family, who have settled in 'Milton-Northern', a Lancashire cotton town. Mr Hale is a Hampshire clergyman who has given up his living because he can no longer conform to the liturgy of the Church of England. He plans to set up as tutor to instruct not only the children of the mill-owners but the masters themselves, many of whom lack a formal education. He is accompanied by his wife and his daughter, Margaret.

Thornton, a self-made man who believes that the suffering everywhere apparent is but 'the natural punishment of dishonestly-enjoyed pleasure', is describing the growth of the cotton trade:

The whole machinery—I don't mean the wood and iron machinery now—of the cotton trade is so new that it is no wonder if it does not work well in every part all at once. Seventy years ago what was it? And now what is it not? Raw, crude materials came together; men of the same level, as regards education and station, took suddenly the different positions of masters and men, owing to the motherwit, as regards opportunities and probabilities, which distinguished some, and made them far-seeing as to what great future lay concealed in that rude model of Sir Richard Arkwright's. The rapid development of what might be called a new trade, gave those early masters enormous powers of wealth and command. I don't mean merely over the workmen; I mean over purchasers—over the whole world's market . . . The men were rendered dizzy by it. Because a man was successful in his ventures, there was no reason that in all other things his mind should be well-balanced. On the contrary, his sense of justice, and his simplicity, were often utterly smothered under the glut of wealth that came down upon him; and they tell strange tales of the wild extravagance of living indulged in on gala-days by those early cotton-lords. There can be no doubt,

137

too, of the tyranny they exercised over their work-people. You know the proverb, Mr Hale, 'Set a beggar on horse-back, and he'll ride to the devil',—well, some of these early manufacturers did ride to the devil in a magnificent style—crushing human bone and flesh under their horses' hoofs without remorse. But by-and-by came a reaction; there were more factories, more masters; more men were wanted. The power of masters and men became more evenly balanced; and now the battle is pretty fairly waged between us . . .'

'Is there necessity for calling it a battle between the two classes?' asked Mr Hale. 'I know, from your using the term, it is one which gives a true idea of the real state of things to your mind.'

'It is true; and I believe it to be as much a necessity as that prudent wisdom and good conduct are always opposed to, and doing battle with ignorance and improvidence. It is one of the great beauties of our system, that a working-man may raise himself into the power and position of a master by his own exertions and behaviour; that, in fact, every one who rules himself to decency and sobriety of conduct, and attention to his duties, comes over to our ranks; it may not be always as a master, but as an overlooker, a cashier, a book-keeper, a clerk, one on the side of authority and order.[4]

CONFLICT

Under the conditions of emerging capitalism in the early nineteenth century the bitter strife and the egoism that appalled Margaret Hale and her father also served greatly to accelerate the development of the new powers of production. The regimentation to which they were subjected in the new factories, and the tyranny of the masters, forced the workers to combine to protect their most elementary needs. After decades of struggle in which the whole repressive machinery of the state was thrown into the scale on the side of the masters, the balance of forces was to some extent restored when trade unions were legalized in 1824. The masters then retaliated by speeding up mechanization in order to free themselves, in turn, from the 'tyranny' of the most powerful, because most highly organized, skilled craftsmen. James Nasmyth (1808–90), the inventor of the steam hammer, and himself a great employer, notes that one of the effects of strikes is a large increase in the number of self-acting machines.[5]

The bitter competition between the capitalists themselves also forced them along the same road. The rapid expansion which resulted did not, however, proceed at an even rate. It took the form of a series of spurts, interrupted by relapses. In these crises the weaker were purged from the capitalist ranks and the survivors emerged strengthened to start the round again at a higher technical level. Hence the violent contradictions that mark the period between Waterloo and the Great Exhibition. Between 1815 and 1851 there were four major economic crises, from 1815 to 1816, 1825 to 1826, 1837 to 1842, and 1847 to 1848. Severe but less general dislocations occurred in 1819–20, 1829 and 1831–2. At all these times of depressions, the distress of the workers, so vividly described by Mrs Gaskell, Mrs Trollope, Dickens, Disraeli and other contemporary writers, added fuel to the political struggle. The Radical movement for parliamentary reform, in which capitalists and workers still formed an uneasy alliance against the landlords, had two peaks—in 1819–20 and 1829–32. Chartism, the first independent political movement of the industrial workers, attained its widest influence and fought its most determined battles in 1837–42, and flared up again in 1847–48. And yet, during this whole period of strife and waste and bitter distress the production of coal increased fivefold, and of pig-iron tenfold. The import of raw cotton increased fifteenfold. But the most striking example of industrial expansion was the creation of the British railway system, precisely during the age of the Chartists. In less than a generation from the opening of the thirty-one-mile-long Liverpool and Manchester Railway in 1830 the mileage of railways available for public use rose from less than one hundred to nearly nine thousand miles in 1854.

GOLDEN CHAINS

It was this ever increasing expansion of its material basis that enabled the new capitalist economy to escape, for the time being, from the consequences of its own internal contradictions. But it also enabled the new England—Elizabeth Gaskell's 'Darkshire'—to triumph over the last remnants of the old. With the relegation of the mail coach to feeder sevices to the new main lines, and the run-down of the canals, eighteenth-century ways of life virtually disappeared. Samuel Smiles was not exaggerating when he wrote at the age of 91, 'The iron rail proved a magicians' road. The locomotive gave a new celerity to time. It virtually reduced England to a sixth of its size. It brought the country nearer to the town, and the town to the country. . . It energized punctuality, discipline, and attention; and proved a moral teacher by the influence of example.'[6]

But the railways also proved a moral teacher in a sense very different from that stressed by Smiles. Most of the earliest public railroads, including the Surrey Iron Railway authorized in 1801, had been feeders to canals and river navigations. Few or none of them competed with the canal or coach owners. But in the first quarter of the nineteenth century the steam locomotive was developed as a substitute for the horse in the coal-fields of the Midlands and the North-East. Its decisive advantage over all other rivals was demonstrated conclusively by its

139

successful use, first on the Hetton Colliery Railway, and then on the Stockton and Darlington, opened in 1825. Shortly afterwards, the promoters of the Liverpool and Manchester Railway sought power to use locomotives exclusively on a line designed not to connect a coal-mine to the nearest river or canal, but to convey goods and passengers between two great centres of population and manufacture, and over a route hitherto monopolized by the canal and coaching interests. Canals, turnpike trusts, coaching concerns and horse-breeders took fright. Even iron-mongers, fearing the railways would cause a shortage of iron, were up in arms. Very soon, every conservative interest in the country was clamouring lest the new mechanical monster should undermine their monopolies or destroy their privileges.

The bitter controversies in Parliament and the Press which accompanied the fight for the Liverpool and Manchester Bill and for all its more important successors in the 1830s, and in which both sides entered the field with armies of lawyers, experts, journalists and caricaturists (Figs. 73 and 74), became the final battles between two economic systems and two incompatible ways of living. But they were only mock battles after all. The real issue had already been decided. After an enormous amount of time, energy and money had been wasted, and after each major railway Bill had been thrown out of Parliament at least once, the most apparently embittered opposition invariably vanished quite suddenly. The lawyers, experts, journalists and caricaturists pocketed their fees. The landlords consoled themselves for the spoliation of rural England with the inflated compensation they had succeeded in extorting from the railway companies. And the British rail-ways were saddled from the start with non-productive overhead costs, far higher than those of any other system in the world.

During the later 1830s and '40s the legal battles continued with equal violence, but their character gradually changed. From last-ditch engagements between the opponents of railways and their promoters, they became gang-fights between railway companies, competing for particular routes. This phase passed through the railway boom of 1836–7 and culminated in the railway mania of 1846–9 and the consequent stock-market crash. Dukes and bishops vied with shopkeepers and manufacturers in paying court to the 'Railway King', George Hudson (1800–71), in a gamble in railway shares and a scramble for profits which aroused the trenchant indignation of Thomas Carlyle. Hudson, who had started life as a draper's assistant, married his employer's daughter in 1821 and became a partner in the business. In 1827 he inherited a fortune. In 1833 he promoted a bank, which he used to finance his various railway speculations. He gradually obtained control of almost the whole north-east section of the British railway system which he linked up with the London and Birmingham line. When Hudson rigged the market to oblige the Duke of Wellington, whose sister had imprudently invested all her property in a bubble company, the aristocratic prejudice against 'trade' had lost all meaning. Henceforth the moral subjection of the old ruling class to the bourgeoisie was complete. The ladies had perforce to admit the manufacturers' wives and daughters to their drawing-rooms, and only the humble shopkeeper remained to smart beneath their haughty looks.

Though Hudson was exposed as a swindler, when he failed to prevent the passing of an Act authorizing his enemies to construct a direct line from London to York through the eastern counties, he was never convicted for fraud, perhaps because too many people were implicated in his manipulations of stock. Thrice elected Tory M.P. for Sunderland (twice even after his downfall), nominated Tory candidate for Whitby in 1859 and arrested for debt in the same year, he ended his life as chairman of the smoking-room of the Carlton Club.[7]

There was a positive element, however, even in the lively displays, in the banquets, civic receptions and brass-band processions, and in the whole noisy publicity that make the career of a man like Hudson appear like a continuous carnival. They all manifest an exuberant pride in the achievements of the industrial age. Moreover, while many of the artists of the time lost themselves in academic banalities, retired into the picturesque, or else sought an escape from contemporary life in colourful visions of an imaginary past, the straighforward desire to record the achievements of the engineers continued to inspire many unassuming draughtsman and illustrators. The story of the art inspired by the industrial revolution ends, as it began, in the humble sphere of documentation.

RAILWAY DOCUMENTARIES

The earliest known printed illustration of a locomotive appears to be the engraving of 'Catch me who can' on the back of tickets issued by Richard Trevithick for his exhibition off the Euston Road in 1808. The first *published* illustration in history appears to be a crude little woodcut in the *Leeds Mercury* on 18 July 1812. The second is probably the aquatint of 'The Collier' with a Blenkinsop locomotive in the background in George Walker's *Costume of Yorkshire* (Fig. 44). It is dated 1 August 1813, and was included in the first of the ten parts in which this work was originally issued. The circulation of *Costume of Yorkshire* cannot have been very large, so the first illustration of a locomotive to be seen widely in London and the south was probably another woodcut of a Blenkinsop in the *Monthly Magazine* for June 1814.[8] This periodical was founded by Sir Richard Phillips[9] (1767–1840), the radical Leicester bookseller and publisher of many works of popular education in the arts and sciences. A few weeks later, in the August issue, Phillips himself contributed a prescient article on the steam locomotive in which he proves himself to have been one of the first men to realize its significance. Reaching the 'populous, industrious, and opulent village of Wandsworth' during a morning's walk along the Thames from London to Kew, he pauses to admire the Surrey Iron Railway, a horse-line joining Croydon to the river.

'I felt renewed delight'—he wrote—

on witnessing at this place the economy of horse-labour on the iron rail-way; and a heavy sigh escaped me, as I thought of the inconceivable millions which had been spent about Malta, four or five of which might have been the means of extending *double lines or iron rail-ways* from London to Edinburgh, Glasgow, Holyhead, Milford, Falmouth, Yarmouth, Dover, and Portsmouth! A reward of a single thousand would have supplied coaches, and other vehicles . . . and we might, ere this, have witnessed our mail coaches running at the rate of ten miles an hour, drawn by a single horse, or impelled fifteen miles by Blenkinsop's steam-engine! Such would have been a legitimate motive for overstepping the income of the nation, and the completion of so great and useful a work might have afforded *rational* grounds for public triumph in a general jubilee![10]

From this time the Blenkinsop design, with its characteristic gear-wheel meshing in a rack laid parallel to the track, became gradually the national and even the international image of the steam locomotive. It was featured in the *Encyclopaedia Londoniensis* in 1816. The frontispiece of the 3rd, 1822, edition of *Observations on a general Iron Way* by Thomas Gray (1787–1848), shows Blenkinsop locomotives drawing both passenger coaches and goods wagons, supported by a piece of doggerel verse:

> No speed with this, can fleetest Horse compare
> No weight like this, canal or Vessel bear.
> As this will Commerce every way promote
> To this let Sons of Commerce grant their vote.

Gray was the first writer to develop in detail the idea of a national railway system. The first edition of his book is dated 1820. It had run into five editions by 1825, and was widely read.

A transfer of a Blenkinsop locomotive decorates a handsome Leeds jug, the first of a very long and distinguished line of railway mugs, jugs, bowls and plates. A

VII NEWCASTLE ON TYNE *(1823) J M W Turner*

Blenkinsop drawing a coach full of passengers appears on a plate made for the German market and encircled by the legend: 'Dampf Wagen von London nach Bristol'. There is also an early lithograph of German origin showing a Blenkinsop drawing a carriage with a canopy and curtains, full of elegantly dressed passengers. Finally, the Royal Iron Foundry, Berlin, constructed two Blenkinsop locomotives in 1816, one of which features in that company's cast-iron New Year 'card' for that year.[11]

Published illustrations of George Stephenson's early locomotives are scarce. The first appears to be that in the *Repertory of Arts* for May 1817,[12] derived from the patent specification of the previous year. On 18 November 1822 the Hetton Colliery Railway was opened, connecting the colliery to Hetton Staithes, about seven miles away on the Wear, just above the Sunderland Bridge. It was engineered by George Stephenson and used by him as a kind of proving ground for his locomotives. The young Scottish artist, James Duffield Harding (1798–1863), was evidently commissioned to make two small lithographs of the line, one of the colliery with a pair of Stephenson locomotives at work in the yard,[13] and one of the staithes. He also made another and much larger lithograph, a kind of panorama of the whole line, with the great Brusselton incline in the centre, over which the lines of trucks were hauled by a stationary engine and cable. In the distance, on the level parts of the line, Stephenson locomotives with their trains move backwards and forwards, busy as ants. The size of the impressions of all three must have been small, for prints are now very scarce. Harding later became a devotee of the picturesque in the convention of Gilpin and Uvedale Price, and turned his back on industry in all its forms, unless a lithograph he made in 1830 of an outsized ship in full sail passing under one of the rejected designs of the Clifton Suspension Bridge be included under this head. In 1823 another railway pioneer, William James (1771–1837), a colleague of George Stephenson, put a crude little woodcut of a Stephenson locomotive on the cover of his prophetic *Report or Essay to illustrate the Advantage of direct inland Communication.*

The first railway to attract even a modicum of national attention was the Stockton and Darlington engineered by George Stephenson and opened in September 1825. Even so, it is not well documented. The Darlington Art Gallery has a large oil painting of the opening by John Dobbin (*fl.* 1842–88), and there is a related drawing by him in the Science Museum. J. Bousefield of Darlington issued an uninteresting lithograph of the event, published both independently and as an illustration to the 1827 edition of Michael Longridge's *Remarks on the comparative*

Merits of cast Metal and malleable Iron Rail-ways; and Account of the Stockton and Darlington Rail-way. Otherwise there is little.[14] Perhaps the economic crisis that broke out in 1826 damped down public interest. However, from this time the Stephenson locomotive gradually ousted the Blenkinsop from public view. Almost the last appearance of the latter in print is in an engraving on steel by T. Owen after Nathaniel Whittock in Thomas Allen's *A new and complete History of the County of York*, published in 1829–31.[15] Dated 1829, it shows a Blenkinsop passing over a viaduct in front of Christ Church, Leeds.

Surprisingly, even the Rainhill locomotive trials organized by the Liverpool and Manchester Railway on 5 October 1829, for a prize of £500, seem to have elicited little more than passing interest except in the technical press. The winner was George Stephenson's *Rocket*. Runners-up were *Sans Pareil* by Timothy Hackworth (1786–1850) of the Stockton and Darlington, and *Novelty* by John Braithwaite (1797–1870) and the Swedish engineer, John Ericsson (1803–89). In the next hundred years, thanks to Samuel Smiles' not always balanced enthusiasm, *Rocket* gradually came to be regarded not only as the most famous locomotive in the world but even, in popular imagination, the first. Yet contemporary illustrations are rare. The reason is, presumably, that she was less a standard type than a prototype, and her immediate successors, such as *Fury* or *North Star* or *Northumbrian*, were normally chosen as the subject for illustration. The well-known coloured lithograph 'Locomotive Engine "The Rocket", 1830' is a later pastiche.

There appear to be no contemporary illustrations of the Rainhill locomotives beyond technical engravings in the *Mechanics' Magazine*,[16] and a fine lithograph of a train headed by *Novelty* after a drawing by Charles Vignoles. At about this time, however, there began a flow of caricatures, most of them composed to denigrate the age of steam and many of them designed deliberately to shake confidence by introducing the public to a feast of explosions and sudden death. George and Robert Cruickshank (1792–1878; 1790–1856), Henry Alken (1774–1850), Hugh Hughes (1790–1863) and many others joined in the fun. At first they tended to concentrate on steam coaches, till these were driven off the roads by legislation from above and sabotage from below by the coaching interests. Then they turned to railways (Fig. 74). Exceptionally, Robert Seymour (1798–1836), who started off as technical artist before he became a caricaturist and illustrator of Pickwick, contributed charming, humorous head- and tailpieces to *Anecdotes of the Steam Engine* by Robert Stuart (Meikleham), printed in 1829 'with a rolling press moved by a steam-engine'. Seymour's designs combining amorini with steam

144

engines would have appealed to Erasmus Darwin, but they must have seemed oddly old-fashioned to his contemporaries.

If the Stockton and Darlington Railway and the Rainhill trials on the Liverpool and Manchester attracted less attention than might have been expected, the opening of the latter on 15 September 1830 became a national sensation, stimulating the publication of prints in unprecedented quantities, to say nothing of commemorative medals, mugs and jugs, printed handkerchiefs, jigsaw puzzles, peep-shows, and a 'padorama'—containing ten thousand square feet of canvas—in Baker Street. No engineering work had ever been so well documented before. None would be so well documented again till the Crystal Palace in 1851.

To understand the reason, it is necessary briefly to review the position the Liverpool and Manchester had come to occupy in the public mind on the eve of its inauguration. As we have seen, it threatened to bring the whole lucrative structure of monopoly by the canal and coaching interests crashing to the ground. So it was fought, tooth and nail, by every stratagem its opponents could command. Fought in the Lords and Commons so that parliamentary expenses were driven to unheard-of heights; fought by molesting the engineers and surveyors trying, often by stealth and at night, to work out the best route; fought in the public Press; fought by pamphlets and broadsides.

For the sake of peace, it looks as if the directors of the Liverpool and Manchester sought deliberately to discourage publicity in connexion with the Rainhill trials. But the circumstances surrounding the birth of the new line nearly a year and a half later compelled public attention. Its engineering was massive and spectacular. Its downright, pugnacious engineer was a striking figure with what Fanny Kemble called his 'peculiar and very original, striking, and forcible' way of explaining his ideas in broad Northumbrian.[17] Above all, the Liverpool and Manchester set out from the beginning to harness what Thomas Creevey called 'this infernal nuisance—the loco-motive Monster . . . navigated by a tail of smoke and sulphur'[18] to draw passengers as well as goods. (Before this time such regular passenger services as existed relied on the horse, even on the Stockton and Darlington.) Finally, the disastrous and tragic series of accidents that marred the opening ceremony made it necessary to woo public opinion. Accordingly, the directors mounted what would today be called a major public relations campaign, designed to show their undertaking in as favourable a light as possible.

There was another, less obvious, motive for attempting to focus public attention on the new line. The mill-owners of the day had pushed the factory system to its inhumane limit, justifying their policies by economic laws specially designed to prove that suffering and poverty were the inevitable concomitant of manufacturing progress. They sustained their complacency in the face of obvious social breakdown by a conviction that the lower classes were low because of their innate laziness coupled with immorality, drunkenness and irresponsibility. The result, they were indignant to notice, was a threatening, surly undercurrent of hostility. In 1830 Josiah Wedgwood would never have sent his ladies unprotected into the middle of working-class Manchester during a strike. The Rev. Edward Stanley (1779–1849), later Bishop of Norwich and mathematician, ornithologist and reformer, in the description of the opening of the Liverpool and Manchester which he contributed to *Blackwood's Magazine* for November, 1830, noted that the Manchester crowds impatiently waiting for the inaugural trains from Liverpool, jeered at so-called respectable people walking among them, bespattering the more decently dressed with clay and mud.

There can be little doubt that the opening ceremony was designed in part to distract the attention of the people from other and more dangerous topics. Everything—the Duke of Wellington's special car of triumph, decorated in crimson and gold, the flags, the trumpeters and the military band, the eight locomotives, shining in their new paint, and the blue livery of the men on the footplates with the word 'fireman' and the name of their charge picked out on their caps in red, combined to form a splendid spectacle. The whole scene, Stanley observed, had the air of 'a compound of the Lord Mayor's show and Epsom races'. 'It was like the jubilee of the Jews'—he said—'when all grievances were forgotten; enmities and heart-burnings evaporated like smoke, and the very Quakers, throwing aside their gravity, looked as gay as larks, and joined in the general joyousness.'

The ceremony took the form of a cortège of eight trains headed, respectively, by *Northumbrian*, *Phoenix*, *North Star*, *Rocket*, *Dart*, *Comet*, *Arrow*, and *Meteor*. George Stephenson himself was at the regulator of *Northumbrian*, which drew the Duke of Wellington's car and the coaches reserved for directors and their friends. Although the first train was not due out till 10.30, the crowds began to assemble, in their best and brightest clothes, as soon as it was light. The weather at first was fair, but with a blustering wind. Within a few hours, 400,000 spectators packed the route, occupying every vantage-point, perched on top of the half-built chimneys at Liverpool, packed into grand-stands along the line, clinging to the sails of a windmill, lining the banks and cuttings.

At one point, high above the grim and grimy crowd of scowling faces, Fanny

146

Kemble records that a loom had been erected, at which sat a tattered, starved-looking weaver, 'evidently sent there as a *representative man*, to protest against this triumph of machinery, and the gain and glory which the wealthy Liverpool and Manchester men were likely to derive from it'.[19]

At twenty to eleven the signal gun was fired. The trains moved out, slowly at first, so that the spectators could enjoy their 'novelty, beauty, and splendour', then faster, into the 'awful chasm' of the Olive Mount cutting (Fig. 66). 'No words', said Stanley,

can convey an adequate notion of the magnificence (I cannot use a smaller word) of our progress. At first it was comparatively slow; but soon we felt that we were indeed GOING, and then it was that every person to whom the conveyance was new, must have been sensible that the adaptation of locomotive power was establishing a fresh era in the state of society: the final results of which it is impossible to contemplate.

'The most intense curiosity and excitement prevailed'—wrote Fanny Kemble—'and . . . enormous masses of densely packed people lined the road, shouting and waving hats and handkerchiefs as we flew by them. What with the sight and sound of these cheering multitudes and the tremendous velocity with which we were borne past them, my spirits rose to the true champaigne height . . .'

'The long continuous lines of spectators'—observed Stanley—'. . . seemed to glide away, like painted figures swiftly drawn through the tubes of a magic lantern.' 'In the rapid movement of these engines'—he noted later, from the side of the line:

there is an optical deception worth noticing. A spectator observing their approach, when at extreme speed, can scarcely divest himself of the idea, that they are not enlarging and increasing in size rather than moving. I know not how to explain my meaning better, than by referring to the enlargement of objects in a phantasmagoria.[20] At first the image is barely discernible, but as it advances from the focal point, it seems to increase beyond all limit. Thus an engine, as it draws near, appears to become rapidly magnified, and as if it would fill up the entire space between the banks, and absorb everything within its vortex.

Perhaps it was some optical effect that confused the economist, William Huskisson (1770–1830), during a pause for watering the locomotives at Parkside, seventeen miles out from Liverpool. Standing between the up line and the down near the Duke of Wellington's car, he was cut down by *Rocket* and fatally injured. *Northumbrian* was hastily brought up and Huskisson was sent forward to Eccles. The engine went on to collect a surgeon, but nothing was of avail. Huskisson died that evening.

After the accident, the Duke wished to cancel the proceedings and to return to Liverpool. However, he was persuaded by the directors to complete the journey to Manchester for fear, they said, that the restless crowds, of alarming size, would get out of hand. James Scott Walker, one of the engineers associated with the line, has another explanation for the decision to proceed, namely that the directors feared that the value of their property might be affected if the procession did not go on to Manchester, so demonstrating the practicability of the locomotive.[21] It was their duty, they felt, to complete the ceremony. Completed it was, but with great confusion and delay. The trains got back to Liverpool six hours late, after dark and in the pouring rain. It had been a disastrous day. But the railway age was launched.

To create the image of the Liverpool and Manchester Railway the directors were fortunate in enlisting the help of one of the greatest publishers of the day, Rudolf Ackermann (1764–1834), famous for the splendour of his books of topography and travel. Ackermann was the son of a Saxony coach-builder who, as a young man, had settled in London as a coach-designer. Marrying an English wife, he set up a publishing and bookselling business in the Strand in 1795, combined with an art school. In 1805 he had become sufficiently well known to be entrusted with the preparation of Lord Nelson's funeral car.

From the beginning of the century, in a gradually mounting volume, there flowed from his printery and workshops a series of magnificently illustrated books. Their titles included such celebrated works as the *Microcosm of London* (1808–10) by Rowlandson and Pugin, Pyne's *Microcosm* (1822–4), Nash's *The Royal Pavilion at Brighton* (1826), *The University of Oxford* (1814), *The University of Cambridge* (1815), Papworth's *Select Views of London* (1816), *Public Schools* (1816), and *The History of Westminster Abbey* (1812). Ackermann published books of travel and distributed them to every quarter of the world, books on furniture, on gardening, on decoration and on architecture, and many works of instruction in painting and engraving. The Abbey bibliographies list about 188 separate works published by Ackermann and his successors, Ackermann & Co., between about 1800 and 1860, more than half issued before 1830. (In this total, *The World in Miniature*, 1821–7, in forty-three volumes, and that delightful illustrated periodical, *Repository of Arts*, in forty volumes from 1809 to 1829, are included as single items.) The earlier volumes were illustrated mainly by aquatints, the later by lithographs.

Ackermann took the principles of the division of labour established by the eighteenth-century print makers and developed them to a pitch of great excellence, combining fairly large editions with standards of illustration that have never been equalled, let alone surpassed. In doing so, he created an image of his age, one of studied, elegant tranquillity on the surface, with a streak of cheerful coarseness underneath, exemplified by *Miseries of Human Life* (1808) and *Dr Syntax*, both illustrated by Rowlandson. That this image is both superficial and false is evident when it is appreciated that it covers the period of the Napoleonic wars, Peterloo, the Bristol Riots, a succession of economic crises, the rise of Chartism, the first Reform Act and the ruthlessness of an industrial capitalism advancing under the banner of Malthusian determinism.

Ackermann himself was not an artist but a combination of impresario and technologist. He took existing techniques and brought them to perfection. Always on the look out for new ideas, he kept up his interest in old ones, in 1818 taking out a patent for 'axletrees for four-wheeled carriages'. His establishment was one of the first in London to introduce gas lighting. In about 1812 he commissioned Fredrick Christian Accum (1769–1838) to install retorts in his basement. He laid on gas, not only in the public library (Fig. 50) and in his warehouse, printery and workshops, but also in his private apartments, to the total exclusion of all other forms of light. When contrasted with the previous lighting system of candles and lamps, he wrote to Accum in 1815, gas lighting 'bears the same comparison to them as a bright summer sun-shine does to a murky November day'. So delighted was he with the effect that he published in 1815 what must be one of the most elegant textbooks in the English language, Accum's *A practical Treatise on Gas-Light*, illustrated by seven coloured aquatint plates, four of equipment and three of Regency gas fittings (Fig. 51) of the greatest charm and delicacy.[22]

Not content with taking the technique of aquatint as far as it could be taken, he also established lithography as a fine art and, as we have seen, published a translation of Senefelder's essential textbook in 1819. As a consequence, when the aquatint began to lose its popularity between 1830 and 1840, the firm was able to maintain its lead by changing over to lithography and then to chromolithography.

Only in the choice of artists and designers was Ackermann conservative, preferring to look back to the calm sun-lit objectivity of Sandby or Edward Dayes (1763–1804) or Thomas Malton (1748–1804), one of Turner's masters, or Michael Angelo Rooker. He avoided the slashing line of men like Thomas Gillray (1757–1815), the apocalyptic ravings of John Martin or, on occasions, Francis Danby (1793–1861), and the chiaroscuro of Turner. He preferred the calmer powers of illustration possessed by such artists as W. H. Pyne, J. C. Stadler, Joseph Nash and

Augustus Pugin (1762–1832), the architectural draughtsman and father of the architect, Augustus Welby Pugin (1812–52). Ackermann even tamed Rowlandson, when in his late fifties, and gave him what must have amounted to almost continuous employment.

When an artist had to be chosen to illustrate the Liverpool and Manchester Railway, Thomas Talbot Bury (1811–77) was selected, one of the elder Pugin's pupils since the age of 13. The first engravings in aquatint after Bury's designs are dated 1 February 1831. They were issued in paper covers under the title: *Six Coloured Views of the Liverpool and Manchester Railway* (in fact, the views numbered seven by the addition of an extra plate of 'Coaches &c'). A new edition of thirteen views was issued later in the year, also in paper covers, with the word 'six' dropped from the title (Figs. 66, 67, 69, and 71). There was a reissue in 1832, followed by editions in Spanish and Italian. Finally, almost all the plates were re-engraved for new editions published in 1833 and 1834, in cloth bindings or in paper covers.

The Bury prints were reproduced separately as coloured lithographs, with titles in French, by Engelmann et fils, Mulhouse. There is also a German edition with copies of the Bury plates in uncoloured aquatint, and a French edition with etched copies.

Judging from a few original Bury studies that have survived, his work was often rough and sometimes insipid. Most of the charm and elegance of the final aquatints, beautifully coloured by hand, was introduced by his engravers, G. Pyall and S. G. Hughes, of whom the latter contributed only a few plates. Indeed, for many decades of the nineteenth century, sketchers naturally clumsy or uninspired sometimes acquired a reputation they did not wholly deserve because of silent and unacknowledged improvements contributed by the craftsmen engravers.

Finally, Ackermann issued what were to become the most famous railway prints in history, the two so-called 'long prints' by I. Shaw of Liverpool, late of Soho Square, London, engraved in aquatint by S. G. Hughes. Both are titled 'Travelling on the Liverpool and Manchester Railway', and are coloured by hand. Each consists of two trains, two passenger trains of first-class and second-class coaches on one, and two goods trains on the other, one with miscellaneous goods and the other with cattle. They were issued late in 1831, and reissued with considerable modifications in 1833, and then again in Italian. They were folded into the end of later editions of the Bury views, or issued separately. There is also a slightly smaller issue, with all four trains on one sheet.

I. Shaw also published in 1831 a series of finely detailed etchings in paper wrappers titled: *Views of the most interesting Scenery on the . . . Liverpool and Manchester Railway*. Though three parts were announced, only two were published, each with four illustrations. From their quality it is apparent that he was a fine and sensitive artist, but no other work by him is known.

From the point of view of the management of the Liverpool and Manchester, the Ackermann venture must have been an enormous success. Judging by the numbers of Bury prints still available, even today, great numbers must have been issued. Careful, clear and sunny, the trains are surrounded by prim groups of figures, the ladies in bright skirts and shawls, the gentlemen immaculately dressed, the attendant workmen neatly unobtrusive. Everything is bright and spotless. To the sophisticated, the effect must have seemed not only a little old-fashioned but a little unreal, a kind of railway minuet sixteen years after the introduction of the waltz. But to the public of Lancashire they must have seemed splendidly reassuring and optimistic.

An amusing side-issue is the number of changes that were made to the plates, both to remove errors and to add new features as the various works were brought to completion. The most troublesome case was that of Plate I: 'The Tunnel'. The Liverpool and Manchester Act stipulated that steam was not to be used in the two tunnels at the Liverpool end of the line, and at first the trains were lowered through them or drawn up by cable. Yet the first impression of Plate I shows a locomotive drawing four trucks through the bright gas-lit interior of the tunnel leading down from Edgehill station to the warehouses at Wapping. It was hastily withdrawn, and a second impression issued with the chimney of the locomotive blotted out, but not the smoke or the circular front of the boiler. And there is no sign of a cable. So more work was done on the plate. Even in the third impression, the boiler is still dimly visible, but cables have been added. It was not till the fourth impression that all signs of the locomotive were removed. In the 1833 impression the front truck of a loaded train of goods wagons, unmistakably hauled by cable, bears a glowing lamp as prominent as the eye of Polyphemus. Such were the anxieties over 135 years ago of the precursors of today's public-relations officers.

There was a direct commercial incentive to circulate the Bury prints and the Shaw 'long prints' abroad. The Spanish and Italian versions of the originals, and the copies and imitations in French and German, prepared the ground for the promotion of railways all over Europe, the greater number to be built by British contractors and powered by British locomotives.

The Bury prints themselves represent one of the later applications of aquatint in the field of industrial documentation. Graceful and delicate though it was, the process was soon to be ousted by the lithograph, itself brought to perfection partly by the efforts of Ackermann & Co. Already most of the local and commercial illustrations of the Liverpool and Manchester were lithographs, some of them crude. Although the minor provincial artist, Andrew Nichol, used aquatint for his *Five Views on the Dublin and Kingstown Railway*, published in 1834, David Octavius Hill (1802–70) selected lithography for the splendid illustrations to his *Glasgow and Garnkirk Railway*, published in 1832 (Fig. 77).

Ackermann & Co. obviously found aquatint the best way of dealing with a series of cardboard discs they published in 1833 for use with the 'Phantascope', a precursor of the cinema invented in 1832 by the blind Belgian physicist, Professor J. A. F. Plateau (1801–83). Plateau, Bury, and the watercolourist, Thomas Mann Baynes (1794–1854), shared the work between them, and produced moving pictures of conjurers, a hobby horse, and waltzing. But nothing could stem the tide of lithography, steel engraving and wood engraving which between them virtually drove out almost all other methods of reproducing pictures. Bury himself seems to have tried to maintain the position of the aquatint. In this he may have had the support of Ackermann & Co., for, in 1835, they issued a charming forecast, aquatinted by Bury, of what the Thames Tunnel might look like when it was completed (Fig. 54). And as late as 1837 they allowed Bury to embark on what was clearly intended to be a publication, in parts, of views of the newly opened London and Birmingham Railway. Today Bury's London and Birmingham pictures seem as beautiful but as distant as a dream. To the contemporary public they would have looked primly archaic. They must have been a commercial failure as well, for only Part 1 was issued, and that in a small edition. Thenceforward, in collaboration with the younger Pugin, Bury concentrated on the Gothic revival, both as architect and antiquarian. In the former capacity he designed St Barnabas, Cambridge, and the New Lodge at Windsor. In the latter he published *Remains of Ecclesiastical Woodwork* in 1847 and *A Historical Description of the Styles of Architecture* in 1849. As an industrial topographer he was superseded by one of the greatest of all artists of industry—John Cooke Bourne (1814–96), whose two great folios of lithographs, *Drawings of the London and Birmingham Railway* (1839) and *The History and Description of the Great Western Railway* (1846), reflect the jubilant self-confidence of the early railway age.

JOHN COOKE BOURNE

John Cooke Bourne[23] was the son of a Hatton Garden hatter descended from a long line of Staffordshire countrymen. His second Christian name, Cooke, appears frequently at this time in the Bourne genealogy. There is a strong family tradition that the Bournes and the Cookes were friends and that the engraver, George Cooke (1781–1834), was John Cooke Bourne's godfather. Bourne's talents seem to have developed early, and he became a pupil of John Pye (1782–1874),[24] one of Turner's favourite engravers, who had a special skill in rendering in line the effects of light and shade, and who was a master of chiaroscuro in translating colour into black and white.

By 1832, when Bourne was 18, he was already a highly proficient draughtsman. By 1836 he was making sensitive pencil and wash drawings in the Lake District with something of the vision of Girtin, by whose work he may have been influenced. Meanwhile, in London, less than a mile from where he lived with his father and brother, both of them hatters and furriers at 19 Lamb's Conduit Street, Robert Stephenson was cutting a swath for the London and Birmingham Railway from Euston through the streets and tenements of Camden Town to the mouth of the tunnel under Primrose Hill, and thence north to Birmingham.

Dickens described the digging of the great Camden Town cutting in *Dombey and Son*, first published in parts from 1846 to 1848. Horrified by the turmoil and confusion, he found the sight almost unbearable: 'The first shock of a great earthquake'—he wrote—

had, just at that period, rent the whole neighbourhood to its centre. Traces of its course were visible on every side. Houses were knocked down; streets broken through and stopped; deep pits and trenches dug in the ground; enormous heaps of earth and clay thrown up; buildings that were undermined and shaking, propped by great beams of wood. Here, a chaos of carts, overthrown and jumbled together, lay topsy-turvy at the bottom of a steep unnatural hill; there confused treasures of iron soaked and rusted in something that had accidentally become a pond. Everywhere were bridges that led nowhere; thoroughfares that were wholly impassable; Babel towers of chimneys, wanting half their height; temporary wooden houses and enclosures, in the most unlikely situations; carcasses of ragged tenements, and fragments of unfinished walls and arches, and piles of scaffolding, and wildernesses of bricks, and giant forms of cranes, and tripods straddling above nothing. There were a hundred thousand shapes and substances of incompleteness, wildly mingled out of their places, upside down, burrowing in the earth, aspiring in the air, mouldering in the water, and unintelligible as any dream. Hot springs and fiery eruptions, the usual attendants upon earthquakes, lent their contributions of confusion to the scene. Boiling water hissed and heaved within dilapidated walls; whence, also, the glare and roar of flames came issuing forth; and mounds of ashes blocked up rights of way, and wholly changed the law and custom of the neighbourhood.

In short, the yet unfinished and unopened railroad was in progress, and from the very core of all this dire disorder, it trailed smoothly away, upon its mighty course of civilization and improvement.

It is illuminating to compare Dickens's bewilderment and irony with the admiration displayed by some of the great artists of the day for the engineering feats to be seen on every hand. Only a year or so before the publication of *Dombey and Son*, Turner had exhibited 'Rain, Steam, Speed' at the Royal Academy in 1844. Based on observations he had made, in torrential rain, leaning out of the window of a train crossing Maidenhead Bridge on the Great Western, the resulting picture is one of the great tributes of the Victorian age to steam. At a humbler but more lucid level, Bourne depicted the building of the London and Birmingham Railway, including the great cutting that had disturbed Dickens so much, with controlled enthusiasm.

Bourne was sponsored by John Britton (1771–1857), the son of a small Wiltshire farmer, and successively cellarman, solicitor's clerk, journalist and antiquarian. Invited to write a popular guide to Wiltshire, Britton was taken up by the Marquis of Lansdowne and given the run of the library at Bowood. He became one of the most celebrated and prolific antiquarians and topographers of the day, combining a love of ancient buildings with a passion for the products of industry, extolling the virtues of cast-iron as a building material and frequently assuming the role of a railway promoter.

From Britton we learn that Bourne first began to execute drawings of the London and Birmingham excavations in 1836. These were intended as 'subjects of professional study, as scenes and compositions replete with picturesque effect and artistic character'.[25] At first there was no idea of publication. The drawings were made *con amore*, as Britton put it. Bourne's more developed work has affinities with the drawings of George Scharf (1788–1860) who also made studies of the works at Camden Town. He also owes much to *Views of the Old and New London Bridges*, a volume of etchings published in 1833 by his godfather's son, Edward . . . William Cooke (1811–80), with whom he is believed to have been on close and friendly terms. But Cooke's etching needle could not compete with the fluency of Bourne's pencil and brush.

As Bourne's drawings of the Euston end of the London and Birmingham Railway accumulated in number, they also increased in interest. His isolated observations grew into a chronicle of order growing out of disorder. Finding that his drawings both amused and informed 'many amateurs and men of science', Bourne sent specimens to Britton, who was immediately and deeply impressed by them. He recommended that they should be lithographed. He felt certain that their intrinsic interest, combined with their beauty, would ensure the success of their publication. There was also another and pressing reason for getting out material putting the London and Birmingham in a favourable light. As Britton wrote on 2 April 1839 to Richard Creed, Secretary of the line:

Fully aware that we have jealous and fastidious critics to deal with, both in the houses of parliament, & out of them, I wish to remove, or at least to check, the tide of prejudice against us, & display our powers, capabilities, & efforts.[26]

As a first step, Bourne produced well over fifty magnificent and highly finished wash drawings. These have been preserved and are now on view at the Railway Museum at Clapham. He was enthralled by the masterpieces of engineering and architecture that were hoisting themselves out of the sticky London clay. He was convinced that faithful delineations of their construction would 'gratify both the lover of the picturesque and the man of science', as well as 'all persons who derive pleasure in contemplating the increasing importance of the commerce, manufactures, and arts of Great Britain'. He defied Gilpin's thesis that in the picturesque 'the arts of industry are rejected', and that one could never on any account introduce into a landscape the 'industrious mechanic'. For Bourne, the vistas of excavation, tunnel, and viaduct were best shown off by 'the picturesque accompaniments of Machinery, Implements, Workmen, etc.'[27] To lend human interest to his more formal drawing, he filled his sketchbooks with lively and often humourous notes and studies of the engineers and navvies (Figs. 81, 82).

Ignoring the advice of another protégé of Britton, Samuel Prout (1784–1852), that figures should be used mainly 'as an honest means of introducing lights, darks, and colours', and to give scale and proportion, Bourne treats the men swarming over the workings as intrinsic to the whole design, assigning to each figure both function and purpose. Never straining accuracy, he chose his sites so skilfully that every element within his field of vision falls into its own logical place. Nothing is superfluous, but nothing is omitted. Each scene has a sense of imminent but arrested action. Everything is endowed with a certainty that lends order to the apparent confusion Dickens found so painful at Camden Town (Figs. 83–86).

Bourne handled his engineering themes with a power and vigour hitherto reserved by Piranesi for the architectural prodigies of classical Rome. Under his lucid eye, the railway cut like a lash across the face of the countryside that his contemporaries, such as James Duffield Harding, Samuel Prout and William Leitch (1804–83), liked to populate with noble, unhurried peasants, pursuing their simple tasks in idyllic surroundings.

Bourne selected thirty-six of his drawings for publication. Though, according to Britton, he had never previously made any drawings on stone, he executed the work himself and with conspicuous success. Creed gave permission for specimens to be hung up before publication at the various stations along the line, and on 11 July 1838 Bourne wrote to Captain Moorsom, the other secretary, at Birmingham, asking for his co-operation in giving the work publicity.[28]

A Series of Lithographed Drawings on the London and Birmingham Railway was first published in four parts by Bourne himself from Lamb's Conduit Street jointly with Ackermann. Each part cost £1 1*s* 0*d*. The first part came out on 1 September 1838, in paper covers, and the second on 20 December. The third and fourth parts were published together in July 1839, with a topographical and descriptive account by Britton. To his annoyance, this had been much reduced in length to economize on paper and printing. Shortly afterwards the four parts were issued in a single volume, with the title shortened to: *Drawings of the London and Birmingham Railway*. It elbowed Bury's trim *Six Coloured Views* into undeserved obscurity.

The work received uniformly good reviews. The *Birmingham Journal* pronounced the pictures to be 'well entitled to a favourable place in the library of the studious, as well as in the drawing-room of the idle'. *The Spectator* considered the pictures represented 'new features of beauty to the English landscape painter'. Other notices were equally flattering. Nevertheless, the confident expectations of author and reviewers were not fulfilled, and no further major work of the kind was issued by Bourne for several years. The art patrons of the day wished for anything rather than to be reminded of the social and technological revolution going on all round them. As a result, perhaps, of a kind of deliberate campaign to suppress Bourne's unwelcome enthusiasm for engineering as a subject for art, the standard works of reference, crammed with the names of his peers and, often, his inferiors, afford him no mention. Even his son, who died as recently as 1962, knew very little about him beyond his dates.

Yet there is one piece of evidence, not only that Bourne was proud of his achievement, but that he had discriminating supporters. For there exists a thin book, bound in full crimson Morocco, gilt, entitled *Subscribers to Bourne's Sketches of the London and Birmingham Railway*. It contains the holograph signatures of leading engineers, business men, land-owners and financiers. The first name is that of Baron Wharncliffe, who was later to preside over the Committee of the Lords appointed to consider the Bill of the Great Western Railway, and after whom Brunel named his great viaduct across the Brent Valley between Paddington and Maidenhead. Wharncliffe is followed by the signatures of the Dukes of Grafton, Buccleuch and Sutherland. Robert Stephenson is there, with Philip Hardwick, architect of the Euston Arch, Joseph Bramah, inventor of the hydraulic press, Richard Creed, Secretary of the London and Birmingham Railway, the Honourable East India Company and 63 other names.

For the next few years next to nothing is known of Bourne's activities, save for a few single lithographs, mainly of railway works, and a volume of lithographs of Cairo after stiff conventional drawings by Robert Hay, published in 1840. It appears that he became associated with Charles Cheffins (1777–1844), whose name crops up frequently as a railway architect, printer, publisher and cartographer. There are also vague indications that he may have worked as an engineering draughts-man, probably in association with Cheffins. If so, he did not identify his work. He also became a highly proficient but rather ethereal watercolourist.

At about this time there began a steady flow of railway pictures by other artists, and a few illustrated books, of which the most important are *Views of the Newcastle and Carlisle Railway* (Newcastle, 1837), consisting of steel engravings after drawings by James Wilson Carmichael (1800–68) (Fig. 46) with descriptions by the engineer to the line, J. Blackmore, and *Views of the Manchester and Leeds Railway* (1845), consisting of a series of prim lithographs by Athur Fitzwilliam Tait (1819–1905) (Fig. 90) with a description by Edwin Butterworth.

Carmichael was a Newcastle artist, best known as a marine painter, and a member of that vigorous school of watercolourists, landscape painters, illustrators and drawing masters that had grown up in Newcastle since the time of Bewick. It included Thomas Miles Richardson (1784–1848) with his five sons, not to mention his grandchildren and other relatives. Between them, the Newcastle artists depicted countless railway subjects, as might be expected from the historical association of the north-east coast with the birth of the railway system, and the splendid bridges and viaducts which are such a predominant feature of the region.

Tait was a landscape and animal painter who studied art at the Royal Institution, Manchester. He emigrated to the United States in 1850.

In 1845, or even earlier, Charles Cheffins commissioned Bourne to execute a series of wash drawings of the Great Western Railway. Though these were transferred to the stone by Bourne with his usual scrupulous fidelity and published by David Bogue in 1846 in *The History and Description of the Great Western Railway*, they were produced entirely under the direction of Cheffins, who also financed the whole venture.[29] It is a magnificent study of the railway as a going concern, and is the second and final railway book by Bourne. As he explained in the preface, he intended his direct, powerful drawings to display the stations, bridges, tunnels and viaducts to the passengers who were whirled past them so rapidly that, otherwise, they had no chance to appreciate their worth.

Bourne's Great Western pictures echo the sweep and swagger of Isambard Kingdom Brunel's great broad-gauge railway, striking up the Thames Valley from Paddington over the Wharncliffe Viaduct (Fig. 92) through Reading to Didcot, skirting the Berkshire Downs by Wantage, plunging into the ringing cavern of the Box Tunnel (Fig. 88), and on through Bath to the vaulted wooden roof of its terminus at Bristol, Temple Meads. The very frontispiece breathes confident achievement. *Acheron*, her copper haystack boiler gleaming, bursts in full steam from the gloom of a tunnel into the sparkling light of day (Fig. 89). Above the portal, as if carved for all eternity in the living stone, are the words: 'The Great Western Railway by J. C. Bourne.' Never before or since has anyone interpreted the simplicity, boldness and drama of great engineering with such deliberation and such verve.

The book was published in the spring of 1846 at the height of the Railway Mania, as the wild, speculative boom in railway shares came to be called. By the autumn of that year the first signs of doubt and anxiety began to make themselves felt, and the serene calm of Bourne's vision must have begun to appear a little false. The caricaturists began to direct their malicious darts not at the railways themselves but at the speculators trying to convince a distraught John Bull of the merits of countless bubble companies. By 1846 they invariably assumed the features of King Hudson, whose doings filled many pleasant pages of *Punch*. The crash came in 1849 when thousands of people were ruined. In the same year Alfred Crowquill (1805–72) devoted a strip-cartoon pamphlet to Hudson, *How he Reigned and how he Mizzled, A Railway Raillery*. Crowquill is the pseudonym of Alfred Henry Forrester, who, as a young man, was closely associated with the Stock Exchange and so could be expected to have particularly strong feelings on the subject.

Bourne had devoted the whole of his great creative powers to depicting the

VIII NANT-Y-GLO IRON WORKS (*c. 1788*) *att. George Robertson*

railways considered as splendid and heroic enterprises, so his disillusion must have been great when he came to realize the fraudulent manipulations that surrounded their administration. What may have been his last railway picture, a watercolour painted in 1847 and now in the Clapham Transport Museum, shows the Anker Viaduct outlined dimly through a bluish haze. Occupying the attention in the foreground is a group of peasants, touched in with an irrelevant affection even Samuel Prout might have envied.

In the Autumn of 1846 the engineer, Charles Vignoles (1793–1875), heard that Czar Nicholas I proposed to have a road bridge thrown across the Dnieper at Kiev. He immediately prepared a set of drawings for a chain suspension bridge of six spans based on information supplied to him from Russia. He mounted them on silk, bound them in full Morocco gilt emblazoned with the arms of Russia, and set out for Moscow in January, 1847.[30] Once there he prepared four more volumes, similarly bound, of drawings for other bridges. All of them have survived in the library of the Obrazov Institute of Railway Engineers in Leningrad.[31]

Vignoles evidently took Bourne with him and several of the volumes contain drawings by him, signed and dated 1847, and designed to elucidate Vignoles' plans and elevations for the benefit of the Czar. The Kiev volume has five drawings in watercolour, mounted side by side so that they can be opened out to yield a single panoramic view. They are executed in a style, for Bourne, unexpectedly broad.

As soon as the Kiev drawings were finished, Vignoles commissioned two elaborate models of the proposed bridge from Jabez James of Southwark. The Czar installed one in the Winter Palace. The other went to the Great Exhibition of 1851, the catalogue entry being accompanied by a coloured lithograph after a view by Bourne.

The Czar awarded the Kiev contract to Vignoles in September, 1847, and work started in the following March. Bourne was appointed 'resident artist', and there have survived from this period a number of delicate, charming but on the whole conventional watercolours of the Kremlin, the Lavra Monastery at Kiev, the floating bridge across the Dnieper which Vignoles' bridge superseded, and a plethora of barges, mules and peasant women, their heads in coloured kerchiefs— all the trappings his contemporaries mobilized to shut out the technological upheavals that were turning their world upside down.

After 1849 the standard of pictorial documentation of the railways diminished sharply. William Dawson, the Exeter watercolour painter and lithographer, was one of the last artists seriously to devote his energies to a series of illustrations of a particular railway, in this case a set group of lithographs in colour of the South Devon, issued in 1848 (Fig. 93).

Dawson was one of a large and talented group of artists who, at this time, devoted themselves to recording every aspect of English topography. For the most part they are unrecognized and their work unrecorded. Dawson's publisher, W. Spreat of Exeter, was one of a similar band of artist publishers who made a speciality of topographical works and guide-books.

Dawson's first published work appears to be the illustrations for an account of the great landslips which took place near Lyme Regis in December 1839 and February 1840. His next known work was prepared in 1846, apparently for publication, and is now in the library of the Institution of Civil Engineers. It consists of an album titled: *South Devon Atmospheric Railway . . . with Sketches on either Side of the Line. Part 1.* It deals with the route from Exeter to Totnes in twenty-five large pages, each embellished by three watercolour strips nearly two feet long, the centre one consisting of a map of the line, the two outside ones being panoramic delineations of the scenery on either side. They combine charming, evocative studies of life along the line with an account of Brunel's system of atmospheric traction by which a train was attached to a piston passing through a cast-iron pipe laid between the rails. The train, outside the pipe, was attached to the piston, inside, by an arm passing through a longitudinal slit rendered airtight by a continuous flap valve. Steam engines, housed in handsome Italianate brick buildings sited at intervals along the line, created a vacuum ahead of the piston which was impelled along by the pressure of the atmosphere, drawing its train behind it.

Dawson's album is one of the most beautiful and sensitive of all the illustrations of the railway age, poised at a moment of calm, just before the markets broke, when it seemed possible to combine the industrial with the idyllic, at least in the West Country. The work was never published, no doubt because the atmospheric system failed almost as soon as it was completed.

From this time onwards public interest shifted from the railways themselves to the great bridges that carried them high above valley floor and ocean tide to the outlying parts of the system. The reason may have been that, at a moment when the very foundations of economic life seemed dangerously precarious, the bridges were reassuringly firm and solid—Robert Stephenson's great tubular bridges across the Conway and the Menai Strait (Figs. 94, 95) and his double-decked High Level Bridge across the Tyne at Newcastle; Brunel's masterpiece, the Saltash Bridge across the Tamar (Fig. 49); John Millers' Ballochmymle Viaduct on the Glasgow

160

and South Western; Kennard's Crumlin Viaduct over Ebbw Vale and, nearer home, the brick spans of William Cubitt's Welwyn Viaduct (Fig. 91). To this partial list of railway bridges must be added two road bridges which, to judge from the wealth of pictures they inspired, had a place in the public mind equal to that of any of the railway bridges—Telford's great suspension bridge over the Menai Straits, opened in 1826 and the last link in his highroad from London to Holyhead (Figs. 41 and 42), and Brunel's Clifton Suspension Bridge, completed in 1864 (Fig. 43), but derived from a much earlier design (Fig. 40).

Of the artists who turned out engravings and lithographs of these great engineering works in such profusion, perhaps only one can compare with John Cooke Bourne, George Hawkins (1810–52). His masterpieces are a series of tinted lithographs of the building of the Stephenson tubular bridges over the Conway and the Menai Strait. Some of them appeared in the Atlas of Plates to Edwin Clark's *The Britannia and Conway Tubular Bridges* (1850). Other, larger lithographs were issued separately. Hawkins, who established himself as an architectural draughtsman and lithographer in the forties, once again exhibits that combination of archaeological and technical interests that distinguished the documentary movement from the start. His lithographs after other artists' drawings include not only railway and engineering subjects but also the plates, after drawings by William Richardson (*fl.* 1842–77), for the Rev. Edward Churton's *Monastic Ruins of Yorkshire*, published in 1843. His record of the construction of the Britannia and Conway Bridges, of which some of his original pencil sketches are preserved in the National Museum of Wales, begins with the building of the massive piers. He then shows in detail how the great tubes were constructed on wooden platforms on the bank, how they were floated into position with the tide and finally raised by means of powerful hydraulic presses (Fig 95).

The great bridges were not the only spectacular engineering feats that stirred public imagination in the 1840s and '50s. For example, the opening of the elder Brunel's Thames Tunnel, which finally took place in 1843 (work having been interrupted for seven years after an inrush of water in 1828), was greeted with an outburst of popular prints, medals and handkerchiefs, although that vast undertaking did not come up to expectations financially and was converted into a railway tunnel in 1869.

Brunel's son, Isambard Kingdom, also became celebrated for spectacular feats of engineering, providing endless opportunites both for sardonic humour and respectful awe. The battle of the gauges, between the younger Brunel, who had persuaded the directors of the Great Western to adopt the seven-foot gauge, and George Stephenson, who advocated a gauge of 4 ft 8½ in. which is now standard, provoked a flood of pamphlets and parliamentary inquiries. The ill-fated atmospheric railway and the transatlantic steamship service, starting in April 1838 with a race between the *Sirius* and Brunel's s.s. *Great Western*, designed to prolong the main line of her namesake all the way to New York, provided ample material for illustrator and caricaturist alike. In 1843 Brunel launched the *Great Britain*, an iron ship of 3,000 tons propelled by screws. (The problem of forging the huge shaft that would have been required for the paddles originally planned, inspired Nasmyth to design his steam hammer.) Finally Brunel staggered his contemporaries by designing a Leviathan of more than 27,000 tons displacement, the *Great Eastern*, which began to tower over the mudbanks of the Thames in John Scott Russell's shipyard at Millbank after 1852 (Fig. 98). She was launched, with great difficulty, in 1858.

When Brunel died, on 15 September 1859, the *Morning Chronicle* said of him: 'The history of invention records no instance of grand novelties so boldly imagined and so successfully carried out by the same individual. He was less successful when he was less bold. . . . Brunel could make an engineering epic, but not an engineering sonnet. When he could not be grand he was nothing at all . . .'[32]

Meanwhile, Bourne seems to have lost all interest in the great works of engineering springing up all round him. Disappointed, perhaps, by the relative failure of his book on the Great Western, he seems to have decided to capture the public fancy in another way, and dedicated himself, equally unsuccessfully, to an attempt to master more conventional subjects. Vignoles' bridge over the Dnieper was opened in 1853, and it is to be presumed that Bourne returned to England before the Crimean War. However, nothing more is heard of him till 1860, when he reverted for a moment to his old style with a spirited account of the fitting out of *Bacchante* at Portsmouth. Though these drawings were marked for the *Illustrated News*, they do not appear to have been published. In 1863 the Royal Academy accepted a watercolour from him for the first and only time, 'Old Houses of Hastings', an agreeable study in the style of Birket Foster.

By now he had accumulated means, either gained in Russia or, as his family believed, inherited from one of the Cookes. In 1866 he married a young woman aged 25, Catharine Cripps, the daughter of an official at Buckingham Palace, and settled down in Teddington. He devoted the rest of his life to photography and the production of watercolours and oil paintings, some of them elaborately worked up from studies made in Russia. Perhaps in a kind of desperation to attract attention, his work progressively degenerated into a sugary and polychromatic parody of his former vision. With a taste for heavy, ornate furniture, austere in manner and a firm disciplinarian, he died, a disappointed man, in February 1896. His only obituary is the laconic description on his death certificate—'Artist (Painter)'.

In spite of the neglect he suffered from his contemporaries, Bourne's name is still alive. His 'creative treatment of actuality' has exercised a compelling influence on many historians of economics, transport and technology (Fig. 96).

THE CRYSTAL PALACE

The enterprise that summed up the whole epoch was the Great Exhibition of All Nations—the Crystal Palace, opened on 1 May 1851. To hear the authentic voice of British capitalism in the hour of its greatest triumph it is necessary to turn only to the chapter on the construction of the building, contributed by Sir Matthew Digby Wyatt (1820–77), Secretary of the Executive Committee, to the *Official Descriptive and Illustrated Catalogue*.[33]

'Had circumstances determined'—he wrote—

that the present industrial position of England should have been represented by the building alone, while other nations should have been allowed to indicate the scope of their resources by a display of choice specimens of all the varied branches of productions to which their efforts had of late years been directed, it is singular to remark how few elements, essential to her commercial success, would have been lost sight of. The courage of her citizens would have been manifested in the vastness of the scheme, their energy, determination, and strength, in the surprising rapidity with which every operation had been carried on.

The happy condition of the liberty of the subject would have been attested by the circumstance of its having been in the power of the people alone to will the existence of so vast a structure; while the fact that the whole expenses had been provided for without in any way trenching on the national resources, would have evidenced at once the wealth and the spirit of enterprise common to every class of society.

That it should have been possible in any country to have so speedily collected such a vast quantity of materials, without previously sounding the note of preparation, would have furnished strong evidence of the abundance of its native resources, and conveyed some faint idea of the extent of the stores of raw material kept ever ready to supply the exigencies of sudden demand. That that raw material should have been moulded into forms so various, so complex, and so original, in so short a time, would argue that such a result could alone have been effected by the natives of a country in which a knowledge of the principles and practice of mechanics and machinery had been long deeply studied and widely diffused. The facility with which the machinery employed must have been brought to bear upon the masses of raw material supplied, would have evidenced a power to produce, and to elaborate matter into manufacture, of the very highest order; while the grace with which

163

the charm of decoration has been superadded, to so utilitarian a structure, would have served to show, that, mindful as the English habitually are, of the practical and economical, they are by no means indifferent to the beautiful in the Fine Arts.

The author turns next to the social system in which all this was achieved. He mentions 'the perfection to which the practice of connecting commercial co-operation in supply, and mutual reliance in money and time bargains, with the methodical organization of labour, has been carried in England at the present time', and then continues:

The firm through whose exertions the building has been erected, in itself presents an excellent model of the commercial constitution necessary to produce such great works with rapidity. While of its heads, one is remarkable for high scientific attainments, another possesses singular commercial aptitude, together with minute knowledge of the working details of his business. Others again, bring to the common stock of intelligence a precise knowledge of legal and monetary transactions, together with experience acquired in many years' connection with speculations of great magnitude. The principal superintendents and foremen set in operation by this intellectual motive power, are each adapted to the particular duties they may be called upon to perform, and act precisely as the various portions of a well-devised machine, being at the same time maintained in as perfect control. Through these agents the labour of the artisan, skilled in his own department, profoundly ignorant in others, is brought into useful operation; and thus thousands are combined to realise the will of one directing mind. But for the perfect system of discipline, which frequent practice in directing the labour of masses of workmen has now made general throughout England, it would have been impossible to have fashioned, in so short a time, so novel and so vast a structure as the Temple of Peace, the gates of which may, we trust, be thrown open to the world at large, for many years to come.

The Crystal Palace of Joseph Paxton (1801–65) was 1,848 feet long and 140 feet high. Its cubic content was 33 million feet. It contained 2,300 cast-iron girders weighing 3,500 tons, 358 wrought-iron trusses weighing 550 tons, and 900,000 superficial feet of glass. The site for the building was obtained on 30 July 1850, and the first column fixed on 26 September. The completed structure was opened on 1 May 1851. The number of workers employed rose from thirty-nine in the first week of September to 2,260 in the first week of December, and rarely fell below 2,000 until the end of March. Their methods of work had been so carefully thought out, and the whole operation was so well organized, that in one week eighty men fixed no less than 18,000 panes of glass. In its admiration for this symbolic achievement, and in the noise and colour of the great fair, England for a time forgot the agonies and struggles of the hungry 'forties. Forgotten, too, were the plague-ridden slums in all the great centres of industry which made the average age of death in a town like Manchester 38 years for 'professional persons and gentry, and their families', 20 years for 'tradesmen and their families', and 17 years for mechanics, labourers, and their families', while the corresponding ages in rural Rutlandshire were 52, 41, and 38.[34]

The contemporary illustrations of the Crystal Palace and its exhibits are legion, carried out in every conceivable medium and by every possible technique. It is by far the best documented event of the nineteenth century, and the golden age of the chromolithograph (Fig. 99). The two great folios, *The Industrial Arts of the Nineteenth Century* by Sir Matthew Digby Wyatt and Dickinson's *Comprehensive Pictures of the Great Exhibition of* 1851, have never been surpassed. Issued in forty parts between 1851 and 1853, and then in two folio volumes, the latter consists of fifty-five magnificent illustrations after Joseph Nash (1808–78), a topographical artist well known for his *The Mansions of England in the Olden Time* (1839), Louis Haghe (1806–85), and David Roberts (1796–1864).

But of all the illustrated works one stands out—a special edition of fifteen copies of *Reports of the Juries*, published in 1852 in four huge quarto volumes, bound in full crimson morocco gilt by Rivière, with the entwined monogram of Victoria and Albert tooled in gold on the front, and with end-papers of purple watered silk. More striking than their sumptuous make-up is the fact that they are illustrated not by chromolithographs but by specially inserted photographs by William Henry Fox Talbot, F.R.S. (1800–77) (Figs. 100–102). A gift to him from the Royal Commissioners, and in turn presented by Fox Talbot to a select list of recipients, these great books represent the opening of a new stage in the development of documentary art, comparable in importance with the position held by Paxton's palace of iron and glass in the history of architecture. For this pointed the way to structures such as the roof spans of St Pancras Station by W. H. Barlow (1812–1902) and York by Thomas Prosser (Figs. 103, 104) and the sections of iron-ribbed tunnel of the Metropolitan Railway, of lesser span but carrying greater loads (Fig. 105).

8 NEW-FANGLED MEN

The horse, in moving along the top of the embankment, draws the rope attached to the wheelbarrow round two pulleys, and thereby raises the barrow of earth up the sloping board, together with the labourer who holds and guides it. This is a dangerous occupation, for the man rather hangs to, than supports the barrow, which is rendered unmanageable by the least irregularity in the horse's motion. If he finds himself unable to govern it, he endeavours, by a sudden jerk, to raise himself erect; then, throwing the barrow over one side of the board, or 'run', he swings himself round and runs down the other. Should both fall on the same side, his best speed is necessary to escape the barrow, which, with its contents, comes bounding down after him. Although . . . each labourer was precipitated down the slopes several times; such, from continual practice, was their sure-footedness, that only one fatal accident occurred. A moving platform was invented by the engineer to supersede the necessity of thus risking life and limb, but the workmen, who considered it was designed to lessen their labour and wages, broke it.[1]
JOHN BRITTON

FIVE YEARS after the Great Exhibition, in April 1856, a banquet was held in London to celebrate the anniversary of *The People's Paper*, edited by the Chartist leader, Ernest Jones (1819–69). The first toast fell to Karl Marx (1818–83), representing the foreign refugees. Among other things, he said:

There is one great fact, characteristic of this, our nineteenth century, a fact which no party dares deny. On the one hand, there have started into life industrial and scientific forces, which no epoch of the former human history ever suspected. On the other hand, there exist symptoms of decay, far surpassing the horrors recorded of the latter times of the Roman empire. In our days everything seems pregnant with its contrary; machinery gifted with the wonderful power of shortening and fructifying human labour, we behold starving and overworking it. The new-fangled sources of wealth, by some strange weird spell, are turned into sources of want. The victories of art seem bought by a loss of character.

166

At the same pace that mankind masters nature, man seems to become enslaved to other men or to his own infamy. Even the pure light of science seems unable to shine but on the dark background of ignorance. All our invention and progress seem to result in endowing material forces with intellectual life, and in stultifying human life into a material force. This antagonism between modern industry and science on the one hand, modern misery and dissolution on the other hand; this antagonism between the productive powers and the social relations of our epoch is a fact, palpable, overwhelming, and not to be controverted. Some parties may wail over it; others may wish to get rid of modern arts in order to get rid of modern conflicts. Or they imagine that so signal a progress in industry wants to be completed by as signal a regress in politics. On our part, we do not mistake the shape of the shrewd spirit that continues to mark all these contradictions. We know that to work well the new-fangled forces of society, they only want to be mastered by new-fangled men— and such are the working men. They are as much the invention of modern times as machinery itself . . .[2]

NOVELS OF WORKING-CLASS LIFE

Of the 'first-born sons of modern industry', as Marx called the English working men later in his speech, the great novelists of the period, unfortunately, give only an inadequate picture. Not that they tried to evade the issue. Precisely in the age of the Chartists the writers made a serious effort to understand the condition and outlook of the working people. The ground had long been prepared by the political journalists in the Radical and Chartist camps who followed in the wake of Cobbett, and it was covered in a memorable way in the great blue books of the 1840s and '50s. Even before the most stirring of these, the *First Report of the Commissioners for Inquiry into the Employment and Condition of Children in Mines and Manufactories* and Edward Chadwick's *Report . . . into the Sanitary Condition of the Labouring Population*, had both appeared in 1842, Mrs Frances Trollope (1780–1863) made the sufferings of the children in the cotton mills the theme of her novel, *The Life and Adventures of Michael Armstrong, the Factory Boy*, published in 1840 (Figs. 64, 65). Stirred by what she found in the cotton towns, Mrs Trollope chose the novel form in the hope that it would more effectively arouse the conscience of the ruling classes. For, like Dickens, she was profoundly disturbed by the Chartist struggle that reached its climax while she was writing. She believed, however, that it was the duty of the workers to win their cause by reason and logic alone, without taking direct action and without questioning the essential doctrines underlying the society of which they found themselves a part. Accordingly, as she explains in the preface, she felt herself compelled to abandon her plan to write a sequel in which a grown-up Michael Armstrong would embark on those 'perfectly constitutional struggles for the amelioration of the sufferings of his class', because she considered so many working-class reformers had not only perpetrated 'scenes of outrage and lawless violence' but supported doctrines 'subversive of every species of social order'.

Sybil, published by Benjamin Disraeli (1804–81) in 1845, is the archetype of the novel of political propaganda as analysed in the *Communist Manifesto* in 1848:

In order to arouse sympathy, the aristocracy was obliged to lose sight, apparently, of its own interests, and to formulate its indictment against the bourgeoisie in the interest of the exploited working class alone. Thus the aristocracy took their revenge by singing lampoons on their new master, and whispering in his ears sinister prophecies of coming catastrophe.

In this way arose feudal socialism: half lamentation, half lampoon; half echo of the past, half menace of the future; at times, by its bitter, witty and incisive criticism, striking the bourgeoisie to the very heart's core, but always ludicrous in its effect, through total incapacity to comprehend the march of modern history.[3]

Nevertheless, an exciting echo of real life animates Disraeli's novel, in spite of its pasteboard characters and preposterous plot concerning a Chartist leader who turns out in the end to be the rightful heir of a great estate, stolen from his family at the time of the dissolution of the monasteries by the ancestors of the grasping Whig now in possession. Its limitations only become glaring in comparison with Mrs Gaskell's portrayal of the workers in *Mary Barton* (1848) and *North and South* (1855). As the wife of a Unitarian minister in Manchester, Elizabeth Gaskell had every opportunity for studying the daily problems of working-class life, and she counted many Chartists among her friends. Hence she had in an eminent degree what Disraeli lacked, a thorough first-hand knowledge of the workers. She expressed her sincere admiration of them to the end of her life, not only in words but in deeds, for she was tireless in organizing relief during the cotton famine of 1862. Her championship of the mill-girls and her denunciation of the Cinderella-mentality which made so many of them dream of escaping from their class only to lead them into prostitution, made her a fearless and warm-hearted friend of the oppressed. The chapter in *Mary Barton* where John Barton describes his visit to London as a Chartist delegate surely deserves to be treasured as one of the most precious literary possessions of the British working class. Nevertheless, Elizabeth Gaskell failed to appreciate the great constructive achievement of the workers in building up their own independent organizations. For she makes the trade union into a sinister conspiracy that drives John Barton, maddened by hunger and suffering, to political assassination. In *North and South*, it is true, Mrs Gaskell shows herself much better informed. In the great strike against Thornton and his fellow mill-owners, the union seeks to gain the sympathy of the public by a policy of strict non-violence. Although this is frustrated and the strike lost through the lack of discipline of a section of the workers, the hard struggle of the union to build up a spirit of disciplined co-operation is denounced as a new form of tyranny. This, and not merely the system of exploitation, is made responsible for the suicide of the weakling Boucher. In the end Nicholas Higgins, the staunch trade unionist, and John Thornton learn to appreciate each other's good qualities and to work together, without abandoning their opposed points of view. Mrs Gaskell's conclusion is that the class struggle and strikes will remain, but that much suffering can be avoided by greater candour and sympathy between masters and men.

Between the publication of *Mary Barton* and *North and South* there appeared *Yeast* (1848) and *Alton Locke* (1850) by Charles Kingsley (1819–75), *Shirley* (1849) by Charlotte Brontë (1816–55), and Dickens' *Hard Times* (1854). None of these writers approach Mrs Gaskell's insight into contemporary working-class life. For all its sincerity, Kingsley's 'Christian Socialism' was broadly based on the outlook of the middle class. Like Carlyle's cult of the hero, which grew steadily more reactionary from the publication of *Past and Present* in 1843 to *Latter-Day Pamphlets* in 1850, it was fundamentally conservative. Even Charlotte Brontë's stirring picture of the workers' struggle in *Shirley* is moved back to the days of the Luddites, depicting therefore not contemporary workers but their ancestors, the craftsmen, in their desperate resistance to subjection by the machine. Dickens was so obviously out of his depth when he tried to deal with the conditions of the industrial north that the failure of *Hard Times*, evident from its grating, caricature-like form, is scarcely surprising.

None of these writers understood what was the distinguishing, unprecedented feature in the outlook of the new industrial workers—their acceptance of the machine and their determination to build a new and better life by co-operating in its use. That the Victorian novelists failed to see this is the more remarkable, since they were so brilliant in depicting the middle and upper classes. The women writers, in particular, were acute and subtle in observing the changing relationships between the various sections of those classes. What more felicitous than the formidable Mrs Cadwallader in *Middlemarch*, whose 'feeling for the vulgar rich was a sort of religious hatred: they had probably made all their money out of high retail prices. . . . Such people were no part of God's design in making the world.'[4] The new masters were as much the products of modern industry as the new workers.

Although what seemed their vulgar manners disturbed the hierarchy of rank and birth, and shocked the sensibilities of the gentry (and of the writers trained in the traditions of the gentry), the landlords and the new capitalists were not irreconcilable. Both lived by other men's labour, and the quarrels between them merely concerned the redistribution of the spoils they extorted from the working population. Both had fundamentally the same outlook. Not so the workers. When, therefore, the Victorian novelists stepped out of their elegant drawing-rooms, or even out of the suburban semi-detached villas, into the back-to-back cottages in the industrial slums, it was as if they had floundered into an alien civilization with language, customs and morals as unintelligible to them as Polynesian totemism to the early missionaries.[5]

'SELF-HELP'

The simplest way to appreciate the difference in outlook between the two new classes in nineteenth-century society, the capitalists and the industrial workers, is to glance at the writings of Samuel Smiles (1812–1904). In the *Lives of the Engineers* (1861–2), and in such works as *Industrial Biography* (1863) and *Men of Invention and Industry* (1884), that tireless publicist for the new middle-class ethic paints a fascinating picture of human achievement. It is a sort of heroes' gallery devoted to the arts of peace and, as such, consciously opposed to the feudal glorification of the arts of war. On page after page, brilliantly gifted men rise from the ranks and, struggling against all sorts of adverse conditions, become great inventors, engineers, and captains of industry. There is a pleasing radicalism about Smiles. Again and again he points out how many key inventions came from the workshop and not from the study. He chooses his heroes by preference from those great engineers, like James Brindley or George Stephenson, who did, in fact, start as workers. The qualities that enabled these men to rise in the world he finds admirable in themselves: intelligence, perseverance, application, foresight— virtues which Smiles summarizes in such works as *Self-Help* (1859), *Character* (1871), *Thrift* (1875) and *Duty* (1880). Proud of their achievements, Smiles' heroes resent interference in the conduct of their affairs. They expect their employees to display the qualities by which they themselves have risen to be masters. At this point a discord inevitably creeps into Smiles' epic tale. Having pursued his career through struggles and hardship, the hero at last sets up his own business and opens a factory. He prospers. Orders flow in. He is on excellent terms with his workers. Then suddenly—trouble! The workers resent the employment of un-

170

skilled labour on some particular job they regard as skilled. The conditions of apprenticeship customary in their trade (but according to the employer now out of date, because the technique has changed) must be observed, or they will go on strike to enforce the principle of the closed shop. In short, they act in a way which a Smiles hero, say a Nasmyth or a Fairbairn, cannot but regard not only as an infringement of his right 'to do what he likes with his own' but also as an attempt to curtail the liberty of those workers who might otherwise be inclined to follow the road of self-advancement. There was no possible means of reconciling these two points of view. Each was the expression of material conditions from which neither party could escape. The ideology of self-help alone could fit the capitalists for the ruthless competition they had to face. The need for interdependent solidarity was the bitter lesson the workers learned in the factory, where each was at the mercy of his masters unless all acted together.

Thornton was right in stating that all workers who achieved advancement must abandon their fellows to enter the masters' camp, however humble their reward might be. Moreover, the doctrine of self-help as preached to the workers by Samuel Smiles was an illusion, for even if every worker had been a devoted follower of Smiles, only a negligible minority could possibly have succeeded in rising above its station. Neverthless, self-help of a kind was as necessary to the workers as to the budding capitalists. It took many bitter disappointments before the workers ceased to believe that the Queen or the Prince Consort or Parliament would help them if only they knew the truth. The refusal of Parliament to accept the Charter petition of 1839 brought the final and most cruel awakening (Elizabeth Gaskell makes it the turning-point in John Barton's career). But the kind of self-help that alone could improve the workers' lot, or even enable them to maintain their standards, was the exact opposite of that taught by Smiles. It implied that each worker should fight for himself by fighting side by side with his comrades, all for all, instead of the capitalist war of all against all. It implied the organization of a united working class.

THE ENGLISH NAVVY

How true this was is shown by the experience of one special group of workers, the navvies, who were regarded by the middle classes with a kind of awe-struck admiration as the very cream of the sturdy and independent British working man (Figs. 80, 81 and 82). Samuel Smiles, himself the secretary of the South Eastern Railway and who was largely following earlier railway writers such as John Francis and Frederick Williams, paints this picture of the navvy:

The labourers who executed these formidable works were in many respects a remarkable class. The 'railway navvies', as they were called, were men drawn by the attraction of good wages from all parts of the kingdom . . . and some of the best came from the fen districts of Lincoln and Cambridge, where they had been trained to execute works of excavation and embankment . . . Their expertness in all sorts of earthwork, in embanking, boring, and well-sinking—their practical knowledge of the nature of soils and rocks, the tenacity of clays, and the porosity of certain stratifications—were very great; and, rough-looking as they were, many of them were as important in their own department as the contractor or the engineer.

During the railway-making period the navvy wandered about from one public work to another—apparently belonging to no country and having no home. He usually wore a white felt hat with the brim turned up, a velveteen or jean square-tailed coat, a scarlet plush waistcoat with little black spots, and a bright-coloured kerchief round his herculean neck, when, as often happened, it was not left entirely bare. His corduroy breeches were retained in position by a leathern strap round the waist, and were tied and buttoned at the knee, displaying beneath a solid calf and foot encased in strong high-laced boots. Joining together in a 'butty-gang', some ten or twelve of these men would take a contract to cut out and remove so much 'dirt'—as they denominated earth-cutting—fixing their price according to the character of the 'stuff', and the distance to which it had to be wheeled and tipped . . . Their powers of endurance were extraordinary. In times of emergency they would work for twelve and even sixteen hours, with only short intervals for meals . . . They displayed great pluck, and seemed to disregard peril. Indeed the most dangerous sort of labour—such as working horse-barrow runs, in which accidents are of constant occurrence—has always been most in request amongst them, the danger seeming to be one of its chief recommendations.[6]

Such was the navvy as he appeared to Samuel Smiles, a warm-hearted member of the Victorian middle class with radical leanings who had played an active part in the agitation for the repeal of the Corn Laws when he was a newspaper editor at Leeds. He appeared in the same light to Ford Madox Brown (1821–93) who made him the central figure in his great allegorical composition 'Work', (Fig. 115). It is an attractive and sympathetic picture, but it does not penetrate beyond the outer shell of appearances. To appreciate the reality it is necessary to turn to the statement Henry Mayhew (1812-87) took in 1849 on a bitterly cold night from a navvy, sheltering in the Refuge for the Houseless at Playhouse Yard, Cripplegate. His Odyssey gives a truer picture of the real cost of the great railway-building campaigns than the story of Hudson or even that of Stephenson. Mayhew's navvy 'was a fine, stoutly built fellow, with a fresh-coloured open countenance, and flaxen hair—indeed, altogether a splendid specimen of the Saxon Labourer. He was habited in a short smockfrock, yellow in parts with clay, and he wore the

172

heavy high lace-up boots, so characteristic of the tribe'. But they 'were burst, and almost soleless with long wear'. This is what he had to say:

I have been a navvy for about eighteen years. The first work that I done was on the Manchester and Liverpool. I was a lad then. I used to grease the railway wagons, and got about 1s 6d a-day. There we had a tommy-shop, and we had to go there and get our bit of victuals, and they used to charge us an extra price. The next place I had after that was on the London and Brummagem. There I went as a horse-driver, and had 2s 6d a day. Things was dear then, and at the tommy-shop they was much dearer. . . What the contractors, you see, can't make out of the company, they fleeces out of the men. . . If we didn't eat and drink at the tommy-shop we should have no work. . . . I went to work on the London and York. Here we had only 2s 9d a day, and we had only four days' work in the week to do besides . . . I stopped on this line (for work was very scarce, and I thought myself lucky to have any) till last spring. Then all the work on it stopped, and I dare say 2000 men were thrown out of employ in one day. They were all starving, the heap of them, or next door to it. I went away from there over to the Brummagem and Beechley branch line. . . . I left the Brummagem and Beechley line, about two months before Christmas before last, and then I came to Copenhagen-fields, on the London and York—the London end, sir; and there I was till last March, when we were all paid off, about 600 on us; and I went back to Barnet. Whilst I was there, I hurted my leg, and was laid up a month. I lived all that time on charity; on what the chaps would come and give me. One would give a shilling, another sixpence, another a shilling, just as they could spare it; and poorly they could do that, God knows! I couldn't declare onto the sick fund, because I hadn't no bones broken. Well, when I come to look for work, and that's three weeks agone, when I could get about again, the work was all stopped, and I couldn't get none to do. . . I went to a lodging-house in the Borough, and I sold all my things—shovel and grafting-tool and all, to have a meal of food. When all my things was gone, I didn't know where to go. . . . If I could get any interest, I should like to go away as an emigrant. . . . This country is getting very bad for labour; it's so overrun with Irish that the Englishman hasn't a chance in his own land to live. Ever since I was nine years old I've got my own living, but now I'm dead beat, though I'm only twenty-eight next August.[7]

GODFREY SYKES AND JAMES SHARPLES

Just as the novels of the 1840s and '50s on working-class themes are full of interest, despite their limitations, so are the contemporary paintings that provide equally valuable records. Henry Perlee Parker's painting of miners has already been mentioned (Plate I). 'The Dinner Hour: Wigan' (Fig. 113), by Eyre Crowe (1824–1910), is similar in spirit and execution.

More attractive, because less self-conscious and more objective, is a group of small oil paintings by Godfrey Sykes (1825–66), an engraver and designer of Sheffield plate. He was at home among the quaint old-fashioned workshops of that city, where little had changed since the eighteenth century. His romantic views of water-driven tilt-hammers, smiths' shops and grinders' hulls are generally supported by well-observed groups of workers. The Sheffield City Art Gallery, where most of these pictures are preserved, also has preliminary watercolour sketches for some of them. They were evidently taken on the spot and show how very much smaller these workshops actually were than they appear in Sykes' finished pictures (Fig. 107). When Alfred Stevens (1817–75) came to that town in 1850–1 to work as as industrial designer for the firm of Hoole, he appointed Sykes as his assistant. Ten years later Sykes came to London to take part in the decoration of the South Kensington Museum.[8]

There exist, also, two engravings that show an engineering workshop as seen through the eyes of a worker employed in it. These are the work of James Sharples (1825–92),[9] a lifelong member of the Amalgamated Society of Engineers. Sharples was born at Wakefield in Yorkshire, one of thirteen children. His father was a blacksmith. When he was 10 years old he got his first job as a smith's boy in Kay's Phoenix Foundry at Bury, where his father was working in the engine shop. From six in the morning to seven or eight at night he heated and carried rivets for the boiler-makers. In his spare time he managed to learn to read and his mother later taught him to write. His talent for drawing was discovered when he helped his foreman in chalking out designs on the workshop floor. His elder brother, Peter, who later emigrated to Canada and became a railway engineer, encouraged him to practise figure and landscape drawing and to copy lithographs. At sixteen he attended a drawing class for six months, one evening a week, at the Bury Mechanics' Institute, where he was taught by a genial barber and signwriter called Billy Binns. Then he got hold of a copy of John Burnet's *A Practical Treatise on Painting* (1827). Although he still had a great difficulty in reading, he studied this work assiduously early in the morning and late at night.

At the age of 18 he felt able to start experimenting in oils. He made himself an easel and a palette and invested in brushes and paints, walking eighteen miles to Manchester and back to buy them. After finishing a still-life and a landscape, he began his most important work, 'The Forge', on a canvas of fifty-two by thirty-eight inches in 1844. To help him overcome his difficulties with anatomy, his brother bought him Flaxman's Anatomical Studies and posed for him. James volunteered to undertake the heavier kinds of work at the factory, because the material required for large engine parts or mill-gear took longer to heat. This gave him time to study Brook Taylor's *New Principles of Linear Perspective*, published

174

in 1719, and to draw exercises from it on the sheet-iron casing in front of the hearth. Under such conditions 'The Forge' was finished in the autumn of 1847, after about three years of spare-time work.

In the same year Sharples painted a portrait of his father and a group portrait of his foreman, James Crossland, with his wife and child (Fig. 109). His fee for the latter was £18. James Crossland, in wing collar and black choker, is seated, his right hand on an open book on a table. Others are piled up. Of these, one is the *Practical Mechanic*, Vol. II, and another, a copy of the *Magazine of Science*, with an engraving of Henson's Aerial Steam Carriage. The Crosslands could be lay figures for any Smiles group, the man bent on self-improvement, the women modest and respectable; the man a trifle larger than life, the woman a trifle smaller.

Shortly before, in 1846, Sharples had finished his apprenticeship at the Phoenix Foundry and, encouraged by Zanetti of the firm of Agnew and Zanetti, art dealers of Manchester, he decided to devote himself exclusively to art. He spent the next fifteen months mainly painting portraits, though he also executed a 'Head of Christ', a romantic scene from Gray's *Elegy*, and a large view of Bury in 1848.[10] At the end of this period he returned to the foundry, devoting his creative energies not so much to painting as to designing and engraving. Noticing an advertisement by a Sheffield manufacturer of steel plates for engravers, he ordered one measuring twenty-one by eighteen inches, made himself a press and the necessary tools, and spent ten years of his spare time, from 1849 to 1859, engraving 'The Forge' on steel (Fig. 108). He did not use acid even in the darkest shades, but cut the whole design by hand with the needle. When the plate was at last finished in the autumn of 1859 he took it to London to have it printed. To his suprise it was an immense success. It pleased the critics and was reviewed by all the important periodicals. Thousands of copies were sold. James Sharples, the blacksmith-artist, had become famous overnight.[11]

So far, Sharples' story reads like a chapter out of Smiles, and that is, in fact, where many of the details are to be found. When 'The Forge' was published, Smiles wrote to the artist and got his story from him for inclusion in later editions of *Self-Help*, first published in 1860. What Smiles does not say, however, is that the success of the engraving did not enable Sharples to 'better' himself in the world. He was exploited outrageously by the print-sellers, and what he did earn from the sale of his prints went to support his family during several prolonged periods of illness and unemployment. Nevertheless, Sharples did not lose heart. In about 1865 he started work on 'The Smithy', a companion piece to 'The Forge'. He did not engrave it, but his executors issued prints in 'Goupilgravure' in 1894, a year after his death.

As soon as it was founded the Amalgamated Society of Engineers organized a competition for the best design for its emblem. It was won by Sharples in 1851 and he received the prize of £5. A pentecostal dove hovers over a winged genius on a cornucopia who holds haloes over the heads of two workers, one on each side. One worker declines to repair the broken sword of Mars; the other receives a scroll from an angel of peace. On each side again, forming, as it were, the base of a pyramid, two slaves demonstrate that unity is strength by the legendary bundle of sticks. All these figures are grouped on a plinth with three embrasures, the outer ones containing portraits of Crompton and Arkwright in contemporary dress, the centre one a bust of Watt in a toga. Supporting them all, a manufactory, its side cut away to reveal its inner workings in doll's-house detail, surmounts the legend BE UNITED AND INDUSTRIOUS (Fig. 110).

At a time when the arts had long forsaken the classical myths and figures so loved by Erasmus Darwin and so despised by Wordsworth, the workers of mid-Victorian England still used the old mixture of allegory and engineering detail to express their deep and genuine emotions in a true folk art that decorated the walls of countless workers' homes.

The great craft unions were not only effective fighting organizations. They also exhibit to an eminent degree that element in the workers' outlook stressed by Marx in his address at the People's Paper banquet, their pride in the new forces of production and their confidence in their own ability to master those forces. While the more primitive attitude of hostility to the machine was still widespread, even in the Chartist period, and was expressed, for example, in the poem on 'King Steam' by Edward P. Mead of Birmingham, reprinted in Engels' *Condition of the Working Class in England in 1844*, a proud interest in technical progress is evident in some of the miners' songs of the period.

The same spirit of pride animates such working drawings as those made by John Nuttall, already mentioned, and it is the essence of James Sharples' art. To quote his own words, 'The Forge' represents 'the interior of a large work-shop such as I have been accustomed to work in, although not of any particular shop'. The meticulous care with which the tools, ranged along the wall or lying on the floor, are drawn reflect the craftsman's pride in his job. One can be quite certain that an engineering shop of the 1840s looked exactly like this. But it is in the figures that Sharples' art differs most significantly from the sentimental or

176

romantic attitude of his middle-class contemporaries. Although there is nothing else like them in English painting, they are surprisingly similar to Millet's heroic peasants. Classical simplification is combined with realistic detail to express the heroism of the first-born sons of modern industry.

CASHBOX AESTHETICS

It required the broad canvas of the Victorian novel and its deep human sympathy to trace the progress of the individual through the shifting social relationships of this vigorous age, and its triumphs and disasters. On the other hand, the decline of English painting after Turner and Constable is related to the new standard of values established by the triumphant capitalists. Accustomed to the common level of market-place, they often lacked all appreciation of qualities that did not immediately suggest costliness. Minutely detailed copies of commonplace objects, either very large or very small (for both required enormous amounts of painstaking labour), banal sentiment, and heavy gold frames amply satisfied the normal taste of the newly rich, and their older landed partners in the ruling class often followed their example in this as in most other things. 'The painters, such were the financial inducements, became purveyors of the patrons' tastes, caterers in fact. . . . Nothing recondite or surprising (and certainly nothing naked or sordid) was wanted, and the careers of the Victorian painters showed a regular pattern from high promise to pot-boiling and replica painting.'[12] The calculated ostentation in furnishings, food and drink which the businessman affected in order to impress the world with his unlimited command of credit is amply documented by the furniture illustrated in the catalogue of the Great Exhibition of 1851.

FORD MADOX BROWN

Pre-Raphaelite art as a whole, with its jewel-like colouring and nostalgic medievalism, is perhaps best understood in terms of the drab monotony and ugliness of the industrial towns in which it found its chief admirers.[13] On the other hand, Ford Madox Brown, a friend and sympathizer, but not a member of the Pre-Raphaelite brotherhood, had more positive links with contemporary realities. His importance in the present context lies in the fact that some of his pictures express experiences that go to the roots of English life. His famous picture, 'Work' (Fig. 115), for instance, painted between 1852 and 1865, with its chiselled outlines, motionless atmosphere and bright colours, has a monumental quality, like a stained-glass

177

window. At first sight the four navvies, shovelling earth out of a deep excavation in Heath Street, Hampstead, carrying bricks or resting for a drink, have the same splendid physique, picturesque clothes and proud disdain for the rest of the population as those described by Smiles. But, unlike that writer, Brown shared the navvies' view of their status. They occupy the centre of his composition, which symbolizes modern society. They provide the foundation that sustains all other ranks. While harvesters sleep in the shadow by the roadside and thus supplement the working group, all other grades flutter round it like butterflies. They range from the intellectuals, like Thomas Carlyle and the Rev. Frederick Dennison Maurice (1805–72), lounging against the rail on the right, to the beggar clothed in fantastic rags carrying a basket of wild flowers on the left. The programme of this grand composition was largely coloured by Carlyle's denunciation of capitalist society and by the ideas of the Christian Socialists and other middle-class friends of the workers; indeed, at the time he was painting it, Brown himself was giving art classes at the Workingmen's College.

The fact that, at the same time, Brown was also painting 'The Last of England' (Fig. 116) proves that he was also aware of that other side of the workers' experience which Mayhew's navvy revealed. Into it Brown put everything he felt when he saw his friend, the poet and sculptor Thomas Woolner (1825–92), off to Australia on the emigrants' ship at Tilbury.

Ford Madox Brown greatly influenced the work of a whole group of artists, mainly living in the provinces—'Iron and Coal' (Fig. 112), for instance, by William Bell Scott (1811–90), one of a series of eight murals he was commissioned to paint in 1861 to decorate the new picture gallery of Sir Walter Trevelyan at Wallington Hall, Northumberland. It presents a fascinating view of Tyneside, just after the opening of Robert Stephenson's High Level Bridge, which can be seen in the distance. All the local industries are represented, and the three hammermen are portraits of men from the works of Robert Stephenson & Co., locomotive builders. The newspaper in the corner records the victory of Garibaldi at Caserta in 1861.

But in Brown's own last and most surprising work, twelve murals in the Manchester Town Hall, scarcely a trace of the Pre-Raphaelite manner intrudes. Painted between 1886 and 1891, they are unlike the historical cycles that are found in so many civic buildings of the Victorian age. In the first place, seven out of the twelve subjects have a direct bearing on the history of education, science, or industry. That reproduced in Fig. 114 is 'The Opening of the Bridgewater Canal in 1761'. Other subjects are John Kay, the inventor of the flying shuttle, escaping from his home in 1753 before it was wrecked by other weavers who feared being put out of work by his invention, and John Dalton pursuing his epoch-making chemical experiments. At the same time these low, wide panels with their unusual foreshortenings and distortions reveal a striving for a new form that points, ultimately, to Stanley Spencer (1891–1959).

Parallel with the development of this realist wing at a time dominated by the Pre-Raphaelites, the interest in social documentation had also been strengthened by the emergence of a new kind of pictorial reporting which followed the foundation of the *Illustrated London News* in 1841. The illustrators of this paper, who included such superb draughtsmen as Constantin Guys (1802–92), were in constant touch with developments in industry and the labour movement (Fig. 111).

Towards the end of the 'sixties a whole group of young artists, including Frank Holl (1845–88), Luke Fildes (1844–1927), and Hubert Herkomer (1849–1914), as well as followers of Brown, were painting work and other 'social problem' pictures. Most of them contributed to the *Graphic*, founded in December 1869, and their full-page drawings of factories, mines, refuges for the homeless, *émigré* ships, and of individual workers, were also published separately in the *Graphic Portfolio*.

The work of this school also had a widespread influence abroad. Vincent Van Gogh (1853–90), for example, who worked in the London branch of his uncle's firm, the Goupil Galleries, from 1873 to 1875, and visited England again for eight months in 1876, was thoroughly acquainted with it. In a list of his most treasured possessions which he sent to his brother Theo, in June 1882, he mentioned specifically a folder containing 'the large pages of *Graphic*, *London News*, *Harper's Weekly*, *Illustration*, etc.' The whole, he says, forms an interesting series of 'sketches of London life, types of the people, from the opium-smokers . . . to the most elegant ladies' figures and Rotten Row or Westminster Park. To these are added similar scenes from Paris and New York, so the whole is a curious "tale of those cities" '. Another folder has 'Irish types, miners, factories, fishers, etc.' Among the English artists Van Gogh mentions are Luke Fildes, Boyd Houghton, Hubert Herkomer, Frank Holl and Frederick Walker (1840–75).[14]

By 1892 many Continental artists were painting the kind of social themes that interested the illustrators of the *Graphic*. In France the tradition of the work pictures of Jean François Millet (1812–75) and Gustave Courbet (1819–77) was continued by the *plein-air* painters such as Jules Bastien-Lepage (1848–84) and Léon Augustin Lhermitte (1844–1925), and also on occasions by most of the Impressionists. The same social preoccupation characterizes the work of both the

179

Dutch painter, Joseph Israels (1824–1911), and his pupil, Max Liebermann (1847–1935). In 1875, Adolf Menzel (1815–95) composed his famous picture of a rolling mill.[15] In the 'eighties, Constantin Meunier (1831–1905) began his grand series of paintings and sculptures of industrial workers. Before the end of the century both Aimé Jules Dalou (1838–1902) and Auguste Rodin (1840–1917) had modelled hundreds of brilliant sketches and motion studies of all kinds of workers for their projected monuments of labour. Alexander Steinlen (1859–1923), an outstanding figure among the socially conscious graphic artists of the late nineteenth and early twentieth centuries in France, arrived in Paris in 1882. Thus Ford Madox Brown and the English reporter-illustrators form the link between the documentary art which reflected the industrial revolution and the later trend in art on the Continent which came to reflect in its turn the growing influence of Socialism. However, such subtle but direct approaches towards realism were not the only aesthetic evaluations of the industrial revolution in the second half of the nineteenth century.

GUSTAVE DORÉ, JAMES MACNEIL WHISTLER AND JULES VERNE

William Blanchard Jerrold (1826–84), a journalist with vaguely liberal radical leanings, and Gustave Doré (1832–83) succeeded in confusing the critical issues of the time in one of the most striking pieces of social reporting in the whole nineteenth century, *London, A Pilgrimage*, published in 1872. In this work, Jerrold and Doré proposed to show 'how the conglomerate millions act and react upon each other . . . till the ingenious man is lost in wonder over the infinite methods which Competition has invented of earning a leg of mutton . . .'[16] They planned to approach London life, not as historians or topographers, but as 'pilgrims, wanderers [and] gipsy loiterers.'[17] 'Waking London'—Jerrold explained—'is, indeed a wonderful place to study, from the park where the fortunate in the world's battle are gathering roses, to the stone-yard by Shadwell where, at daybreak . . . the houseless, who had a crust and a shake-down in the casual ward, turn to the dreary labour by which it is to be paid.'[18]

To Jerrold the ulcerated ferocity of the London slums had primarily a romantic or even an aesthetic appeal. 'Every twisting or backing of a cart; every shifting of the busy groups suggests a happy combination of lines and light and shade.'[19] Of those who manoeuvred the carts or assembled in such picturesque groups, 'he who falls from honest, methodical, skilled labour . . . must earn his shilling or eighteenpence a day as boardman or dock labourer; or he must withdraw to the workhouse, or starve;' or become a criminal.[20]

Gustave Doré[21] was the son of an engineer of the Département des Ponts et Chaussées of Strasbourg. From his earliest childhood he practised with a pencil. At the age of 16 he witnessed the Revolution of 1848 in Paris and was deeply disturbed by what he saw, though he afterwards displayed no political preferences for one side or the other. In a short time he became famous as an incredibly fecund, imaginative, rapid and slightly facile draughtsman and caricaturist. Yet, in spite of his success, he was an embittered, frustrated man. Disdaining his own natural talent, he thought of himself as a painter in the grand tradition. Huge canvasses of religious and historical subjects accumulated in his studio. The French critics laughed at them, and they failed to sell.

As an illustrator, Doré followed John Martin and illustrated both the Bible and *Paradise Lost*. However, where Martin is reflecting the anxiety of his age, Doré seems to be expressing his own personal anxiety and animosity. His masterpiece is Dante's *Inferno*, first published in 1861. It is evident that he identifies himself with Dante and Vergil, who are present in almost every illustration. Perhaps the pain and punishments he reveals in such alarming detail represent his revenge on the world at large for withholding approval of his works.

At the invitation of Jerrold, Doré came to England in 1869 to begin the illustrations of *London*. In the final version, while Jerrold's style owes something of its colour to Dickens but substitutes sanctimonious moralizing for Dickens' creative vision, Doré's drawings have an extraordinary power and bravura, but also a kind of over-dramatized unreality. Engraved partly on wood and partly on steel, they are crowded, energetic and often frenzied. By night and by day, in the parks and in the opium dens, in the ballrooms of 'May Fair' and in Newgate Prison, at the Derby and in Rotherhithe, from the Choir of Westminster Abbey to the whelk-stalls of Houndsditch, the people of London go restlessly about their pleasures and their toil. The society ladies are as light and ephemeral as gossamer, the working women as brawny as pugilists. Doré is obsessed by the spectacle of deprivation and misery to the partial exclusion of human observation and character.

For Bourne's lucid affection for the railway navvies, Mahew's compassion for the predicament of the poor, and Dickens' hot indignation, Doré substituted an element of morbid hysteria. The identity of art and industry of earlier times has disappeared from his work. Under the contradiction of man's increasing mastery of technology in a society lacerated by unemployment, crime and poverty, his vision has failed him.

Though Doré's contemporary, James MacNeil Whistler (1834–1903), was a witness of the same scenes of urban and industrial life that Doré observed with such virtuosity, he declined to include them in his delicate vision. In the 'eighties, he delivered the famous lecture he called 'The Ten O'Clock' with the thesis that Nature is usually wrong:

The sun blazes, the wind blows from the east, the sky is bereft of cloud, and without, all is iron. The windows of the Crystal Palace are seen from all points of London. The holiday-makers rejoice in the glorious day, and the painter turns aside to shut his eyes . . .
   And when the evening mist clothes the riverside with poetry, as with a veil, and the poor buildings lose themselves in the dim sky, and the tall chimneys become campanili, and the warehouses are palaces in the night, and the whole city hangs in the heavens, and fairy-land is before us . . . Nature who, for once, has sung in tune, sings her exquisite song to the artist alone . . .[22]

Though he may not have been aware of it, Whistler had been anticipated by Sir Robert Rawlinson (1810–98), a civil engineer who believed he could convert tall chimneys to campanili without the aid of an evening mist. Trained by Robert Stephenson, he was appointed chief engineering inspector to the Local Government Board in 1848. In 1858 he published *Designs for Factory Furnace and other tall Chimney Shafts*, consisting of a short introduction and 24 plates lithographed in colour by C. F. Kell. In 1159 there were many tall towers in Pisa, he observes. 'The towers of Asinelli and Garisenda, at Bologna, show how tall-chimney-like they were in appearance . . . The trade requirements of modern times necessitate the building of tall chimneys; and Manchester (in chimneys) can match (for numbers) the numerous tall towers of Pisa, as the manufacturing towns of England can match the other cities of Italy. May we hope that it will become fashionable to strive after grace and ornament . . . There is great beauty in a vertical line.'
   Rawlinson's designs include a detached chimney shaft in common brick, sorted, set and pointed in alternating bands of two colours, intended for the Wigan water-works but unhappily not executed; a ventilating-tower with terra-cotta cornices and an open cast-iron roof; and a detached chimney-shaft with castellated finish-ings suitable for an old county town. Till this day, such monuments to Italian and oriental taste pierce the skyline of our cities, gracing many a pumping station and sewage works. 'Why should modern architects shrink from using "white, black, red, brown" or any other colour,' demands Rawlinson, 'if monotony can be prevented, and the eye and mind gratified?' Why indeed?
   Of all the writers and artists of the late nineteenth century who observed with

dismay their environment transformed by the industrial revolution, Jules Verne (1828–1905)[23] had a vision of the potential of science and technology as bizarre and fantastic as it was imaginative. Underlying his novels of science and travel lay a growing conviction that the machinery of the new industrial age could be brought under control only by the training of a managerial élite.

'O my imagination, my imagination,' cried Jules Verne, 'neither a Crampton locomotive, nor an electric spark, nor a tropical cyclone can keep pace with you.'[24]

Trained as a lawyer, Jules Verne decided to become a professional writer in 1862, encouraged by Alexandre Dumas. By 1865 he was into space-travel with *From the Earth to the Moon*. In 1867 he went on the maiden voyage of Brunel's 'Great Eastern'. His most famous novel, *Twenty Thousand Leagues under the Sea*, came out in 1870. It is the story of a silent, inscrutable, passionate engineer, Captain Nemo, who built the submarine 'Nautilus' and mastered the lower reaches of the oceans.

Of greater significance in the present context is Robur, the garrrulous, truculent, provocative designer and commander of the 'Albatross', a multiple helicopter with 74 horizontal propellers revolving on tall, slender spindles. *Robur le Conquérant* was first published in 1886 and shortly afterwards issued in England under the title *The Clipper of the Clouds*.

After planting a black flag bearing a golden sun surrounded by stars on the highest minaret of St Sophia, the cross of St Peter's, the Eiffel Tower, the Statue of Liberty and a few other places, equally prominent, Robur made his *début* by addressing the Weldon Institute in Philadelphia, a centre of the lighter-than-air school of aeronauts:

Citizens of the United States! My name is Robur. I am worthy of that name! I am forty years old although I look but thirty, and I have a constitution of iron . . . You see before you an engineer whose nerves are in no way inferior to his muscles. I have no fear of anything or anybody . . . When I have decided on a thing, all America, all the world, may strive in vain to keep me from it.[25]

With these words he launched an attack on the past, present and future of lighter-than-air craft and all that the Weldon Institute stood for, subsequently kidnapping the president and secretary and taking them in the 'Albatross' on a fantastic journey round the world.

At the end of the adventures, Jules Verne asks himself the rhetorical question: 'And now, who is this Robur? . . . Robur is the science of the future. Perhaps the science of tomorrow! Certainly the science that will come!'[26]

Robur returned in 1904, in *The Master of the World*. This time he has a machine combining the properties of a submarine, aeroplane and automobile and called 'Epouvante'. It gives him undisputed power over the whole world. 'Let the Old and New Worlds understand that they can do nothing against me and that I can do anything against them,' he states in a manifesto. 'I sign this letter: MASTER OF THE WORLD.' The mad Robur rises from the sea in the 'Epouvante' and makes for an electric storm. Amid the crash of thunder it is just possible to make out his last words: 'I . . . Robur . . . Robur . . . Master of the World'.[27] The lighting strikes. The 'Epouvante' is destroyed.

The year is 1905. Jules Verne is 77. Enfeebled, deaf and nearly blind, he is on his death bed. Einstein is about to publish his Special Theory of Relativity. The Curies have isolated radium. The Wright brothers have taken off from Kitty Hawk. Marconi has sent a signal across the Atlantic . . . In our nucleonic age it is left to the historians to assess the achievements of the age of coal and iron and steam and of the great artists who were concerned with its images.

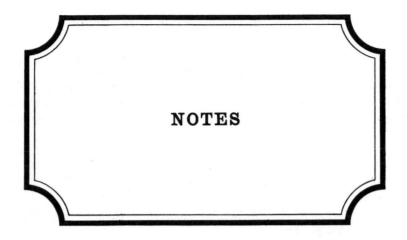

NOTES

Throughout this work, both author and editor have used the standard reference works: *The Dictionary of National Biography*, Bryan's *Dictionary of Painters*, Bénézit's *Dictionnaire des Peintres* and Thieme-Becker's *Kunstler-Lexikon*. More specialized works consulted include Colonel M. H. Grant's *The Old English Landscape Painters* and Roget's *A History of the Old Water Colour Society*. The author's death deprived him of a number of other more recent but equally invaluable works, among them Ellis Waterhouse's *Painting in Britain 1530–1790*, Iolo Williams' *Early English Watercolours*, the three Abbey bibliographies, and *A History of Technology* edited by the late Dr Charles Singer and others, and quoted below as *Hist. Technology*. In the bibliographical references that follow, unless otherwise stated, the place of publication is London.

To provide general background to the first chapter, Klingender drew on the following:

G. N. Clark: *Science and Social Welfare in the age of Newton*, Oxford, 1937.

J. G. Crowther: *The Social Relations of Science*, 1941.

G. W. Daniels: *The Early English Cotton Industry*, Manchester, 1920.

M. Dobb: *Studies in the Development of Capitalism*, 1946.

A. Wolf: *A History of Science, Technology and Philosophy*, 1935–8.

1. *The Revolution in Technique*

[1] Defoe, *A Tour thro' the whole Island of Great Britain, 1724–7*, Vol. 1, pp. ii–iii.

[2] Cleveland: *Poems, Orations, Epistles*, 1650, p. 10.

[3] Defoe, *op.cit.*, vol. 3, letter 1, p. 191.

[4] J. U. Nef, *The Rise of the British Coal Industry*, 1932, vol. 1, p. 20.

[5] The title of his patent of 1630.

[6] The credit may belong, not to Savery, but to Edward Somerset, second Marquis of Worcester (1601–67), who included an obscure description of an hydraulic machine 'for driving up water by fire' in his *Century of Inventions*, published in 1663. See A. E. Musson's

introduction to the reprint of H. M. Dickinson's *A Short History of the Steam Engine*, Cambridge, 1963.

[7] Samuel Smiles, *Lives of the Engineers*, 1861–2, vol. 3, pp. 9–10.

[8] L. T. C. Rolt, *Thomas Newcomen*, Dawlish, 1963, *passim*.

[9] Nef, *op. cit.*, vol. 1, p. 20; vol. 2, p. 357. Klingender quoted figures from L. C. A. Knowles's *The Industrial and Commercial Revolution in Great Britain during the nineteenth Century*, 1924, p. 71. Figures based on Nef's more exacting researches have been substituted.

[10] J. R. Harris, 'The Employment of Steam Power in the Eighteenth Century', *History*, vol. 52, No. 175, June, 1967, pp. 139; 144. Klingender drew his estimate of the number of engines at work from John Lord, *Capital and Steam Power, 1750–1800*, 1923. Lord's figures are now known to be far too low.

[11] *A descriptive Poem, addressed to two Ladies, at their Return from viewing the Mines near Whitehaven*, 1755, p. 11n.

[12] Based on a table of 'Important Events in Pure and Applied Science' at the end of H. W. Dickinson's *A Short History of the Steam Engine*, Cambridge, 1938.

[13] Quoted by H. W. Dickinson, *Matthew Boulton*, Cambridge, 1937, p. 113.

[14] Lord, *Capital and Steam Power, 1750–1800*, 1923, pp. 167–71.

[15] Quoted by David MacPherson, *Annals of Commerce*, 1805, vol. 3, p. 114. The statement must be taken with reserve, for Wood had commercial reasons of his own to inflate the import figures.

[16] T. S. Ashton, *Iron and Steel in the Industrial Revolution*, Manchester, 1924, pp. 235–4, 238–40. For excellent accounts of the products and processes of the iron industry, see Raymond Lister, *Decorative Wrought Ironwork in Great Britain*, 1952; *Decorative Cast Ironwork in Great Britain*, 1960. See also: W. K. V. Gale, 'Wrought Iron: A Valediction', *Trans. Newcomen Soc.*, vol. 36, 1963–4, pp. 1–11.

[17] For the Darby family and their work, see Arthur Raistrick, *Dynasty of Iron Founders*, 1953.

[18] Ashton, *op. cit.*, pp. 98, 236. The output for 1825 and 1858 is from J. A. Hobson, *The Evolution of Modern Capitalism*, 1926 (revised ed.), p. 87.

[19] John Theophilus Desaguliers, F.R.S., *A Course of Experimental Philosophy*, vol. 2, 1844, p. 467. (Vol. 1 was published in 1734.)

[20] The letters are in the Boulton & Watt Collection at the Birmingham Reference Library. See also: E. Kilburn Scott, *Matthew Murray*, Leeds, 1928, pp. 33–43.

[21] Sir William Fairbairn, *Useful Information for Engineers*, 2nd series, 1860, p. 212.

[22] For Brindley, see Smiles, *op. cit.*, vol. 1, pp. 307–476; Hugh Malet, *The Canal Duke*, Dawlish, 1961. Klingender stated that Brindley 'worked for little more than a worker's wage', echoing Smiles, who harped on his supposed poverty. The later researches of Malet suggest that he became, in fact, quite well off.

[23] Defoe, *op. cit.*, vol. 3, letter 1, p. 38.

[24] Defoe, *op. cit.*, 3rd ed., 1742, vol. 3, p. 67.

[25] Nevertheless, the schoolboys may have been misled. The evidence for the story is

slender, and put forward, apparently for the first time, and without much conviction, by William Hutton, *The History of Derby*, 1791, pp. 199–200.

[26] G. N. Clark, *Science and Social Welfare in the age of Newton*, Oxford, 1937, p. 38.

[27] M. W. Flinn, *Men of Iron. The Crowleys in the early Iron Industry*, Edinburgh, 1962, *passim*.

[28] John Dyer, *The Fleece*, 1757, p. 101.

[29] William Hutton, *An History of Birmingham*, 3rd ed., 1783, p. 63.

[30] A. W. Skempton, 'Canals and River Navigations before 1750', *Hist. Technology*, vol. 3, pp. 459–68; Malet, *op. cit.*, pp. 27–30 and *passim*.

[31] Smiles, *op. cit.*, vol. 1, p. 449.

[32] Arthur Young, *A Six Months Tour through the North of England*, 1770, vol. 3, pp. 265, 288–9.

[33] Aikin, *A Description of the Country from thirty to forty miles round Manchester*, 1795.

[34] Smiles, *op. cit.*, vol. 1, pp. 345–61; Charles Hadfield, *British Canals*, 1959, *passim*.

[35] *The Life of John Metcalf, commonly called Blind Jack of Knaresborough*, York, 1795, *passim*; Smiles, *op cit.*, vol. 1, pp. 208–34.

[36] For general information on these and other early cast-iron bridges, see John Gloag and Derek Bridgewater, *A History of Cast Iron in Architecture*, 1948, pp. 82–111; S. B. Hamilton, 'Building and Civil Engineering Construction', *Hist. Technology*, vol. 4, pp. 455–62. For Paine's contribution to bridge building, see Alfred Owen Aldridge's *Man of Reason*, 1960, pp. 108–17.

[37] Young, *op. cit.*, vol. 3, p. 312.

2. *Under the Banner of Science*

[1] Milton, *Paradise Lost*, 1686, Book 9, lines 679–83.

[2] Young, *A Six Months Tour through the North of England*, 1770, vol. 3, pp. 14–15.

[3] Yalden, *To Sir Humphry Mackworth on the Mines late of Sir Carbery Price*, 1710, pp. 4–5.

[4] Waller, *Essay on the Value of the Mines, late of Sir Carbery Price*, 1698. From the 'Epistle Dedicatory'.

[5] Mackworth last appeared before the public with a project similar to the one that came to be known as 'The South Sea Bubble'.

[6] Also quoted by Thomas Wright, *Caricature History of the Georges*, 1867, pp. 45–48.

[7] The B.M. catalogue suggests 1750 as the date of publication. Klingender's attribution of 1718–25 is more convincing.

[8] Moore, *The History or Narrative of the great level of the Fenns, called Bedford Level*, 1685, pp. 71–81.

[9] *Ladies Diary*, 1725, pp. 18–19; 1726, p. 10. The lady readers must have had agile and informed minds, for each issue is packed with all kinds of mathematical, mechanical, astronomical and literary enigmas, puzzles, and rebuses.

[10] *Ibid.*, 1721, pp. 21–22.

[11] The quotations that follow are drawn, respectively, from pp. 7, 9, 10, 12, 15.

[12] Dyer, *The Fleece*, 1757, p. 103.

[13] *Ibid.*, pp. 77–78.

[14] *Ibid.*, pp. 87–88.

[15] *Ibid.*, pp. 111–12.

[16] *Ibid.*, p. 99. See also pp. 86–87.

[17] *Boswell's Life of Johnson*, ed. Hill and Powell, 1934–50, vol. 2, p. 453.

[18] For an excellent account of the revolution in agriculture, see Sir John Russell, *A History of Agricultural Science in Great Britain, 1620–1954*, 1966.

[19] Useful guides to this vast subject are: John Parker Anderson, *The Book of British Topography*, 1881; Arthur Lee Humphreys, *A Handbook to County Bibliography*, 1917; Ronald Arnold Aubin, *Topographical Poetry in XVIII-Century England*, New York, 1936; *Scenery of Great Britain and Ireland in Aquatint and Lithography, 1770–1860*, from the library of J. R. Abbey (privately printed), 1952.

[20] *A Descriptive Poem* . . .pp. iii-iv.

[21] *The Torrington Diaries*, ed. C. Bruyn Andrews, 1934, vol. 1, respectively, pp. 290, 7, 302.

[22] See generally: Edward Malins, *English Landscaping and Literature*, 1966.

[23] See generally: Irene Parker, *Dissenting Academies in England*, 1914.

[24] There appears to be no adequate general history of the literary and philosophical societies of the eighteenth and nineteenth centuries. But see: Douglas McKie, 'Scientific Societies to the End of the Eighteenth Century', *The Philosophical Magazine*, July 1948, pp. 133–43; Eric Robinson, 'The Derby Philosophical Society', *Annals of Science*, 1953, vol. 9, pp. 359–67.

[25] For Roscoe, see M. W. Brockwell's Preface to *Catalogue of the Roscoe Collection*, Walker Art Gallery, 1928.

[26] Clive D. Rudkin, *Thomas Spence and his Connections*, 1927, pp. 36, 41–42.

[27] From an early, unpublished draft of *The Wealth of Nations*, reproduced by William Robert Scott in *Adam Smith as Student and Professor*, 1937, pp. 325–6. This work is also the source of the biographical details of Smith, quoted below, and much information on Scottish intellectual life. See also: Roy Pascal, 'Property and Society. The Scottish Historical School in the eighteenth century', *Modern Quarterly*, 1928, vol. 1, no. 2, pp. 167–79.

[28] Adam Smith, *An Inquiry into the Nature and Causes of the Wealth of Nations*, ed. Edwin Cannan, 1950, 6th ed., vol. 1, p. 14.

[29] Smith, *op. cit.*, vol. 1, pp. 10–11. For the omitted passage from the first draft, see Scott, *op. cit.*, p. 336.

[30] Scott, *op. cit.*, p. 338.

[31] Smith, *op. cit.*, vol. 1, p. 18.

[32] Scott, *op. cit.*, pp. 344–5.

[33] Smith, *op. cit.*, vol. 2, p. 260.

[34] *Ibid.*, pp. 267–8, 270.

[35] Scott, *op. cit.*, pp. 337–8.

[36] *James Nasmyth Engineer. An Autobiography*, ed. Samuel Smiles, 1885, 3rd ed.,

pp. 28–30; J. and W. H. Rankine, *Biography of William Symington*, Falkirk, 1862, *passim*. A lithograph of Alexander Nasmyth's steamboat by Charles Cheffins after a drawing by John Cooke Bourne, copied without acknowledgement from the original by Alexander Nasmyth, is in Bennet Woodcroft's *A Sketch of the Origin and Progress of Steam Navigation*, 1848, facing p. 32.

[37] Cited by R. H. Campbell, *Carron Company*, Edinburgh, 1961, p. 39.

[38] *A Series of Original Portraits and Caricature Etchings by the late John Kay*, 1837.

[39] For the Lunar Society, with much biographical detail, see: Robert E. Scholfield, *The Lunar Society of Birmingham*, 1963. For an account differing considerably from Scholfield in matters of fact, date, and membership, see also Eric Robinson, 'The Lunar Society: Membership and Organisation', *Trans. Newcomen Soc.*, vol. 35, 1962–3, pp. 153–77.

[40] Ernst Krause, *Erasmus Darwin. With a preliminary Notice by Charles Darwin*, 1879, p. 211.

[41] Desmond King-Hele, *Erasmus Darwin*, 1963, *passim*.

[42] The first combined edition came out in 1791, followed by a second combined edition in the same year, and a third in 1795. These were quartos. The first combined edition has a plate engraved by Blake after Fuseli titled 'Fertilisation of Egypt'. The 3rd, 1795, edition has a second Blake-Fuseli plate titled 'Tornado'. The extracts cited are from the 1st combined edition of 1791 unless otherwise stated. The pagination is very confused.

[43] Walpole. *Letters*, ed. Mrs Paget Toynbee, 1903–5, vol. 15, p. 110.

[44] Vol. 2, p. 501.

[45] *Botanic Garden*, I, pp. 26–27.

[46] *Ibid.*, I, pp. vii–viii.

[47] *Ibid.* Both quotations extracted from I, 'Contents of the Notes', I, pp. 212–13.

[48] *Ibid.*, II, pp. 41–49, *passim*.

[49] *Ibid.*, II, pp. 56–58.

[50] *Ibid.*, I, Additional Notes, p. 22.

[51] *Ibid.*, I, pp. 29–30.

[52] *Ibid.*, I, p. 26n.

[53] *Ibid.*, I, p. 178n.

[54] *Ibid.*, I, 180n; pp. 178–9.

[55] *Ibid.* Images selected from a 'Catalogue of the Poetic Exhibition', II, pp. 176–8.

[56] *Ibid.*, II, p. vi.

[57] *Ibid.*, II, pp. v–vi.

[58] Wordsworth, *Poetical Works*, ed. de Selincourt, Oxford, 1947–54, vol. 1, pp. 12–13n.

[59] *Ibid.*, vol. 2, p. 396. The phrase 'the language really used by men' comes from the preface to the 2nd, 1800, edition of *Lyrical Ballads*. The same sentiment is expressed, more clumsily, in the 1st, 1798, edition: 'the language of conversation in the middle and lower classes of society'.

[60] *Poetry of the Anti-Jacobin*, 1880, 2nd ed., pp. 115, 119.

[61] Horner, *Memoirs and Correspondence*, ed. Leonard Horner, 1843, vol. 2, p. 2. Also quoted by Smiles, *Lives of Boulton and Watt*, 1865, p. 385.

3. *Joseph Wright of Derby*

[1] *The Botanic Garden*, 1795, 3rd ed, II, 'The Loves of the Plants', pp. 19–20. Though the combined title-page in the British Museum copy is that of the 3rd ed. of 1795, the separate title-page of 'The Love of the Plants' is that of the 4th ed., dated 1794. The stanzas quoted do not occur in earlier editions.

[2] For Staffordshire pottery see: G. W. and F. A. Rhead, *Staffordshire Pots and Potters*, 1906; W. B. Honey, *English Pottery and Porcelain*, 1952, 4th ed.

[3] Campbell, *op. cit.*, 1961, pp. 14, 77.

[4] H. W. Dickinson, *Matthew Boulton*, Cambridge, 1937, chap. 3.

[5] J. F. Hayward, *English Cutlery*, V. and A. Museum, 1956.

[6] George Unwin, *Samuel Oldknow and the Arkwrights*, Manchester, 1924, chap. 1.

[7] Honey, *op. cit.*, *passim*.

[8] *Letters of Josiah Wedgwood*, ed. Lady Farrer, 1903, vol. 2, p. 257.

[9] Honey, *op. cit.*, p. 87. For Wedgwood, see Eliza Meteyard, *The Life of Josiah Wedgwood*, 1855–6; Samuel Smiles, *Josiah Wedgwood, F.R.S.*, 1894.

[10] For an illuminating account of the proliferation of such problems in the nineteenth century, see: Quentin Bell, *Schools of Design*, 1963.

[11] *Letters*, *op. cit.*, vol. 2, p. 382.

[12] *Ibid.*, vol. 2, pp. 315–16.

[13] *Ibid.*, vol. 2, pp. 365–71.

[14] *Ibid.*, vol. 2, pp. 380–1.

[15] Eliza Meteyard. *The Life of Josiah Wedgwood*, 1865, vol. 2, p. 442.

[16] Sir Walter Gilbey, *Life of George Stubbs, R.A.*, 1898, p. xix. Stubbs is said to have painted a picture of Hercules and the Cretan Bull to show the Academicians he knew as much about the human figure as about animals.

[17] For Stubbs, see: Gilbey, *op. cit.*; Walter Shaw Sparrow, *George Stubbs and Ben Marshall*, 1929; Ruthven Todd, *Tracks in the Snow*, 1946. For a Stubbs iconography, see the illustrated catalogue of a Stubbs exhibition held at the Whitechapel Art Gallery in 1957.

[18] *Signature*, 1940, no. 13, pp. 15–32.

[19] For Wright, see: William Bemrose, *The Life and Works of Joseph Wright, A.R.A.*, 1885; S. C. Kaines Smith and H. Cheyney-Bemrose, *Wright of Derby*, 1922; Todd, *op. cit.*; *Joseph Wright of Derby*, an illustrated catalogue of the Arts Council Exhibition in 1958, with an introduction by Benedict Nicolson. See also two catalogues of Wright exhibits in the Corporation Art Gallery, Derby, in 1883 and 1934, both in the Art Library of the V. & A. Museum.

[20] Kaines Smith, *op. cit.*, pp. 82–83.

[21] For de la Tour, see: S. M. M. Furness, *Georges de la Tour of Lorraine*, 1949.

[22] Bemrose, *op. cit.*, pp. 30, 122.

[23] *Torrington Diaries*, vol. 2, p. 196.

[24] For the passage that follows, Klingender drew on: Paul Brandt, *Schaffende Arbeit und bildende Kunst im Altertum und Mittelalter*, Leipzig, 1927.

[25] For much information on this subject and many excellent reproductions, see: von Heinrich Winkelmann, *Der Bergbau in der Kunst*, Essen, 1958; René Evrard, *Les Artistes et les Usines à Fer*, Liège, 1955; *Das Eisen in der Kunst*, a portfolio of reproductions issued by Phoenix-Phimrohr of Düsseldorf; *Forschung und Technik in der Kunst*, a catalogue of an exhibition at Ludwigshafen am Rhein in the spring of 1965.

[26] For the van Valckenborch brothers, see: Evrard, *op. cit.*; Jacques Stiennon, *Les Sites Mosans de Lucas et Martin van Valkenborch. Essai d'Identification*, Liège, Société Royale des Beaux Arts, 1954.

[27] *Hist. Technology*, vol. 3, p. 707, and plates 28–31. *Forschung und Technik in der Kunst* has some reproductions in colour.

[28] Charles ffoulkes, 'A Craft Picture by Jan Bruegel', *The Burlington Magazine*, 1911, vol. 19, pp. 41–48. Another version with the title 'Fire', one of a series of four panels showing the 'elements', Earth, Air, Fire and Water, was formerly among the Astor pictures at Cliveden. It was sold at Christie's on the 23 June, 1967 (Lot 9). The illustrated catalogue attributes it, not only to Jan Brueghel and van Balen, but also to Jan van Kessel (1648–1698), a landscape painter in the manner of Ruisdael with a penchant for winter scenes.

[29] For the le Nains, see: Paul Jamot, 'Sur les Frères le Nain', *Gazette des Beaux Arts*, 1922, vol. 5, pp. 129–36, 219–33, 293–308; 1923, vol. 7, pp. 31–40, 157–66.

[30] Bemrose, *op. cit.*, pp. 85, 121.

[31] *Ibid.*, p. 96.

[32] For Hilleström, see: Sixten Ronnow, *Pehr Hilleström och hans Bruks-och Bergverk-smalningar*, Stockholm, 1929; Evrard, *op. cit.*

[33] For Defrance, see: Charles Gobert, *Autobiographie d'un Peintre Liègois*, Liège, 1906; Evrard, *op. cit.*

4. *Documentary Illustrations*

[1] *Felix Farley, Rhymes*, by Themaninthemoon, Bristol, 1826, p. 86.

[2] One of the best general accounts of the various processes of reproducing pictures is *How Prints Look*, by William M. Ivins. First published by the Metropolitan Museum of Art in 1943, it is now issued as a paperback by the Beacon Press, Boston, Mass. For wood-cutting and engraving, see: Douglas Percy Bliss, *A History of Wood-engraving*, 1928. For engraving and etching on metal, see: Arthur M. Hind. *A History of Engraving and Etching*, 1923, 3rd ed. For lithography, see: Elizabeth Robins and Joseph Pennell, *Lithography and Lithographers*, 1915; Wilhelm Weber, *Saxa Logmintur Steine Reden. Geschichte der Lithographie*, Heidelberg, 1961.

[3] Hind. *op cit.*, pp. 211, 223.

[4] Ed. 1791, Part I, add. notes, pp. 6–7; Part II, pp. 127–8.

[5] Pierre Ami Argand (1750–1803). The Swiss inventor of the conventional oil lamp with a glass chimney. Patented in Britain in 1784, it was taken up by Boulton and Watt.

[6] Louis Bertrand Castel (1688–1757). Jesuit mathematician and physician. He invented an 'ocular clavecin' in which the notes produced coloured ribbons to represent their

nuances. See: Castel, 'Nouvelles Expériences d'Optique et d'Acoustique', *Mémoires pour l'Histoire des Sciences et des beaux Arts*, August 1735, art. 79, pp. 1444–82; art 103, pp. 2018–53. Diderot also refers to him. See: *Dialogues by Denis Diderot*, trans. Francis Birrel, 1927, p. 58.

[7] Husband of Susannah, daughter of Josiah Wedgwood, and father of Charles Darwin.

[8] R. M. Burch, *Colour Printing and Colour Printers*, 1910, pp. 51–58.

[9] H. M. Dickinson, *Matthew Boulton*, Cambridge, 1937, pp. 104–7.

[10] Burch, *op. cit.*, pp. 174–202.

[11] J. L. Roget, *A History of 'The Old Water-Colour Society'*, 1891, vol. 1, pp. 28–30. See also: Abbey, *Scenery*, pp. 343–4.

[12] For the evolution of the watercolour, see: S. T. Prideaux, *Aquatint Engraving*, 1909. See also: Roget, *op. cit.*, 1, pp. 23–24 and *passim*.

[13] When Grierson coined the phrase, or where, does not seem to be known. He first applied the word 'documentary' to film when reviewing Robert Flaherty's *Moana*, in the *New York Sun* in February 1926. The definition came later. *Grierson on Documentary*, ed. Forsyth Hardy, 1966, p. 13.

[14] P. J. Booker, *A History of Engineering Drawing*, 1963, p. 214. For examples of mechanical drawings generally see, *inter alia: Transactions of the Newcomen Society*; A. Wolf, *A History of Science, Technology and Philosophy*, 1935–8; William Barclay Parsons, *Engineers and Engineering in the Renaissance*, Baltimore, 1939; *Hist. Technology*.

[15] Roget, *op. cit.*, vol. 1, pp. 11–12.

[16] The demand for encyclopaedias and technical dictionaries of all kinds appears to have been as great in Britain during the eighteenth century as in France. The range of titles is enormous and includes John Harris's *Lexicon Technicum* (1704); Ephraim Chambers' *Cyclopaedia* (1728); the *Encyclopaedia Britannica* (1771), constantly reissued till the present day; Abraham Rees' *The New Cyclopaedia; or, Universal Dictionary of Arts and Sciences*, issued in parts from 1802 and completed in 1820 in forty-five volumes of text and plates; John Wilkes' *Encyclopaedia Londoniensis* (1810–29), with its many plates engraved on wood by J. Pass and often beautifully coloured, and *Encyclopaedia Metropolitana* (1817–45) on a system devised by Coleridge, who contributed not only the prospectus but a number of articles. The whole subject is treated in detail by Robert Collison: *Encyclopaedias; their History throughout the Ages*, New York, 1964.

[17] *A Memoir of Thomas Bewick written by himself*, Newcastle upon Tyne, 1862, pp. 51–59.

[18] Cited in the introduction to *A Catalogue of the . . . Engineering Designs* (1741–1792) *of John Smeaton, F.R.S., preserved in the library of the Royal Society*, 1950, Newcomen Soc. Extra Publication no. 5, p. xiii.

[19] J. H. C. Warren, 'John Nuttall's Sketch Book', *Trans. Newcomen Soc.* 1930–1, vol. 9, pp. 67–89.

[20] Hugh W. Davies, *Bernhard von Breydenbach and his Journey to the Holy Land, 1483–4*, 1911.

[21] For Ralph Allen's railway, see: Arthur Elton, 'The Pre-History of Railways', *Proc. Somersetshire Archaeological Soc.*, 1963, vol. 107, pp. 39–56.

[22] 3rd ed., 1736, p. 16. First published in 1734.

[23] For the Sandbys, see: William Sandby, *Thomas and Paul Sandby*, 1892, p. 12.

[24] The Rev. Stebbing Shaw, *The History and Antiquities of Staffordshire, 1798–1801*, vol. II, pl. XVII, facing p. 117.

[25] Bisset, *Poetic Survey*, 1800, p. 12.

[26] Klingender took a special interest in the subject, making a small collection of tokens and contributing an article on them to *The Architectural Review* in February 1943. For an excellent summary with a bibliography, see: Peter Mathias, *English Trade Tokens*, 1962.

5. *The Sublime and the Picturesque*

[1] The citations from Burke are from J. T. Boulton's scholarly edition of *A Philosophical Enquiry into . . . the Sublime*, 1958. Page references have been omitted, since the passages quoted can be easily identified from the index.

[2] William Gilpin, *Three Essays to which is added a Poem, on Landscape Painting*, 1792, pp. 7–8. The poem is separately paginated.

[3] For William Gilpin, see: Carl Paul Barbier, *William Gilpin*, Oxford, 1963.

[4] Gilpin, *Three Essays*, p. 36.

[5] *Ibid.*, p. 8.

[6] Gilpin, *Observations, relative chiefly to Picturesque Beauty . . . particularly the Mountains, and Lakes of Cumberland, and Westmoreland*, 1786, vol. 2, p. 44.

[7] Gilpin, *Three Essays*, p. 10.

[8] Sir Uvedale Price, *An Essay on the Picturesque*, 1796, vol. 1, pp. 213–14.

[9] *Ibid.*, pp. 66–67.

[10] Rotha Mary Clare, *Julius Caesar Ibbetson*, 1948, plate 46.

[11] Price, *op. cit.*, p. 63.

[12] E. T. MacDermot, *History of the Great Western Railway*, revised ed., 1964, vol. 1, p. 56; J. C. Bourne, *The Great Western Railway*, 1846, p. 54, and plate, 'Tunnel No. 2 near Bristol'. Christopher Hussey's *The Picturesque*, 1927, is a masterly account of the whole subject.

[13] Arthur Young, *Annals of Agriculture, and other useful Arts*, 1785, vol. 4, pp. 166–8.

[14] For Robertson, see: James Moore, 'Fresh Light on some Watercolour Painters of the British School', *Walpole Soc.*, 1917, vol. 5, pp. 54–59.

[15] Anna Seward, *The Poetical Works*, ed. Sir Walter Scott, Edinburgh, 1810, vol. 2, pp. 314–15.

[16] *Ibid.*, p. 218.

[17] *Rep.* Sydney D. Kitson, *The Life of John Sell Cotman*, 1939, facing p. 48.

[18] de Selincourt, vol. 1, pp. 16–18.

[19] *Memoirs of the late Thomas Holcroft*, 1816, vol. 1, pp. 46–50.

[20] For de Loutherbourg, see: William T. Whitley, *Artists and their Friends in England*

1700–1797, 1928; W. J. Lawrence, 'Philippe Jacques de Loutherbourg', *The Magazine of Art*, 1895, pp.17 2–7. For his stage work, see also: Dougald MacMillan, *Drury Lane Calendar 1747–1776*, Oxford, 1938; Allardyce Nicoll, *A History of English Drama, 1660– 1900*, Cambridge, 1952–9, vol. 3, *passim*; George Winchester Stone, *The London Stage*, Southern Illinois University Press, 1962–5, part IV, *passim*.

[21] Cited in: R. Crompton Rhodes, *The Plays and Poems of Richard Brinsley Sheridan*, 1928, vol. 2, p. 240. In the body of the play, Sheridan states that de Loutherbourg's 'miraculous power' is universally acknowledged, p. 211.

[22] Gilpin, *Three Essays*, 'Poem on Landscape Painting', p. 3. For Gilpin's theories, see: *Nature, representing the Effect for a Morning, a Noontide, and an evening Sun*, 1810, and J. H. Clark, *Practical Illustration of Gilpin's Day*, 1824.

[23] Charles Baudelaire, *Oeuvres Complètes*, ed. Gautier-Le Dantec, Paris, 1918–43, 'Curiosités Esthétiques', vol. 5, p. 87.

[24] Quoted by W. T. Whitley, *op. cit.*, vol. 2, p. 352.

[25] Ephraim Hardcastle (i.e. W. H. Pyne), *Wine and Walnuts*, 1823, chap. 2, pp. 281– 304.

[26] Olive Cook deals with de Loutherbourg, considered as a precursor of the cinema, in *Movement in Two Dimensions*, 1963, pp. 28–31.

[27] Hussey, *op. cit.* p. 4.

[28] Cited by Hussey, *op. cit.*, p. 16.

[29] Kitson, *op. cit.*, p. 41.

[30] For Turner, see: Jack Lindsay, *J. M. W. Turner—a Critical Biography*, 1966.

[31] Ford Madox Hueffer, *Ford Madox Brown*, 1896, pp. 127–8.

[32] Quoted in John Rewald, *Camille Pissarro. Letters to his Son*, 1944, p. 151n.

6. *The Age of Despair*

[1] John Britton, *Autobiography*, 1850, vol. 1, pp. 128–9. (Large paper ed.)

[2] Wordsworth, *Poetical Works*, ed. de Selincourt, vol. 2, pp. 395–7.

[3] For Trevithick, see: H. W. Dickinson and Arthur Titley, *Richard Trevithick*, Cambridge, 1934.

[4] For Trevithick's experiments with locomotives, see: Dickinson, *op. cit.*, pp. 63–70, 105–13; C. F. Dendy Marshall, *A History of Railway Locomotives down to the end of the year 1831*, 1953, pp. 9–27.

[5] Dickinson, *op. cit.*, pp. 90–105. See also: David Lampe, *The Tunnel*, 1963.

[6] For machine-tools, see: L. T. C. Rolt, *Tools for the Job*, 1965.

[7] J. L. and Barbara Hammond, *The Rise of Modern Industry*, 1925, p. 183.

[8] *The Census of Great Britain in 1851*, 1854, p. 88, table 2.

[9] W. Stanley Jevons, F.R.S., *The Coal Question*, 1906, 3rd ed. revised, p. 270.

[10] Harry Scrivenor, *History of the Iron Trade*, 1854, new ed., pp. 136, 295. The figure for 1801 is the average between those for 1796 and 1806.

[11] Sydney J. Chapman, *The Lancashire Cotton Industry*, Manchester, 1904, p. 144. The

figure for 1801 is taken from Andrew Ure, *The Cotton Manufacture of Great Britain*, 1861, vol. 1, p. 200, table 5. The Ure estimate for 1831 is a good deal less than that by Chapman, and their figures generally cannot be easily reconciled.

[12] P. B. Shelley, *Poems*, ed. C. D. Locock, 1911, vol. 1, pp. 36–37.

[13] From a biographical notice added by Edward Hailstone to his facsimile edition of *The Costume of Yorkshire*, published at Leeds in 1885. The plates of this edition are chromolithographs by Ernst Kauffman of Lahr, near Baden, taken from the original drawings, then in the hands of Hailstone.

[14] Josiah Wedgwood, *Letters*, ed. Katharine Eufemia Farrer, 1903, vol. 2, pp. 420–5.

[15] Robert Owen, *A New View of Society*, 1831. Quoted by E. Royston Pike, *Human Documents of the Industrial Revolution in Britain*, 1966, pp. 38–39.

[16] T. Robert Malthus, *An Essay on the Principle of Population*, 1803, 2nd ed., p. 531.

[17] William Cobbett, 'Mechanics Institution', *Weekly Political Register*, 1825, vol. 58, col. 436. Quoted by G. D. H. and M. Cole, *The Opinions of William Cobbett*, 1944, p. 289.

[18] Shelley, *op. cit.*, vol. 1. Preface to 'The Revolt of Islam', p. 37.

[19] Byron, *Don Juan*, ed. T. G. Steffan and W. W. Pratt, Austin (Texas), 1957, vol. 3, p. 472.

[20] John Keats, *Letters*, ed. Maurice Buxton Forman, Oxford, 1947, 3rd ed., p. 407.

[21] William Blake, *Complete Writings*, ed. Keynes, 1966, p. 323.

[22] Vol. 16, pp. 464–76.

[23] For Hazlitt on Malthus, see: *The Collected Works of William Hazlitt*, ed. A. R. Wallace and Arnold Glover, 1902, vol. 4.

[24] Vol. 2, pp. 292–300.

[25] *Quarterly Review*, December, 1812, vol. 8, p. 322. Southey is reviewing Patrick Colquhoun's *Propositions for ameliorating the Condition of the Poor*. His review was reprinted in his *Essays Moral and Political* (1832) under the title, 'On the State of the Poor, the Principle of Mr Malthus's Essay on Population, and the Manufacturing System'. The *Quarterly* changed sides and, in 1817 (vol. 17, pp. 369–403), published a highly favourable review of the 5th ed. of Malthus by the Rev. John Bird Sumner (1780–1862), later Archbishop of Canterbury.

[26] [Thomas Allsop], *Letters, Conversations and Recollections of S. T. Coleridge*, 1836, vol. 1, pp. 135–6. Reprinted in *The Table Talk and Omnia of S. T. Coleridge*, ed. T. Ashe, 1884, p. 318.

[27] Wordsworth, *op. cit.*, vol. 5, pp. 268–9.

[28] *Ibid.*, p. 469.

[29] *Ibid.*, pp. 270–1.

[30] *Ibid.*, pp. 274–6.

[31] *Ibid.*, p. 292.

[32] *Ibid.*, pp. 271–2.

[33] *The Condition of the Working-Class in England in 1844*, ed. 1892, p. 284.

[34] Sir Gavin de Beer, F.R.S., *Charles Darwin*, 1963, pp. 98–99. Klingender cites the view, supported by many earlier authorities, that Darwin obtained the idea of natural

•

selection of variations from Malthus. De Beer shows that Darwin had already grasped the importance both of variation and of selection by the time he read Malthus, to whom he owed only the realization that the high rate of mortality exacted by nature resulted in pressure.

[35] He provided the frontispiece for Gideon Mantell's *The Wonders of Geology* (1838), and Thomas Hawkins' *The Book of the great Sea Dragons* (1840), the latter a ferocious mezzotint, engraved by Martin himself. It is reproduced by Ruthven Todd in *Tracks in the Snow*, 1946, facing p. 100. For Martin generally, see Thomas Balston: *John Martin*, 1947. Mary L. Pendered, *John Martin, Painter*, 1923; Todd, *op. cit.*, pp. 94–122.

[36] Quoted by Balston, *op. cit.*, p. 107.

[37] Samuel Smiles, *The Life of Thomas Telford*, 1867, new ed., pp. 297–8.

[38] Quoted by Balston, 'John Martin', *The Library*, 1934, 4th series.

[39] Blake, *op. cit.*, p. 483.

[40] Thomas Balston, *The Life of Jonathan Martin, Incendiary of York Minster, with some Account of William and Richard Martin*, 1945.

[41] *Sezincot House*, n.d. [c. 1819]. Martin's etchings were aquatinted by Frederick Christian Lewis, sen. (1779–1856), and there is a set of each in the British Museum Print Room. However, neither appears to have been issued to the public. Lewis was engraver to the court and responsible for aquatinting Girtin's *Picturesque Views of Paris*, published in 1803.

[42] Isambard Brunel, *The Life of Isambard Kingdom Brunel*, 1870, pp. 46–58; Celia Brunel Noble, *The Brunels Father and Son*, 1938, pp. 106–10; L. T. C. Rolt, *Isambard Kingdom Brunel*, 1957, pp. 51–59. Brunel's original drawings are preserved at Swindon Railway Museum.

[43] Balston, *op. cit.*, pp. 205–6.

[44] *Lancashire Illustrated*, 1831, p. 70.

[45] Hair's *Sketches of the Coal Mines in Northumberland and Durham* was first published in 1839 with an engraved title-page, but apparently without a text and with only twelve plates. The 1844 edition incorporates the original title-page with a vignette of a horse-gin, and a separate, printed title-page, dated 1844—*A Series of Views of the Collieries in Northermberland and Durham*. There are forty-four etchings, including the frontispiece and the original title-page. Most of these are executed by Hair himself, but a few are etchings after his drawings by J. Brown, J. E. Nicholson and L. J. Davies. Some of them are dated 1844. Very inferior impressions, with new titles and shorn of the names both of artist and engraver, were used as illustrations to W. Fordyce's *A History of Coal, Coke, Coal Fields . . . Iron, its Ores, and Processes of Manufacture*, 1860. No doubt Fordyce had purchased the plates, to each of which he added his own name as publisher.

[46] William Howitt, *Visits to remarkable Places; Old Halls, Battle Fields, and Scenes illustrative of striking passages in History and Poetry*, 1842, pp. 86–87.

[47] *Historical Romances of the Author of Waverley*, Edinburgh, 1821–7; *The Monastery*, 1821, vol. 1, p. 48.

[48] Hair, *op. cit.*, ed. 1844, p. 7n.

[49] Howitt, *op. cit.*, p. 303.

[50] Hair, *op. cit.*, respectively, p. 44n, p. 40n.

[51] *Pickwick Papers*, chap. 49; *The Old Curiosity Shop*, chap. 45.

[52] Balston, *John Martin*, 1947, p. 236.

7. The Railway Age

[1] *Blackwood's Edinburgh Magazine*, November 1830, vol. 28, pp. 824–5.

[2] Quoted by Louise Schutz Boas, *Hariet Shelley*, 1962, p. 103.

[3] Quoted by Elisabeth Beazley, *Madocks and the Wonder of Wales*, 1967, p. 201. Other details have been drawn from M. J. T. Lewis, *How Festiniog got its railway*, 1965.

[4] Gaskell, *North and South*, ed. 1855, pp. 124–6.

[5] James Nasmyth, *An Autobiography*, ed. Samuel Smiles, 1885, 3rd ed., p. 311.

[6] Samuel Smiles. *The Life of George Stephenson*, 1903, p. vii. First published in 1857 and many times revised and re-issued. The words quoted appear for the first time in Smiles' preface to the 1903 edition, issued when he was 91 to mark the centenary of his publisher, John Murray.

[7] Richard S. Lambert, *The Railway King*, 1934, *passim*.

[8] Vol. 37, p. 394.

[9] Phillips. Prominent Leicester radical and anti-Newtonian; imprisoned for selling Paine's *Rights of Man*, 1793; moved to London, 1796, and started *The Monthly Magazine*; publisher of many works popularizing science and education; Sheriff of London and knighted by George III, 1807.

[10] Vol. 38, p. 118, 'A Morning's Walk to Kew'. Reprinted in a volume of the same title, 1817.

[11] Rep. C. F. Dendy Marshall, *Early British Locomotives*, 1939, p. 34.

[12] Vol. 30 (2nd series), facing p. 238. The illustration was also issued separately.

[13] Rep. C. F. Dendy Marshall, *A History of British Railways*, 1930, facing p. 26.

[14] A coloured lithograph with the title 'Opening of the First English Rail-Way between Stockton and Darlington, Sept. 27th, 1825' is not contemporary and was perhaps issued in connexion with the Railway Jubilee in 1875. Even the Dobbin painting is not free from suspicion.

[15] Vol. 4, facing p. 40. Rep. Dendy Marshall, *op. cit.*, p. 30

[16] 1829, vol. 12, 14th November. There are also in existence at least two coloured lithographs purporting to show the Rainhill trials. One is titled: 'Race of Locomotives at Rainhill, near Liverpool, in which George Stevenson's [sic] "Rocket" won, 1829'. Neither is contemporary. Both were perhaps issued in 1875.

[17] Frances ('Fanny') Anne Kemble, *Record of a girlhood*, 1878, vol. 2, p. 164.

[18] *The Creevey Papers*, 1905, ed. Sir Herbert Maxwell, Bt., p. 429.

[19] Kemble, *op. cit.*, vol. 2, p. 197.

[20] *Phantasmagoria*. A term coined in 1802 by the lanternist, Philipsthal, to describe a display by which the projected images could be made to increase or diminish in size by manipulating the lens.

21 *An accurate Description of the Liverpool and Manchester Railway*, Liverpool, 1830, p. 45.

22 Accum, *Practical Treatise*, 1815, 1st ed., p. 72. Three more editions followed in 1815, 1816 and 1818. Thomas Boys then took over, publishing *Description of the Process of Manufacturing Coal Gas* in 1819, with a 2nd ed. in 1820, both beautifully illustrated by aquatints.

23 For an illustrated account of Bourne's life, see: Arthur Elton, 'The Piranesi of the Age of Steam', *Country Life Annual*, 1965, pp. 38–40.

24 *Gentleman's Magazine*, 1838, vol. 10 (new series), p. 419.

25 John Britton, *The Auto-Biography*, 1850, large paper copy, vol. 1, p. 123; vol. 2, p. 56.

26 British Railways Board, Historical Records, H.L., R/281/3.

27 Introduction (by John Britton) to Part I of *The London and Birmingham Railway*.

28 British Railways, *loc. cit.*, R/281/1.

29 Stated in an M.S. inscription in the copy Cheffins presented to the library of the Institution of Civil Engineers.

30 Olinthus J. Vignoles, *Life of Charles Blacker Vignoles*, 1898, pp. 317–68 *passim*.

31 From information kindly supplied by Mme Larissa Doukelskaya of the Hermitage, Leningrad. The Kieff panorama measures 60·4 × 197·5 cm.

32 Cited by Celia Brunel Noble, *The Brunels*, 1938, p. 245.

33 Vol. 1, pp. 49–50.

34 Edward Chadwick. *Report . . . on an Inquiry into the Sanitary Conditions of the Labouring Population of Great Britain*, 1842, p. 157.

8. *New-fangled men*

1 J. C. Bourne, *Drawings on the London and Birmingham Railway . . . with an historical and descriptive Account by John Britton, F.S.A.*, 1839, p. 20.

2 Karl Marx, *Selected Works*, ed. 1942, vol. 2, pp. 427–9.

3 Quoted in *A Handbook of Marxism*, 1935, pp. 47–48.

4 George Eliot, *Middlemarch*, 1871, vol. 1, p. 99.

5 For a Marxist account of the impact of capitalism on the Victorian novelists, see: Ralph Fox, *The Novel and the People*, 1937. T. A. Jackson's *Charles Dickens; The Progress of a Radical* (1937) is a detailed study of the same relationship in terms of a single author. Discussing *Hard Times*, Jackson stresses its significance as a satire on the Manchester philosophy, but finds its treatment of trade unions and its description of the 'conscientious non-unionist' the one outstanding set of faulty observations in the whole of Dickens.

6 Samuel Smiles, *Lives of the Engineers*, 1861–2, vol. 3, pp. 321–3.

7 Henry Mayhew, *London Labour and London Poor*, 1851–61, vol. 3, pp. 420–1.

8 For Sykes, see: *Cornhill Magazine*, 1912, vol. 32, pp. 464–73; W. Odom, *Hallamshire Worthies*, Sheffield, 1926, pp. 224–5.

9 For Sharples, see: Joseph Baron, *James Sharples, Blacksmith and Artist*, 1893; Smiles, *Self-help*, pop. ed. 1897, p. 194. There is a copy of Baron in the Blackburn Public Library.

[10] Now in the Bury Art Gallery.

[11] 'The Forge' was extensively reviewed in November and December 1859 in such periodicals as the *Art Journal*, the *Athenaeum*, the *Illustrated London News* and the *Manchester Guardian*.

[12] Peter Ferriday, 'The Victorian Art Market', *Country Life*, 16 June, 1966, p. 1578.

[13] For the Pre-Raphaelites, see: Ford Madox Hueffer, *Ford Madox Brown*, 1896. W. M. Rossetti, *Pre-Raphaelite Diaries and Letters*, 1900; William Bell Scott, *Autobiographical Notes*, 1892; Robin Ironside, 'Pre-Raphaelite Paintings at Wallington', *Architectural Review*, December 1942; William Gaunt, *The Pre-Raphaelite Tragedy*, 1942.

[14] Vincent Van Gogh, *Complete Letters*, 1958, vol. 1, p. 384.

[15] Konrad Kaiser. *Adolf Menzels Eisenwalzwerk*, Berlin, 1953.

[16] Jerrold & Doré, *London*, 1872, pp. 17–18.

[17] *Ibid.*, p. 1.

[18] *Ibid.*, p. 117.

[19] *Ibid.*, p. 25.

[20] *Ibid.*, p. 113.

[21] For Doré see: Blanchard Jerrold, *Life of Gustave Doré*, 1891; Blanche Rooseveldt, *Life and Reminiscences of Gustave Doré*, 1885.

[22] Cited by Robert L. Peters, *Victorians on Literature and Art*, New York, 1961, p. 146.

[23] For Verne see: Kenneth Allott, *Jules Verne*, 1940.

[24] Cited by Allott, *op. cit.*, p. 34.

[25] Verne, *Clipper of the Clouds*, ed. 1891, pp. 30–1.

[26] *Ibid.*, p. 192.

[27] Cited by Allott, *op. cit.*, pp. 234; 240–1.

Each entry is arranged as follows: *Title*, in a line to itself.

There follows: *medium, dimension* (in centimetres, height before width), *date* and *artist*. In the case of prints, the name of the engraver or lithographer precedes that of the artist. In the case of illustrations from books, the source is given with number of plate or page. In some cases, the name of the publisher of a print is added. When only part of a picture or print is reproduced, the dimensions refer to the whole area of the original.

There follows an acknowledgement. Entries marked with an asterisk are drawn from sources in the Editor's collection. Finally, there is often a note, reduced to a minimum when subject, artist or engraver is dealt with in the main text.

The following are the principal abbreviations used:

att.   = attributed
eng.   = engraved
fl.   = flourished
lith.   = lithographed
pl.   = plate
pub.   = published
rep.   = reproduced

In the case of prints, after the dimensions one of the following abbreviations is sometimes used:

pm   = Dimensions between plate-marks
ps.   = Dimensions of printed surface, excluding borders, titles, etc.

Lack of such qualifications indicates that the dimensions refer to the size of the paper, not always a satisfactory practice in the case of prints, but sometimes unavoidable.

Tracking down the source of pictures that have become detached from the books of which they originally formed part has been lightened by the indices of the Abbey bibliographies. Many prints, originally issued in and designed for black and white, have been coloured in more recent times by unscrupulous dealers artificially to enhance their value, a practice that still continues. In the notes below, the word 'coloured' after the medium indicates that the colouring appears to be contemporary. Since many prints were taken from two or more plates or stones, in order to add one or more tints or colours, but were also coloured by hand, no attempt has been made to distinguish between those prints, partly or wholly coloured by hand, and those partly or wholly printed in colours. *The principal page reference in the text* is given in brackets at the end of each entry.

COLOUR PLATES

I

*PITMEN PLAYING AT QUOITS
Oil on canvas. 76 × 62·5. *n.d.* (*c.* 1840?).
Henry Perlee Parker (1795–1873).
There is another version of this picture in the Laing Art Gallery, Newcastle-on-Tyne. Parker painted a number of canvases on the theme of pitmen at play. For example, the National Coal Board has a scene of pitmen playing marbles (*Rep.* Winkelmann. *Der Bergbau in der Kunst.* 1958. Facing page 332). 'Pitmen Playing at Quoits' was lithographed by Thomas Fairland (1804–1852), a pupil of Fuseli well known for his spirited rendering of works by artists such as Landseer. (128)

II

*LOCOMOTIVE ENGINE
Line engraving, coloured. 54·3 × 82. 1848.
Eng. by and after John Emslie (1813–75).
Source: *Diagrams of the Steam Engine.* 1848.
James Reynolds.
One of a pair, the other being titled: 'Double Acting Condensing Steam Engine'. They were issued in covers in various forms, sometimes with a text, sometimes without, but always sectioned and mounted.
Emslie was an engraver of maps and book illustrations. (76)

III

*DUNDAS AQUEDUCT, CLAVERTON
Aquatint, coloured. 24·2 × 34·1 (*ps*). 1805.
Eng. I. Hill after John Claude Nattes (*c.* 1765–1822). Source: *Bath, illustrated by a series of Views.* 1806. John Claude Nattes.

Pl. XXVI.
Nothing appears to be known of I. Hill. The aqueduct carries the Kennet and Avon Canal over the Avon between Barthampton and Limpley Stoke. It was built by John Rennie (1761–1821) in 1804. A self-acting railway incline used for bringing down building stone from the crest of the hill can be made out, just above the sail of the barge. The aqueduct is now preserved as a national monument. (81)

IV

*THE PARYS MINE IN
ANGLESEA
Watercolour. 25·5 × 17·6. *n.d.* François Louis Thomas Francia (1772–1839).
This view of the Parys Mine appears strongly to have influenced Sir Robert Ker Porter's view of the Dannemora Iron Mine in Russia (Fig. 52). *Cf.* also Fig. 12. (94)

V

*IRON WORKS, COLEBROOK DALE
Aquatint, coloured. 23·2 × 32 (*ps*). 1805.
Eng. William Pickett (*fl.* 1792–1820) after Philippe Jacques de Loutherbourg (1740–1863). Source. *Picturesque Scenery of England and Wales.* 1805. P. J. de Loutherbourg. *Pl.* II. (99)

VI

BEDLAM FURNACE, NEAR MADELEY
Watercolour. 26 × 47. 1802. John Sell Cotman (1782–1842).
Reproduced by courtesy of Sir Edmund Bacon Bt. (102)

VII

NEWCASTLE ON TYNE
Watercolour. 15·3 × 21·4. 1823. Joseph
Mallord William Turner.
*Reproduced by courtesy of the British
Museum.*
Designed as one of a number of illustrations
for a projected publication in mezzotint to
be called *The Rivers of England*, and to
contain engravings after Turner, William
Collins (1788–1847) and Thomas Girtin
(1775–1802). The first part came out in
1823, Turner's 'Newcastle' being engraved
by Thomas Goff Lupton (1791–1873).
Publication was stopped with the seventh
part in 1827, and all the engravings so far
made were gathered together and issued with
a new title page—*River Scenery by Turner
and Girtin*. This was re-issued with a
similar title page, but undated, in about
1830. Publication was suspended, ostensibly
because 'of there not being sufficient engravers in mezzotint to carry it on with
spirit'. A further reason was, almost
certainly, that the substitution for the first
time of steel plates for copper ones caused
the engravers great technical difficulties.
(From notes by G. Mallord W. Turner in the
Print Room of the Victoria and Albert
Museum.) (102)

VIII

NANT-Y-GLO IRON WORKS
Watercolour. 14 × 20. *n.d.* (*c.* 1788?). *Att.*
George Robertson (1742–88).
*Reproduced by courtesy of the National
Museum of Wales.*
Provenance uncertain. Originally thought to
be a scene of copper works at Swansea and
attributed to Paul Sandby. However, this
location is doubtful on both topographical
and technical grounds and the style is
remote from that of Sandby. The more
recent identification of the scene with the
Iron Works at Nant-y-Glo, and the attribution to Robertson, derived from a pencil note
on the back of the picture, are much more
convincing. The apparatus on the right
appears to be a blast furnace for reducing
iron ore; furnaces in the distance on the left
appear to be puddling furnaces for converting
pig iron to malleable iron of the type introduced by Henry Cort (1740–1800) in 1784.
Robertson painted scenes in the same vein
at nearby Coalbrookdale, on the Severn, in
1788 (e.g. Fig. 14).
It is known that this picture was engraved,
but no example has been traced. The
proprietor of Nant-y-Glo was Richard Crawshay, who also owned the Cyfarthfa Iron
Works at Merthyr and four others. (131)

ILLUSTRATIONS IN BLACK AND WHITE

1

COAL STAITHES ON THE RIVER WEAR
(Detail)
Oil on canvas. 113·5 × 219·3. 1680. Peter
Hartover.
Reproduced by courtesy of Viscount Lambton.
The complete picture shows the Lambton
estates in panorama, Harraton Hall on the
left, Lumley Castle in the distance on the
extreme right, and the coal staithes on the
upper Wear left of centre, with Old Lambton
Hall on the south bank. An endless line of
horses and carts with two wheels is
transporting coal from the north over the
river to the south bank for loading from the
staithes into keels, to be transported down-
stream to Sunderland for shipment to
London and the South.
In the foreground a hawking party and
foxhounds compete for attention, and draw
the eye up to Harraton Hall and the
staithes beyond, bringing scenes pastoral,
industrial and sporting into a single relation.
Christopher Hussey (*Country Life*, 14 April
1966) suggests that the figures, animals
and birds were added by Francis Barlow
(1616–1702) or copied from his engravings.
Nothing is known of Peter Hartover.
In the portion of the picture reproduced,
part of Harraton Hall appears on the left,
and Old Lambton Hall can be made out
just behind the staithes. (5)

2

*A VIEW OF THE UPPER WORKS AT
COALBROOKDALE
Line engraving. 36 × 52·7 (*ps*). 1758. *Eng.*
Francis Vivares (1709–80) after G. Perry
and Thomas Smith of Derby (*d*. 1767).
No. 1 of a pair. No. 2 is titled: 'The South
West Prospect of Coalbrookdale and the
adjacent Country'. Of French descent,
Vivares came to England in 1727 and is well
known for his engravings after Claude. He
also executed a number after Thomas Smith.
G. Perry is almost certainly George Perry
(1719–71), an engineer, who executed 'A
Plan of the Iron-Works at Madeley Wood in
Shropshire' (B.M. Map Room. King's
Topography. 16–9) and established a
foundry business in Liverpool in 1758 (*Trans
Newcomen Soc.* 1934. Vol. 13, p. 49). He
made an extensive topographical and
economic survey of Liverpool, but died before
it could be published. Dr William Enfield
(1741–97), Presbyterian rector of Warrington
Academy, worked up his notes into *An
Essay towards the History of Liverpool*,
Warrington, 1773. (87)

3

*THE SOUTH EAST PROSPECT OF THE
CITY OF BATH (Detail)
Line engraving. 24·1 × 77·8 (*ps*). 1734.
Eng. by and after Samuel and Nathaniel
Buck (*c*. 1696–1779; *d*. 1779 *ante*.).
In the centre foreground can be seen Ralph
Allen's railway from his quarries on Combe
Down to a wharf on the south bank of the
Avon, whence it was ferried across to the
city or lowered into barges for conveyance
down the Avon to Bristol and beyond. (77)

4

PRIOR PARK THE SEAT OF RALPH
ALLEN ESQ.
Line engraving. 25 × 42·3 (*ps*). 1750. *Eng.*
by and after Anthony Walker (1726–65).
Pub. John Bowles and Son, 1752.
*Reproduced by courtesy of Mr Nicholas
Meinertzhagen.*
In some impressions, the publisher's line has
been amended by deleting the date and

replacing the words 'and Son' by a dash. It
is frequently found coloured, usually badly
and invariably recently. Another version
appeared in *The Universal Magazine*, May
1754. (78)

5

*A VIEW OF THE CHELSEA WATER
WORKS (Detail)
Line engraving. 25·6 × 41 (*ps*). 1752. *Eng.*
by and after John Boydell (1719–1804).
The engraving is numbered '5' and is
probably drawn from one of the sets of six
topographical engravings issued by Boydell
at intervals from 1744. This and many other
topographical engravings were re-issued in
1760 in *A Collection of Views in England
and Wales*. (78)

6

THE ENGINE FOR RAISING WATER
(WITH A POWER MADE) BY FIRE
Line engraving. 18·3 × 18·6 (*ps*). 1717.
Eng. by and after Henry Beighton, F.R.S.
(1686–1743).
*Reproduced by courtesy of the Science
Museum.* (75)

7

*STEAM ENGINE NEAR GOSCOTE,
WALSALL, STAFFORDSHIRE
Water colour. 23·1 × 14·6. *n.d.* Peter le
Cave (*fl.* 1780–1810).
According to Lewis' *Topographical Dictionary*
(1835) Messrs Otway and Wennington's iron
foundry at Goscote near Walsall was the
most extensive as well as the oldest in the
district. Cylinders for steam-engines of every
size, as well as cannon and various smaller
articles, were cast there. (86)

8

*A STEAM ENGINE OF 20 HORSE POWER
BY FENTON & CO., LEEDS
Wash drawing. 44·8 × 62 (within wash
border). *c*. 1827. Joseph Clement (1779–1844).
The original for a line engraving by
George Gladwin for *The Steam Engine* (1827)
by Thomas Tredgold. (*Pl.* XIV). For Joseph
Clement, who contributed other equally fine

drawings to the same work, see: Samuel Smiles, *Industrial Biography*, 1863, pp. 236–57; L. T. C. Rolt, *Tools for the Job*, 1965, *passim*. Clement, the son of a Westmorland hand-loom weaver and amateur entomologist, was trained as a thatcher and slater. Building his own screw-cutting lathe in 1804, he became a mechanical engineer. He was taught drawing by Peter Nicholson (1765–1844), mathematician and architect. After a short spell with Joseph Bramah (1748–1814), the manufacturer and inventor, Clement joined the firm of Maudslay Son and Field in 1814. He set up on his own in 1817 as a mechanical draughtsman and mechanic, contributing a series of fine drawings to the Transactions of the Society for the Encouragement of Arts. He made many improvements to machine tools, and was later employed by Charles Babbage (1792–1871) to build his calculating engine. Little is known of Gladwin, who published some engravings of the Royal Pavilion at Brighton. (75)

9

PIT-HEAD OF A COAL MINE WITH A HORSE GIN

Watercolour. 24·7 × 33. 1786(?). Paul Sandby (1725–1809).
Reproduced by courtesy of the National Museum of Wales. (86, 95)

10

PIT-HEAD OF A COAL MINE WITH STEAM WINDING GEAR

Oil on canvas. 95 × 153. (*c.* 1820?.) Artist unknown.
Reproduced by courtesy of the Walker Art Gallery, Liverpool.
A Newcomen engine, adapted to winding, something rarely done on account of various technical difficulties. However, H. W. Dickinson states, in his *Short History of the Steam Engine* (1938, pp. 64–65) that a certain number of such engines were made rotative towards the end of the eighteenth century and continued work well into the nineteenth. They were clumsy but cheap,

and made in large numbers for winding from shallow pits. In the Midlands they were known as 'whimseys'. (95)

11

*THE PENRHYN SLATE QUARRIES

Lithograph. 18·4 × 27·1 (*ps*). 1842. *Lith.* W. Crane. Source: *Picturesque Scenery in North Wales.* 1842, *Pl.* II.
This lithograph does not appear completely to tally with that described in Abbey (Scenery—527) which is said to be unsigned. Nevertheless, there seems to be no doubt that the present illustration comes from *Picturesque Scenery.* W. Crane is described as being 'of Chester'. He was responsible for a number of lithographs of the Liverpool and Manchester Railway and Telford's Menai and Conway Bridges. (95)

12

THE PARYS MINE ON ANGLESEA

Watercolour. 21·6 × 28·6. 1792. Julius Caesar Ibbetson (1759–1817).
Reproduced by courtesy of the National Museum of Wales.
A version of this watercolour was aquatinted by J. Bluck (*fl.* 1791–1819) for J. Baker's *A Picturesque Guide through Wales* (1794–7). In this work, the number of illustrations fluctuates from copy to copy, and Bluck's view of the Parys Mine does not appear in the Abbey collation (Scenery—514) though it is present in the copy at Croft Castle. Miss Rotha Mary Clay reproduces a related picture in oils in her *Julius Caesar Ibbetson* 1948, *Pl.* 30. *Cf.* also Plate IV. (94)

13

*A VIEW OF BOTALLACK MINE IN CORNWALL

Lithograph, coloured. 42·4 × 62·4 (*ps*). 1822. *Lith.* George Scharf (1788–1860) after I. Tonkin of Penzance.
Scharf fought with the British at Waterloo, and came to London in 1816. He was one of the first successful lithographers in Britain, and contributed many illustrations to scientific and geological works. He was responsible for the Scharf Collection in the

British Museum Print Room, an immense
and detailed pictorial record of everyday life
in London, whole pages being devoted to the
types of hat or boot worn by Londoners,
interspersed with more general scenes of
life in the streets. He was the father of Sir
George Scharf (1820–95), another artist
of considerable attainment and the first
Director of the National Portrait Gallery in
London. (95)

14

*AN IRON WORK, FOR CASTING OF
CANNON . . . TAKEN FROM THE
MADELEY SIDE OF THE RIVER SEVERN
Line engraving. 35 × 52 (ps). 1788. Eng.
Wilson Lowry (1762–1824), after George
Robertson (1742–88). Pub. John and Josiah
Boydell. (90)

15

*THE INSIDE OF A SMELTING HOUSE,
AT BROSELEY
Line engraving. 34·8 × 52·3 (ps). 1788.
Eng. and Pub. as in Fig. 14. (90)

16

CYFARTHFA IRONWORKS, MERTHYR
TYDFIL
Watercolour. 21·8 × 30. n.d. (1795?).
Julius Caesar Ibbetson (1759–1817).
Reproduced by courtesy of the Cyfarthfa
Castle Museum, Merthyr Tydfil. (86)

17

*ROLLING MILLS, MERTHYR TYDFIL
Sepia wash drawing. 30 × 48·3. c. 1817.
Thomas Hornor (fl. 1800–44).
Hornor published two works on surveying
in 1800 and 1813. He spent several years
in executing pictorial (sic) delineations of
landed estates in perspective panoramic
views. In the course of this work he
constructed 'an apparatus by which the
most distant and intricate scenery may be
delineated with mathematical accuracy,'
probably some kind of Camera Lucida.
Using this piece of equipment he spent the
summer of 1820 in the lantern of St Paul's
executing a general view of London. At

about this time the Cathedral authorities
erected scaffolding over the dome to remove
the ball and cross. Hornor obtained
permission to place an observatory on top,
and spent a precarious and windy couple
of years making detailed sketches of the
surrounding views on 280 sheets of paper,
with a combined area of 1680 sq. ft. These
he intended to work up into four detailed
engravings of the views to North, South,
East and West from the top of St Paul's,
each supported by a descriptive key-sheet.
He believed they would be of great interest
to surveyors, topographers and property
owners. Finding it difficult to relate
the sketches to the general scheme, he made
a single, comprehensive 'key-sketch' of the
whole which is now in the Crace
Collection (Views, III, No. 99) in the British
Museum.

To enlist subscribers, Hornor published a
prospectus in two editions in 1822 and 1823,
having the title View of London, and the
surrounding Country, taken with mathematical
accuracy from an Observatory purposely
erected over the Cross of St Paul's Cathedral.
It contains an elaborate account of how the
engravings were made and their content.
He hoped to be able to supply them in
monochrome or in impressions coloured
to give the effect of highly finished
drawings. He also intended to issue Select
Views in London and its Vicinity in ten
parts of ten engravings each. Though he
made ready but perhaps did not publish yet
a third edition of the prospectus (described in
Weinreb and Breman Catalogue No. 24,
1967), the whole scheme seems to have
petered out, and there is no sign that
Hornor ever managed to put his work on the
market. It appears that he settled in New
York some time before 1828, where he
executed several panoramic views of that
city before moving to Ossening in 1844.
(131)

18

*THE IRON FORGE BETWEEN DOLGELLI
AND BARMOUTH
Aquatint in sepia. 21·5 × 29·7 (ps). 1776.

Eng. by and after Paul Sandby (1725–1809). Source: *Views in North Wales.* Paul Sandby. 1776. Part 2, *Pl.* XVIII. (68, 71, 79)

19

AN IRON FORGE, VIEWED FROM WITHOUT

Oil on canvas. 105 × 140. 1773. Joseph Wright of Derby (1734–97).
Reproduced by courtesy of the Hermitage.
Purchased directly from the artist's studio in 1774 by Catherine the Great. In the picture of this title dated 1772, in the possession of the late Countess Mountbatten of Burma, the surroundings of the building are not shown, and the effect is at once more conventional and more sentimental. The latter was engraved in mezzotint by Richard Earlom (1743–1822) and published by John Boydell in 1773. (60)

20

*VIEW OF BARTON BRIDGE

Line engraving. 20·4 × 26·1 (*pm*). 1794. *Eng.* Robert Pollard (1755–1838) after John Swertner (1746–1813). Source: *A description of the Country . . . round Manchester.* 1795. John Aikin, M.D. *Pl.* X, facing page 113. (15)

21

*A NAVIGATION AFLOAT IN THE AIR

Line engraving. 12 × 14·6 approx. (*ps*). 1795. *Eng.* Philip Audinet (1766–1837) after Thomas Stothard, R.A. (1755–1834). Source: as in Fig. 20. Vignette on engraved title page. (16)

22

A SOUTH WESTERN PROSPECT OR PERSPECTIVE VIEW OF STOUR PORT

Aquatint. 33·2 × 49·1 (?). 1776. *Eng.* Peter Mazell (*fl.* 1770–1800) after James Sherriff. *Reproduced from a photograph by courtesy of the Waterways Museum, Stoke Bruerne.* Mazell worked for the Boydells and also made the engravings for Cordiner's *Ruins and Romantic Prospects in North Britain* (1792). Nothing appears to be known of Sherriff. (78)

23

*CHARRIOT À CHARBON, DES CARRIÈRES DE NEWCASTLE

Line engraving. 22·3 × 33·2 (*pm*). 1773. *Eng.* Etienne Fessard after William Beilby. Source: *L'Art d'Exploiter les Mines de Charbon de Terre.* 1768–76. Jean Morand. Part 2, *pl.* XXXIV.
Morand's work is part of a series, issued by the Academie des Sciences under the general title, *Description des Arts et Métiers.* (74–5)

24

*A VIEW OF TANFIELD ARCH

Aquatint, coloured. 43·7 × 60·6 (*ps*). 1804. *Eng.* Joseph Constantine Stadler (*fl.* 1780–1812) after Joseph Atkinson.
The Tanfield waggonway was laid in 1712. The Tanfield Arch, over the Beckley Burn, was built in 1726 by George Bowen. The oil painting of the Tanfield Arch by Atkinson was on the London market in 1964. The Science Museum has his water-colour from which the aquatint was derived. (86)

25

*THE IRON BRIDGE OF COALBROOKDALE

Watercolour. 28·4 × 43. c. 1779. Artist unknown.
The style is that of an engineer-draughts-man rather than an artist, and a possible attribution is George Perry (*see* Fig. 2, *note*). (87)

26

*A VIEW OF THE IRON BRIDGE, TAKEN FROM THE MADELEY SIDE OF THE RIVER SEVERN

Line engraving. 34·9 × 52·6 (*ps*). 1788. *Eng.* James Fittler (1758–1835), after George Robertson (1742–88). *Pub.* John and Josiah Boydell. (89–90)

27

THE LIMEKILN AT COALBROOKDALE

Oil on board. 27·4 × 40. c. 1797. Joseph Mallord William Turner (1775–1851). Sold at Sotheby's, 23 November 1966. (No. 86.) Mezzotinted by Frederick Christian Lewis (1779–1856) in 1825. (102)

28
VIEW OF CROMFORD, NEAR MATLOCK
Oil on canvas. 91·4 × 114·2. c. 1793.
Joseph Wright of Derby (1734–97).
Reproduced by courtesy of Mr James Oakes.
Another version of this painting is in the
possession of Mr Booth which appears to be
that originally illustrated by Klingender
(page 177) and dated by him 1789. On
topographical and other grounds, it now
appears that neither is the picture exhibited
in 1789. Both may be dated about 1783. (55)

29
THE TOWN OF LANARK
Aquatint, coloured. 39·4 × 57·4 (ps). 1825
(c. 1784?) *Eng.* by and after I. Clark. *Pub.*
Smith Elder and Co.
Reproduced by courtesy of the Parker Gallery.
I. (or J.) Clark aquatinted a series of airy and
elegant views of Scottish towns in 1824 and
1825, published by Smith, Elder and Co.
Nothing else appears to be known of him. (113)

30
*COTTON FACTORIES, UNION STREET,
MANCHESTER
Steel engraving. 9·8 × 15·3 (ps). 1829. *Eng.*
McGahey after J. Harwood. Source:
*Lancashire Illustrated . . . from original
Drawings by S. Austen, Harwood, [George]
Pyne &c &c.* 1831. Facing page 41.
George Pyne (c. 1800–84) was the son of
William Henry Pyne (1769–1843), the *genre*
and figure painter, and a writer. He
contributed the text of *Lancashire
Illustrated* which first appeared in parts in
1829. It was published by Nicholson & Co.,
a firm which pioneered the production in
bulk of cheap topographical works illustrated
with steel engravings. Nothing appears to be
known of McGahey or J. Harwood, but the
engravings was supervised by Robert Wallis
(1794–1878), the very successful engraver
of Turner's watercolours on to steel. (126)

31
A PHILOSOPHER GIVING THAT LECTURE
ON THE ORRERY, IN WHICH A LAMP IS
PUT IN THE PLACE OF THE SUN

Mezzotint. 48·2 × 58·2 (pm). 1768. *Eng.*
William Pether (1731–c. 1795) after Joseph
Wright (1734–1797). *Pub.* John Boydell.
1768.
*Reproduced by courtesy of the British
Museum.*
The original picture, painted c. 1763–5, is
in the Derby Museum and Art Gallery. (54)

32
AN EXPERIMENT ON A BIRD IN THE
AIR PUMP
Mezzotint. 46·9 × 57·8 (pm). 1769. *Eng.*
Valentine Green (1739–1813) after Joseph
Wright. *Pub.* John Boydell. 1769.
*Reproduced by courtesy of the British
Museum.*
The original picture, painted in c. 1768, is in
the Tate Gallery. (53)

33
THE BLACKSMITH'S SHOP
Mezzotint. 60·7 × 43·1 (pm). 1771. *Eng.*
Richard Earlom (1743–1822), after Joseph
Wright. *Pub.* John Boydell. 1771.
*Reproduced by courtesy of the British
Museum.*
The original picture is in the possession of
the Royal College of Surgeons. (59–60)

34
*EAST VIEW OF THE CAST IRON BRIDGE
OVER THE RIVER WEAR AT
SUNDERLAND . . . PREVIOUS TO THE
CENTRE BEING TAKEN DOWN
Aquatint. 43·7 × 73·8 (ps). c. 1795. *Eng.*
J. Raffield after Robert Clarke.
A companion piece was issued of the
completed bridge from the west side.
Nothing appears to be known of either artist
or engraver. (93)

35
A PERSPECTIVE VIEW OF THE DESIGN
FOR A CAST IRON BRIDGE, CONSISTING
OF A SINGLE ARCH 600 FEET IN THE
SPAN AND CALCULATED TO SUPPLY
THE PLACE OF THE PRESENT LONDON
BRIDGE
Engraving in line and aquatint. 54·8 ×

119·8 (ps). 1801. *Eng.* Wilson Lowry (1762–1824) after Thomas Malton (1748–1804) who was also responsible for the aquatinting.

Lowry executed some of the Coalbrookdale engravings after Robertson (Figs. 14 and 26). Malton was an architectural draughtsman. One of Turner's masters, he executed many watercolours and aquatints of London. The designer of the bridge is Thomas Telford (1757–1834).
Reproduced by courtesy of the Science Museum. (17)

36

*A VIEW OF THE AQUEDUCT AT MARPLE
Aquatint, coloured, 33·7 × 44 (ps). 1803. *Eng.* Francis Jukes (1746–1812), after Joseph Parry (1744–1826).

Jukes was a prolific and popular engraver of topographical, sporting and *genre* works of all kinds. He also specialized in sea pieces. Parry was a Lancashire painter who favoured both marine subjects and portraits. He was above all a recorder of the buildings and back streets of Liverpool and Manchester. (94)

37

*THE LUNE AQUEDUCT
Wash drawing. 36·7 × 53·6. *c.* 1798. Gideon Yates (*fl.* 1897–37).

Designed by John Rennie (1761–1821) and opened in 1797, the Lune Aqueduct carries the Lancashire Canal over the River Lune on its way to Kendal. Yates' view is of the east side. The tablet over the centre arch on the west side bears a verse in Latin and English:

> Old needs are served, far distant
> sites combined:
> Rivers by art to bring new wealth
> are joined. (80)

38

*THE EMBANKMENT, TRAETH MAWR, TRE-MADOC
Aquatint, coloured. 38 × 54 (ps). 1810. *Eng.* Matthew Dubourg (*fl.* 1786–1825) after Horace W. Billington (*d.* 1812). (136)

39

*VIEW OF A STONE BRIDGE AT RISCA
Aquatint, coloured. 39·5 × 56·5. (ps). *c.* 1805. *Eng.* Thomas Cartwright (fl. 1793–1806) after Edward Pugh (*d.* 1813).

The date of the bridge is uncertain, but it was in use by 1805. Built by the engineer, John Hodgkinson, it carried the Sirhowy waggonway from the Sirhowy iron works, over the River Risca, to Newport. The buildings on the far side of the river are the works of the Union Copper Co.

Pugh contributed to H. Whigstead's *A Tour to North and South Wales* (1800), and is well known for his beautiful volume of aquatints *Cambria Depicta; a Tour through North Wales*, published posthumously in 1816. Most of the illustrations for this work were engraved by Thomas Cartwright, of whom nothing appears to be known. Pugh's drawings for the Risca print may have been made at the same time as the drawings for *Cambria Depicta*, and it has been suggested that it was prepared for a companion volume about South Wales which did not mature owing to Pugh's death. However, Cartwright's aquatint is much larger than those for *Cambria Depicta*. (81)

40

*DESIGN FOR A RAILWAY BRIDGE OVER THE WEAR AT SUNDERLAND
Lithograph. 21 × 34·3. *c.* 1830. *Lith.* Isambard Kingdom Brunel (1706–59).

This bears a close resemblance to Brunel's design of 1829 for the Clifton Suspension Bridge. He had commissions in Sunderland in connection with the docks from the early 1830's, and this design no doubt belongs to this period. It was not executed. (161)

41

*THE MENAI BRIDGE
Woodcut. 18 × 23 (within border). 1825. 2nd ed. *Pub.* J. Brown, Bangor.

From the head of a broadside, celebrating the slinging of the sixteenth and last chain, on 9 July 1825. This is the second *ed.* The first was probably published when the first chain was slung, on 26 April 1825. The

bridge, designed and built by Thomas
Telford (1757–1834) was opened in January
1826. (161)

42

*THE MENAI BRIDGE
Lithograph, tinted, 26·7 × 38·1 (ps). n.d.
(c. 1840?). *Lith.* W. Gauci, after a drawing
by Thomas Colman Dibdin (1810–93) after a
sketch by Nathaniel Beardmore, C.E. (1816–72).
Dibdin was a prolific topographical and
landscape artist. Beardmore was an hydraulic
engineer. There were four Gaucis, all related,
who executed and published innumerable
topographical lithographs and pictures
through most of the nineteenth century. (161)

43

*GATEWAY OF CLIFTON SUSPENSION
BRIDGE
Lithograph. 28·8 × 41·1 (ps). 1830. *Lith.*
after a design by Isambard Kingdom Brunel
(1806–59).
The original drawing, signed by Brunel and
dated 18 December, 1830, is in the Railway
Museum at Swindon. A striking feature of
Brunel's design is the Egyptian element in
the decorations. The pylons are surmounted
by sphinxes and clad in cast-iron plaques
illustrating every phase of the construction
of the bridge. All were later abandoned on
grounds of cost. (126, 161)

44

*THE COLLIER
Lithograph printed in colour. 20 × 30 (ps).
1814. *Lith.* Ernst Kaufmann, after George
Walker (1781–1856). Source: *The costume
of Yorkshire . . . being fac-similes of
original drawings.* 1885. *Pl.* III.
Originally issued in 1813–14 in ten parts in
aquatint by Daniel and Robert Havell (*fl.*
1812–37) after George Walker, *The Costume
of Yorkshire* was re-issued in 1885, with
lithographs in colour by Ernst Kaufmann of
Lahr, near Baden, after Walker's original
drawings, then in the possession of the
editor of the new edition, Edward Hailstone
of Walton Hall, Yorkshire. The scene is
Charles Brandling's Middleton Colliery, near

Leeds. The locomotive is one of a number
built by John Blenkinsop (1783–1831) in
1812. He was a 'viewer' or superintendent
at the colliery. (111)

45

*OLD LOCOMOTIVE ENGINE, WYLAM
COLLIERY
Etching. 27 × 37·5. 1843. *Eng.* by and after
Thomas H. Hair (*fl.* 1838–49). Source:
*Sketches of the Coal Mines in Northumber-
land.* 1844. T. H. Hair.
The Wylam Dilly locomotive was built in
1813 for Christopher Blackett by William
Hedley (1779–1843) with the assistance of
Timothy Hackworth (1786–1850). (127–8)

46

*THE DEPOT AT HEXHAM
Pen-and-ink and wash. 12 × 18·2. 1837.
James Wilson Carmichael (1800–68).
Engraved on steel by John Wykeham
Archer (1808–64) for *Views of the Newcastle
and Carlisle Railway*, 1838. Although the
name of the locomotive is indistinct she is in
fact COMET delivered by Messrs Robert
Stephenson & Co. of Newcastle early in
1835. Her tender has been detached and she
is being turned. Archer was a Newcastle
artist who specialized in architectural themes
such as a splendid series of etchings of
Fountains Abbey. (157)

47

*TAFF VALE RAILWAY. QUAKER'S YARD
VIADUCT
Wash drawing. 27·7 × 40·4. 1841. *Att.*
Penry Williams (1798–1885).
The Taff Vale Railway was opened on
28 April 1841. Since the centring of the
arch on the left, carrying the Taff Vale over
the ancient Penydarren plateway, has not
yet been struck, the picture can be dated to
this period. Though Trevithick's locomotive
was put to work on the Penydarren in 1804,
it was withdrawn because it was too heavy
and broke the tram plates. The line was later
strengthened, and locomotives put to work
on it again in 1833, no doubt in connection
with the building of the Taff Vale Railway,

which runs parallel to it. When the latter was opened it fell into disuse, although its course can still be traced. The attribution to the local Merthyr artist, Penry Williams, is based not only on style but also on the fact that only an artist intimately acquainted with the various types of permanent way would have taken such pains to establish that the Penydarren is a plateway.

Williams was born in Merthyr and worked in the Cyfarthfa Iron Works where he would have acquired such knowledge. His artistic leanings were noticed by Sir John Guest and William Crawshay, both local iron masters. They sent him to London to train as an artist in 1824. He went to Italy in 1827, but there is evidence that he returned to Wales on many occasions. Though he executed a number of industrial pictures, now in the Cyfarthfa Castle Museum at Merthyr, his Italian works are of less compelling interest. He did an oil painting of the Quaker's Yard Viaduct in 1845, also in the Editor's collection. (106)

48
*STEAM BOAT ON THE CLYDE NEAR DUMBARTON
Aquatint, coloured. 16·4 × 23·5 (ps). 1817. *Eng.* by and after William Daniell (1769–1837). Source: *Voyage Round Great Britain.* 1814–25. William Daniell. Vol. 3, *Pl.* LXIV. The vessel is the 'Comet' built by Henry Bell. (107)

49
THE OPENING OF THE SALTASH BRIDGE
Canvas. Oil on canvas 29·2 × 50. 1859. Thomas Valentine Robins.
A view from the Devon side of Isambard Kingdom Brunel's masterpiece which carried the main line from Plymouth into Cornwall. The date is 2 May 1859, and the bridge is being opened by H.R.H. The Prince Consort. Albert, his hat raised, is taking the salute from the Royal Yacht. Brunel himself is a dying man, too sick to attend. The only view he had of the completed bridge was lying on his back on a flat truck propelled across it by a locomotive. (160)

50
*ACKERMANN'S LIBRARY FOR WORKS OF ART
Aquatint, coloured. 19·3 × 25·3 (ps). *Eng.* J. Bluck (*fl.* 1719–1819) after Augustus Pugin (1762 or 1769–1832). Source: *Repository of Arts.* 1813. Series 1, Vol. 9, *Pl.* 352.
The room is one of the first to have been illuminated by gas, using fittings designed by Frederick Christian Accum, a pioneer of gas lighting. Pugin was not only a celebrated architect but a prolific watercolourist who executed many topographical and architectural views for Ackermann and who collaborated with Rowlandson on *The Microcosm of London* (1808–11). (149)

51
*GAS LAMPS
Aquatint, coloured. 15·4 × 24·4. 1815. Artist not stated. Source: *A Practical Treatise on Gas-Light.* 1815. F. C. Accum. *Pl.* V, facing page 120. (149)

52
THE DANNEMORA IRON MINE
Aquatint, tinted. 23·6 × 17·7 (ps). 1809. *Eng.* Joseph Constantine Stadler (*fl.* 1780–1812) after Sir Robert Ker Porter (1777–1842). Source: *Travelling Sketches in Russia and Sweden.* 1809. R. K. Porter. Vol. 2, *Pl.* XXXVII. *Cf. Pl.* IV *supra.* James Nasmyth sketched the same scene in 1843. *Rep.* Autobiography, 1885, facing p. 300. (126)

53
*THE HOLLOW DEEP OF HELL
Mezzotint on steel. 26·8 × 20·2. (1826). *Eng.* by and after John Martin (1789–1854). Source: *The Paradise Lost of Milton with Illustrations, designed and engraved by John Martin,* 1827. Vol. 1, facing page 15. *Reproduced by courtesy of the British Museum.* The reference is P. L., Book I, line 314. (126)

54
*THE THAMES TUNNEL
Aquatint, coloured. 28·8 × 37·6 (ps). 1835. *Eng.* John Harris (*d.* 1834) after Thomas Tal-

bot Bury (1811–77). *Pub.* Ackermann and Co. Bury is well known, not only as an architect but as the delineator of the opening months of The Liverpool and Manchester Railway. John Harris is presumably the senior, an illustrator of birds and insects and a marine painter. He is known also as an engraver in aquatint, and the work illustrated must have been almost his final piece, executed at a moment when the aquatint had been almost ousted by lithography, of which his son, John Harris junior (1791–1873) was a skilled exponent.

The Thames Tunnel was not opened until 1843. However, in 1835 work was in full swing after a period rendered stagnant for want of money. This engraving is one of a number put out at this time to regain public interest and confidence. For purposes perhaps of reassurance, the picture suggests, inaccurately, that it will be possible to see right through the tunnel to the open air. (107)

55

AT THE BRINK OF CHAOS
Mezzotint on steel. 26·9 × 19.2 (ps). 1825. *Eng.* by and after John Martin (1789–1854). Source: *The Paradise Lost of Milton with Illustrations, designed and engraved by John Martin*, 1827. Vol. 2, facing page 121. *Reproduced by courtesy of the British Museum.* The reference is P.L., Book X, lines 312 and 347. There is a proof in the B.M. Print Room without the whitish streaks. (122)

56

*THE BANQUET (Detail)
Oils on board. 30·5 × 23·3. 1827. Artist unknown.
Tunnelling under the Thames began on 28 November 1828, from the bottom of a shaft sunk on the north bank. The bore crept forward slowly under a constant threat of an inrush of water. To reassure the public and the shareholders it was decided to hold a dinner in the workings on 10 November 1827. The sides of the tunnel were draped in crimson; the Band of the Coldstream Guards was engaged to play through dinner; the proceedings were illuminated by

chandeliers mounted on decorative urns containing patent portable gas. The guests of honour sat at one table and 100 of the leading workmen at another. At the face, tunnelling continued without cease. Sir Mark Isambard Brunel (1769–1849), the chief engineer, stayed away so that his son, Isambard Kingdom, could receive the honours: already, at the age of 20, he was in dashing command of the undertaking. During the proceedings, the defeat of the Turkish Fleet at Navarino was announced in the presence of Sir Edward Codrington, Commander-in-Chief of the Mediterranean Fleet and an ardent supporter of the Tunnel. James Bandinel of the Foreign Office proposed a toast: 'Down with water and Mahomet—Wine and Codrington for ever!' The workmen toasted their implements and presented Isambard Kingdom Brunel with a pick-axe and spade as symbols of their craft. The artist has given himself the licence to include the elder Brunel, even though he was not present. He is on the extreme left, handing his son a sealed letter. A few weeks later the Tunnel was inundated and all work held up for many weary months while funds were raised with which to make a fresh start. (125)

57

HIGH ON A THRONE OF ROYAL STATE
Mezzotint on steel. 19·3 × 27·7 (ps). 1825. *Eng.* by and after John Martin. Source: *The Paradise Lost of Milton with Illustrations, designed and engraved by John Martin*, 1827. Vol. 1, facing page 37. *Reproduced by courtesy of the British Museum.*
The reference is P.L., Book II, line 1. Martin has converted Milton's 'starry lamps and blazing cressets, fed with naphtha and asphaltus' into flaring coronas of gas. (125)

58

EXPLOSION AND FIRE AT SHIFFNAL
Lithograph. 30 × 40. 1821. *Lith.* by and after Francis Nicholson (1753–1844). Source: *Lithographic Impressions of Sketches from Nature.* 1821. Francis Nicholson.

Reproduced by courtesy of the British Museum.
The title as set out above does not appear in the version illustrated, which has only the words 'Near Wellington, Shropshire'. The legend 'Explosion and Fire at Shiffnal' appears in a slightly different version from another stone featured in *Six Lithographic Impressions of Sketches from Nature*, 1820. (Abbey. Life—161.) (131)

59

THE GREAT DAY OF HIS WRATH
Mezzotint on steel. 26·8 × 41·7 (*ps*). 1850. *Eng.* James Stephenson (1828–86) after John Martin.
Reproduced by courtesy of the British Museum.
An engraving after one of three pictures exhibited by Martin in 1850, each 9 × 13 ft, entitled: 'The Last Judgement', 'The Great Day of his Wrath' and 'The Plains of Heaven'. (Rev. VI 9–17; Isaiah XVIII; Ezek. XXXVIII 20). James Stephenson also engraved the illustrations of *Manchester as it is* (1839). (132)

60

LYMINGTON IRON WORKS, ON THE TYNE
Steel engraving. 9·7 × 15·4 (*ps*). 1832. *Eng.* James Sands (*fl.* 1811–41) after Thomas Allom (1804–72). Source: *Durham and Northumberland Illustrated*. 1832. Facing page 56.
Reproduced by courtesy of the British Museum.
Fisher, Son and Co. published a series of books on English counties: *Westmoreland Illustrated*, *Cumberland Illustrated* and *Durham and Northumberland Illustrated*. They are usually found bound together. They were re-issued in 1847 under the title: *Picturesque Rambles in Westmoreland . . .* etc. (131)

61

*DRAWING THE RETORTS AT THE GREAT GAS LIGHT ESTABLISHMENT, BRICK LANE
Aquatint, coloured. 16 × 21·8 (*ps*). 1821. *Eng.* W. Read. Source: *The Monthly Magazine*. 1821. Vol. 51. Frontispiece. Used also as the frontispiece of *One Thousand Experiments in Chemistry*. 1821. Colin Mackenzie. The publisher of both *The Monthly Magazine* and *One Thousand Experiments* was Sir Richard Phillips (1767–1840). (126)

62

*FACTORY CHILDREN
Lithograph printed in colour. 20 × 30 (*ps*). 1814. *Lith.* Ernst Kaufmann after George Walker (1781–1856). Source: *The Costume of Yorkshire . . . being fac-similies of original Drawings*. 1885. *Pl.* XXXVI. See note to Fig. 44. (112)

63

*CARDING, DRAWING, AND ROVING
Steel engraving. 10·4 × 16·5 (*ps*). 1835. *Eng.* James Carter (1798–1855) after Thomas Allom (1804–72). Source: *History of the Cotton Manufacture in Great Britain*. 1835. Edward Baines Jr. (1800–90). Facing page 182.
Baines was son of the reformer Edward Baines Sr. (1774–1848), proprietor of the *Leeds Mercury* and publisher of topographical works. The latter appointed his son Editor of the *Leeds Mercury* in 1818. Edward Baines Jr. became an economist and sociologist. His *History of Cotton Manufacture* is still a standard work. As the illustration suggests, he took a benign view of child labour and other related problems. (113)

64

*LOVE CONQUERED FEAR
Steel engraving. 14·6 × 10·1 (*ps*). 1839. *Eng.* Thomas Onwhyn (?) (*c.* 1820–86). Source: *The Life and Adventures of Michael Armstrong*. 1840. Frances Trollope. (1780–1863). Facing page 82. (167)

65

*A SERIOUS GENTLEMAN AS OWNS A FACTORY
Steel engraving. 14·8 × 10·2 (*ps*). *Eng.* August Hervieu (*fl.* 1819–58). Source: as in Fig. 64. Facing page 163. (167)

66

*EXCAVATION OF OLIVE MOUNT
Aquatint, coloured. 25·3 × 20·4 (*ps*). 1831.
Eng. H. Pyall after Thomas Talbot Bury
(1811–77). Source: *Coloured Views of the
Liverpool and Manchester Railway . . .
from drawings made on the spot.* 1831. T. T.
Bury. *Pl.* III.
Surprisingly, considering the quality of his
work, very little is known of Pyall. His name
appears on a number of contemporary racing
prints and on some of the plates in Grindley's
*Scenery, Costumes and Architecture . . .
of India,* 1826–30, Moore's *Rangoon
Views, and combined Operations in the
Birman Empire,* 1825–6 and Kinsey's
Portugal Illustrated, 1828. (125)

67

*ENTRANCE OF THE RAILWAY AT EDGE
HILL—LIVERPOOL
Aquatint, coloured. 20·3 × 25·2 (*ps*). 1831.
Eng. H. Pyall after Thomas Talbot Bury
(1811–77). Source: as in Fig. 66. *Pl.* II.
The second impression. The first shows the
base of the left-hand chimney only, sheathed
in scaffolding. (125)

68

BELSHAZZAR'S FEAST
Mezzotint on steel. 46·3 × 71·5 (*ps*). 1835.
Eng. by and after John Martin (1789–1854).
Source: *Illustrations of the Bible.* 1837. John
Martin. *Reproduced by courtesy of the
British Museum.*
From a special proof before letters. (125)

69

*MOORISH ARCH, LOOKING FROM THE
TUNNEL
Aquatint, coloured. 20·4 × 25·1 (*ps*). 1831.
Eng. S. G. Hughes after T. T. Bury.
Source: as in Fig. 66. *Pl.* X.
Nothing is known of Hughes unless he can
be identified with an S. Hughes of Bangor,
who did the original drawing for a litho-
graph by J. Fagan entitled 'The Wonders of
Menai, in its Suspension and Tubular Bridges'.
It was published by Hughes in 1850. (124)

70

GATE OF GRAND CAIRO
Aquatint, coloured. 22·4 × 31·6 (*ps*). 1802.
Eng. Thomas Milton (1743–1827) after
Luigi Mayer (d. 1803). Source: *Views in
Egypt, from the original drawings in the
possession of Sir Robert Ainslie, taken during
his Embassy in Constantinople by Luigi
Mayer.* 1801. *Pl.* XXV, facing page 46.
*Reproduced by courtesy of Maggs Brothers
Ltd.* (124)

71

*RAILWAY OFFICE, LIVERPOOL
Aquatint, coloured. 20·8 × 25·3 (*ps*). 1831.
Eng. as in Fig. 69. Source: as in Fig. 66.
Pl. VIII. (124)

72

THE MOSQUE OF FOUR HUNDRED
PILLARS AT CAIRO
Aquatint, coloured. 22·4 × 31·6 (*ps*). 1802.
Eng. as in Fig. 70. Source: as in Fig. 70.
Pl. XXVII, facing page 48.
*Reproduced by courtesy of Maggs Brothers
Ltd.* (124)

73

*EFFECTS OF THE RAIL ROAD ON THE
BRUTE CREATION
Lithograph. 26·4 × 35·8 (*ps*). 1831. *Anon.*
This is Plate 1, which carries the announce-
ment that Plates 2 and 3 have just been
published. Only Plate 2 is known, on a
similar theme. The design for Plate 1 also
appears on a printed handkerchief. (140)

74

*THE PLEASURE OF THE RAIL-ROAD
Etching, coloured. 22·6 × 33·4 (*ps*). 1831.
Eng. Hugh Hughes (1790–1863).
This, and a companion piece showing a
locomotive mowing down the populace
while the driver and his mate read the
paper, are signed HH in monogram and
identified with Hughes in Francois Brulliot's
Dictionnaire des Monogrammes (1832–3).
He was a Welsh Calvinist turned Plymouth
Brother, a minor topographer and author of
The Beauties of Cambria (1823). (140)

75

*SCIENTIFIC RESEARCHES. NEW
DISCOVERIES IN PNEUMATICS, OR AN
EXPERIMENTAL LECTURE ON THE
POWERS OF AIR
Etching, coloured. 24·5 × 35 (*ps*). 1802.
Eng. James Gillray (1757–1815).
The place is the Royal Institution, founded
in 1799 by Count Rumford (1753–1814) and
Sir Joseph Banks (1743–1820) as a centre for
scientific research and education. The
lecturer is Dr Thomas Garnett (1766–1802),
the first Professor of Natural Philosophy and
Chemistry at the Institution. He is
experimenting on Sir John Coxe Hippisley
(1748–1825). Humphry Davy, Garnett's
successor, is ready with a bellows. Count
Rumford stands near a cabinet of electrical
apparatus on the right. Behind him, almost
out of the picture, can be made out Isaac
Disraeli (1766–1848), the father of Benjamin.
The place is packed with the nobility and
gentry. (108)

76

CHEMICAL LECTURES
Etching, coloured. 22·7 × 32·6 (*ps*). *c.*
1810. *Eng.* Thomas Rowlandson (1756–1827).
Reproduced by courtesy of the British Museum.
The place is the Surrey Institute. The
lecturer is Humphry Davy (1778–1829),
F.R.S., Professor of Chemistry at the Royal
Institution since 1802. On the left, chin on
hand, is the former scientific lecturer at the
Surrey Institute, Frederick Christian Accum,
registering anguished jealousy. Accum was
both a pioneer of chemical analysis and gas
lighting and an ardent propagandist against
the adulteration of food. He was at the same
time inaccurate, truculent and eccentric.
He was the subject of constant lampoons,
and it is only recently that his virtues have
been disentangled from his weaknesses. (108)

77

*OPENING OF THE GLASGOW AND
GARNKIRK RAILWAY
Lithograph. 30·1 × 45·8 (*ps*). 1832. *Lith.*
by and after David Octavius Hill (1802–70).
Source: *Views of the Opening of the Glasgow*

and Garnkirk Railway. 1832.
Hill was one of a number of artists who took
to photography. He is celebrated for his
photographic portraits. (152)

78

*RAILWAY BRIDGES ON THE ANCIENT
PRINCIPLE
Etchings. 19 × 22 (*ps*). 1843. *Eng.* Augustus
Welvy Northmore Pugin (1812–52). Source:
*An Apology for the Revival of Christian
Architecture.* 1843. *Pl.* III. Facing page 10.
Two out of four etchings on Pl. III. (125)

79

*THURGARTON STATION, NOTTINGHAM
AND LINCOLN RAILWAY
Lithograph. 26·1 × 38·8 (*ps*). *c.* 1846.
Lith. W. L. Walton (*fl.* 1834–55).
The architect is J. A. Davies. The N. and
L.R. was opened in 1846, and later absorbed
by the Midland Railway. (125)

80

*PLATE LAYERS ON THE LIVERPOOL
AND MACHESTER RAILWAY
Lithograph. 24·3 × 32·7 (*ps*). 1831. Alfred
B. Clayton. Source: *Views of the Most
Interesting Parts of the Liverpool and
Manchester Railway.* 1831. A. B. Clayton
The published title of this illustration is
'Moorish Arch'. *Views* is a slim 4to with
three lithographs and three sheets of letter-
press. The two other titles are 'Olive Mount
Cutting' and 'View of the Liverpool and
Manchester Rail Road . . . where it crosses
the Duke of Bridgewater's Canal'. (171)

81, 82

*NAVVIES AT WORK ON THE LONDON
AND BIRMINGHAM RAILWAY
Wash and pen-and-ink. Extracted from two
sheets of drawings, each 32·8 × 27. *c.* 1837.
John Cooke Bourne (1814–96). (155, 171)

83

*EARLY STAGES OF THE EXCAVATION
TOWARDS EUSTON
Pencil and wash. 13·6 × 21·5. 1836–7.
John Cooke Bourne.

One of the early sketches. Granby Terrace Bridge will presently be thrown across the middle distance, with the Hampstead Road Bridge at an angle beyond. The building on the left, still standing as these lines are being written, is at the corner of Granby Terrace and Hampstead Road. A plaque records that it was formerly Wellington House where Charles Dickens was educated from 1824–6. The church in the middle distance is St Pancras, with St Paul's (which can still be seen from this point) in the distance to the left. (154)

84
*BUILDING THE STATIONARY ENGINE HOUSE, CAMDEN TOWN
Sepia wash drawing heightened with white. 20·8 × 34·5. 1837. John Cooke Bourne. A view looking north east. The buildings in the distance are the locomotive sheds. Those in the middle foreground will house the winding engines, at first used to lower trains into Euston. There will be two tall chimneys for the boilers, of which only the stumps are completed, one under the sheer-legs crane to the right. There is another, almost identical drawing in the Transport Museum at Clapham. *Lith.* J. C. Bourne. *London and Birmingham Railway.* 1839. *Pl.* VIII. (155)

85
HAMPSTEAD ROAD BRIDGE
Sepia wash drawing heightened with white. 25·6 × 42·8. 1836. John Cooke Bourne. *Reproduced by courtesy of the Transport Museum, Clapham.*
A view looking north under the Bridge. The covered stretch between Hampstead Road Bridge and Granby Terrace Bridge has the beams in position, but they are not yet roofed in. In the foreground are two lengths of rail, chaired and on stone blocks. Not lithographed. (155)

86
PRIMROSE HILL TUNNEL
Wash drawing heightened with white. 23·3 × 33·5. 1837. John Cooke Bourne. *Reproduced by courtesy of the Transport*

Museum, Clapham.
The south face of the Tunnel as seen on 10 October, and practically complete. The two derricks used for lifting stone are still in place. *Lith.* J. C. Bourne. *London and Birmingham Railway. Pl.* XI. (155)

87
KILSBY TUNNEL
Wash drawing heightened in white. 20·3 × 19·6. 1837. John Cooke Bourne. *Reproduced by courtesy of the Transport Museum, Clapham.*
A section of the tunnel below a working shaft through which materials and men are lowered and soil removed. Some months earlier there had been a crisis of confidence in the tunnel's Engineer, Robert Stephenson, who discovered, too late, that in the centre of Kilsby Hill lay a great quicksand. The workings were constantly flooded. Costs rose enormously. A faction of shareholders considered either that the tunnel should be abandoned or another engineer called in. Stephenson convinced the Board of his command of the situation and, finally, completed the longest tunnel yet designed solely for locomotive traffic. Bourne's picture, with its tranquil, cathedral-like lighting, was no doubt intended to reassure. *Lith.* J. C. Bourne. *London and Birimingham Railway. Pl.* XXX. (155)

88
*BOX TUNNEL
Wash drawing heightened with white. 22·6 × 20·2. c. 1846. John Cooke Bourne. *Lith.* J. C. Bourne. *Great Western Railway.* 1846. Perhaps to reassure his readers, Bourne added a small round spot of white in the lithograph to represent daylight at the end of the tunnel. (*c.f.* note to Fig. 54.) (158)

89
*NO. 1 TUNNEL, BRISTOL
Lithograph. 43·8 × 29·4 (*ps*). 1846. *Lith.* by and after John Cooke Bourne. Source: *The Great Western Railway.* Title page. The first tunnel out of Bristol. Later opened out into a cutting. (158)

90
*SUMMIT TUNNEL, MANCHESTER AND
LEEDS RAILWAY
Lithograph. 33·4 × 25·6 (ps). 1845. *Lith.*
by and after Arthur William Tait (1819–
1905). Source: *Views of the Manchester and
Leeds Railway*. 1845. A. F. Tait.
The Transport Museum, Clapham, also has
a run of lithographs by Tait of the London
and North Western Railway. These were
probably issued in a book, but no copy is
known to the editor. (157)

91
*THE WELWYN VIADUCT
Watercolour. 45·7 × 72. 1850. W. Humber.
Lith. Nothing is known of Humber. (160)

92
THE WHARNCLIFFE VIADUCT, GREAT
WESTERN RAILWAY
Lithograph. 29·3 × 42·8 (ps). 1846. *Lith.*
by and after John Cooke Bourne. Source:
The Great Western Railway. Frontis. (158)

93
*VIADUCT OVER THE VALLEY OF THE
ERME AT IVYBRIDGE
Lithograph. 29 × 51 (ps). 1848. *Lith.* by
and after William Dawson. *Pub.* W. Spreat
of Exeter.
One of a series of six. The other titles are:
'Line of the Railway, across the Warren at
Lang [g] stone Cliff'; 'Line of the South
Devon Railway, from Dawlish Sands to Hole
Head'; 'Line of the Railway, up the left
Bank of the Teign'; 'The Marley Viaduct';
'The Slade Viaduct'. They are dated between
August and October, 1848.
    The Ivybridge Viaduct is one of many
such by which Brunel leapt the valleys of
Devon and Cornwall on his engineering
march from London to Penzance. (159)

94
*BRITANNIA TUBULAR BRIDGE OVER
THE MENAI STRAITS
Lithograph, tinted. 37·5 × 58·6 (ps). 1849.
Lith. S. Russell. *Pub.* S. Russell.
A scene taken in 1848 during the construction

of the tubes. The piers they will straddle
can be seen in the distance. Nothing seems
to be known of Russell, except that he also
executed some lithographs of the North
Midland Railway. (160)

95
*BRITANNIA TUBULAR BRIDGE OVER
THE MENAI STRAITS
Lithograph, tinted. 37·9 × 61 (ps). 1849.
Lith. George Hawkins (1810–52). *Pub.* Day
and Son.
A scene taken on 3 December 1849. The
second tube is being floated into position on
a raft, to be raised into position on the piers,
step by step, by hydraulic presses. One of a
set of four. (160)

96
JOHN COOKE BOURNE
Family photograph. *Reproduced by courtesy
of Mr Eric Bourne.* (163)

97
ISAMBARD KINGDOM BRUNEL
Photograph. *c.* 1857. Robert Howlett.
*Reproduced by courtesy of the Institution of
Mechanical Engineers.*
Howlett describes himself as 'of the
Photographic Institution, 155 New Bond
Street'.
    Brunel is standing in front of the
launching chains of the Great Western.
After a formidable struggle to overcome
mechanical, financial and other difficulties,
she was finally floated on 30 January 1858.
    This photograph, and others by Howlett
and J. Cundell, were engraved for a special
'Leviathan Supplement of' *The Illustrated
Times*. By replacing artists' drawings by
photographs, a first step had been taken
towards the complete photo-mechanical
reproduction of pictures. (162)

98
THE GREAT EASTERN ON HER
LAUNCHING CRADLES
Photograph *c.* 1857. Robert Howlett.
*Reproduced by courtesy of the Institution of
Mechanical Engineers.*

The solitary figure on the right with the tall hat is Brunel. (162)

99

*OPENING THE CRYSTAL PALACE: THE FOREIGN NAVE
Chromo-lithograph. 56·2 × 74·8 (ps). 1851. *Lith.* by and after Joseph Nash (1808–78). *Pub.* Dickinson Bros.
The Queen and Prince Albert are leading the opening procession down the nave on 1 May 1851.

No. 2 of a pair. No. 1 is entitled 'The Inauguration'. They are similar in style to, but much larger than, the magnificent chromo-lithographs in Dickinson Bros' *Comprehensive Pictures of the Great Exhibition of 1851.* Nash specialized in medieval buildings and period reconstructions. (164)

100

*VIEW OF THE TRANSEPT, LOOKING SOUTH
Photograph. 1851. William Henry Fox Talbot (1800–77). Source: *Reports of the Juries.* 1852. Vol. 2, facing page 763. (165)

101

*THE EXTERIOR OF THE SOUTH TRANSEPT
Photograph. 1851. William Henry Fox Talbot. Source: as in Fig. 100. Vol. 2, facing page 819. (165)

102

*THE EAST END OF THE CRYSTAL PALACE
Photograph. 1851. William Henry Fox Talbot. Source: as in Fig. 100. Vol. 2, facing page 819. (165)

103

*YORK STATION
Photograph. *Post* 1877. (165)

104

*ST. PANCRAS STATION
Watercolour. 66 × 128. *c.* 1866 (?). Provenance unknown.

Probably an architect's drawing, but with unusual breadth and finish. Perhaps prepared in the drawing office of Sir George Gilbert Scott (1811–78), the architect, or W. H. Barlow (1812–1902), the engineer. The design is close to what was erected, except that the names of the cities the Midland Railway served or hoped to serve, set out in letters of cast iron below the sweep of the roof, did not materialize. It is still possible to obtain a view almost exactly corresponding to the picture. St Pancras was opened in stages from about 1869. (165)

105

*THE METROPOLITAN RAILWAY NEAR PADDINGTON
Chromo-lithograph. 37·3 × 58·8 (ps). 1863. Samuel John Hodson (*c.* 1836–1908).
As first built, the Metropolitan Railway tunnels were adapted for both the broad and narrow gauges, hence the three rails. The line was worked for a time by the Great Western, and one of that company's broad gauge engines is shown taking the spur from what is now the Inner Circle to what was formerly known as Bishop's Road Station, now incorporated into Paddington. (165)

106

*ST. HILDA COLLIERY, SOUTH SHIELDS
Etching. 27 × 37·6. *c.* 1844. *Eng.* J. E. Nicholson after Thomas H. Hair. Source: *Sketches of Coal Mines in Northumberland and Durham.* 1844. T. H. Hair. Facing page 34. (127–8)

107

SHEFFIELD SCYTHE TILTERS
Oil on canvas. 62 × 46·8. 1856. Godfrey Sykes (1825–66). *By courtesy of the Sheffield City Museum.* (175)

108

*THE FORGE
Steel engraving. 32·6 × 43·9 (ps). 1849–59. *Eng.* By and after James Sharples (1825–92). The original painting, made in 1847, is in the Blackburn Art Gallery. (176)

109

*JAMES CROSSLAND AND FAMILY
Oil on canvas. 135·7 × 106·4. 1847.
James Sharples (1825–92).
Of the books on the table, one is *The
Practical Mechanic*, Vol. II, and the other
The Magazine of Science showing an
engraving of Henson's Aerial Steam
Carriage. (176)

110

BE UNITED AND INDUSTRIOUS
Steel engraving. 63·4 × 40·6. 1852. *Eng.*
William Greatbach (*b.* 1802) after James
Sharples.
*Reproduced by courtesy of Mrs Francis
Klingender.*
Greatbach was primarily an illustrator of
almanacks and periodicals, and an engraver
of sentimental and historical pieces. Branches
of the Association of Engineers received an
uncoloured version. Full members received
a version coloured by hand.

111

CHARGING RETORTS AT THE BECKTON
GAS-WORKS
Wood engraving. 29·8 × 22·3 (*ps*). 1878.
Eng. W. J. P. S. after W. Bazett Murray.
Source: *The Illustrated London News.* (182)

112

IRON AND COAL
Mural at Wallington Hall, Northumberland.
189·6 × 189·6. 1861. William Bell Scott
(1811–90).
*Reproduced by courtesy of the National
Trust.*
Wallington Hall was the home of the
Trevelyan family. It is a square, eighteenth-
century house, built round a courtyard. In
the middle of the nineteenth century the
house became a centre for poets, painters
and men of science. Ruskin suggested to Sir
Walter Trevelyan (1797–1879) that the
courtyard should be roofed in. John Dobson
(1787–1865), the architect of the Central
Station at Newcastle-on-Tyne, was engaged.
The courtyard was turned into a picture
gallery. Ruskin did some of the decorations,
but desisted when Lady Trevelyan
criticized some aspect of what he had done.
At the same time, Scott was engaged to
paint a series of eight murals describing
the history of Northumberland, each just
over 6 ft square, and culminating with a
view of contemporary Newcastle. (181)

113

THE DINNER HOUR, WIGAN
Oil on canvas. 73·8 × 105·5. 1874. Eyre
Crowe (1824–1910).
*Reproduced by courtesy of the Manchester
Art Galleries.*
Crowe was primarily a genre painter, but
with an interest in scientific and industrial
subjects. (175)

114

THE OPENING OF THE BRIDGEWATER
CANAL
Mural at Manchester Town Hall. 1886–91.
Ford Madox Brown (1821–93).
*Reproduced by courtesy of The Manchester
Town Hall Committee.*
One of a series of 12 murals on the history
of education, science and industry. (181)

115

WORK
Oil on canvas, arched top. 138·6 × 196.
1852–65. Ford Madox Brown.
*Reproduced by courtesy of the Manchester
Art Galleries.*
The frame is inscribed as follows:

Left: Neither did we eat any man's
          bread for nought; but wrought with
          labour and travail night and day.
Right: Seest thou a man diligent in his
          business? He shall stand before
          Kings.
Centre: I must work while it is day for
          night cometh when no man can
          work.
Below: In the sweat of thy face shalt thou
          eat bread.

Thomas Flint commissioned the artist to
finish the painting in 1856, but died before
it was completed. (173, 180)

116

THE LAST OF ENGLAND
Watercolour. Circular (diam. 33). 1864–6.
Ford Madox Brown. *Reproduced by courtesy of the Tate Gallery.* (180)

117

TOKENS
1 Token issued by John Wilkinson 1787–92 showing Vulcan. 1791.

2 Token issued by John Wilkinson 1787–92 showing tilt-hammer. 1787.
3 Token issued by Basingstoke Canal Co. 1789.
4 Dundee halfpenny showing a glass house. 1788.
5 Coalbrookdale token, showing the inclined plane at Ketley. 1789.
6 Token issued by John Harvey of Norwich, showing a woollen loom. 1792.

219

INDEX

1 *Harraton Hall and the coal staithes on the River Wear* (detail), 1680

2 *A view of the upper works at Coalbrook Dale, 1758*

INDUSTRIAL PROSPECTS

3 *The south-east prospect of the city of Bath* (detail), 1734

4 *Prior Park, near Bath,* 1750

5 *A view of the Chelsea waterworks (detail), 1752*

7 *Goscote Iron Foundry, n.d.*

The ENGINE for Raising Water (with a power made) by Fire.

6 *The engine for raising water by fire, 1717*

8 *Steam engine of 20 horse-power by Fenton & Co, Leeds, 1827*

7

STEAM

8

9 *Pit-head of a coal-mine with a horse-gin, 1786(?), Paul Sandby*

10 *Pit-head of a coal-mine with steam winding gear, c. 1820*

11 *The Penrhyn slate quarries,* 1842

12 *The Parys Mine on Anglesea,* c. 1780–90, Julius Caesar Ibbetson

13 *A view of Botallack mine in Cornwall, 1822*

14 *An ironwork for casting cannon, 1788*

15 *The inside of a smelting-house at Broseley, 1788*

IRON

16 *Cyfarthfa Ironworks, Merthyr Tydfil,* 1795(?), Julius Caesar Ibbetson

17 *Rolling mills, Merthyr Tydfil,* c. 1817

18 *Iron Forge between Dolgelli and Barmouth*, 1776, Paul Sandby

19 *An iron forge*, 1774, Joseph Wright of Derby

20 *Barton Aqueduct,* 1794

21 *A Navigation afloat in the Air,* 1795

22 *A south-west prospect or perspective view of Stour Port, 1776*

23 *A Newcastle coal wagon, 1773*

24 *A view of Tanfield arch, 1804*

25 *The iron bridge at Coalbrookdale, c. 1779*

26 *Another view of the iron bridge, 1788*

27 *The Limekiln at Coalbrookdale*, c. 1797, J. M. W. Turner

28 *Arkwright's cotton mill*, 1783, Joseph Wright

29 *New Lanark*, 1825

30 *Cotton factories, Union Street, Manchester*, 1829

31 *A philosopher giving a lecture on the orrery*, 1768, engraving after Joseph Wright

32 *An experiment on a bird in the air pump*, 1769, engraving after Joseph Wright

33 *The Blacksmith's Shop*, 1771, engraving after Joseph Wright

34 *East view of the cast-iron bridge over the River Wear, c. 1795*

35 *Telford's design for a replacement of London Bridge, 1801*

ENGINEERING WORKS

36 Marple Aqueduct, 1803

37 The Lune Aqueduct, c. 1798

38 *The embankment, Traeth Mawr, 1810*

39 *View of a stone bridge across the valley and river at Risca, c. 1805*

40 *Brunel's design for a railway bridge over the Wear at Sunderland*, c. 1830

41 *The Menai bridge*, 1825, designed and built by Thomas Telford

THE

Menai Bridge,

42 *The Menai bridge,* c. 1840

43 *Proposed Gateway of Clifton Suspension Bridge,* 1830

44 *A collier, and John Blenkinsop's locomotive of* 1812

45 *Old Locomotive Engine, Wylam Colliery,* 1859

46 *The depot at Hexham*, 1837

47 *Quaker's Yard viaduct, Taff Vale railway*, c. 1841

48 *Steamboat on the Clyde*, 1817

SHIPPING

49 *The opening of the Saltash bridge*, 1859

50 *Ackermann's library for works of art,* 1813

GAS LIGHTING

51 *Gas lights,* 1815

JOHN MARTIN

52 *The Dannemora iron mine*, 1809

53 *The Hollow Deep of Hell*, 1826, illustration for 'Paradise Lost' by John Martin

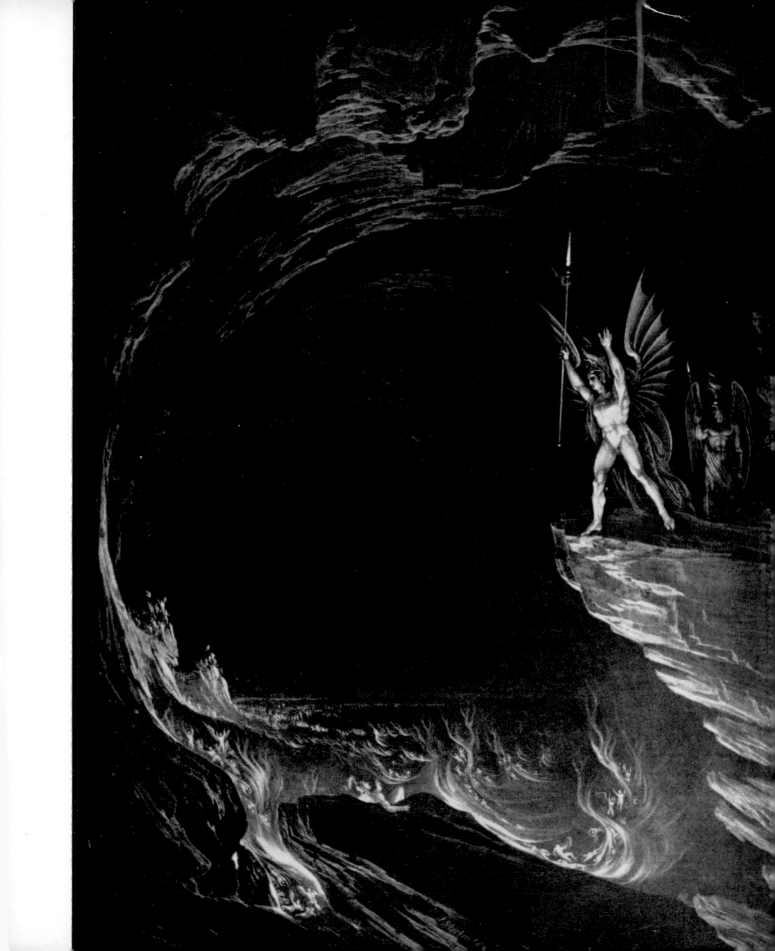

54 *The Thames tunnel,*
1835, after T. T. Bury

55 *At the Brink of Chaos*
illustration for 'Paradise
Lost' by John Martin

56 *The banquet in the*
   Thames tunnel, 1827

57 *High on the Throne of*
   Royal State
   illustration for 'Paradise
   Lost' by John Martin

58 *Explosion and fire at Shiffnal, near Wellington, Shropshire*, 1821

59 *The Great Day of his Wrath*
engraving after John Martin

60 *Lymington ironworks, 1832*

61 *Drawing the retorts at the great
gas light establishment, Brick
Lane, 1821*

62

63

CHILDREN

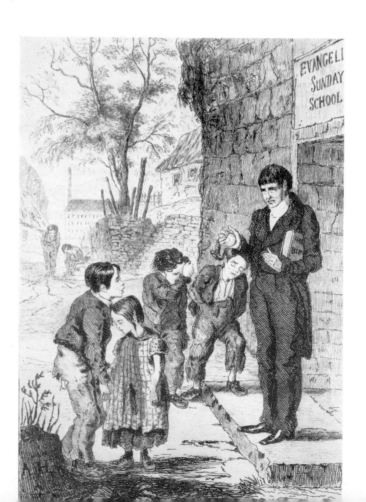

66 *Excavation of Olive Mount, near Liverpool, 1831*

67 *Entrance of the railway at Edge Hill, Liverpool*, 1831

68 *Belshazzar's Feast*, John Martin

69 *Moorish arch, looking from the tunnel,* 1831

70 *Gate of Grand Cairo,* 1802

71 *Railway office, Liverpool, 1831*

72 *The mosque of four hundred pillars at Cairo, 1802*

73 *Effects of the rail road on the Brute Creation, 1831*

74 *The pleasures of the rail road, 1831*

75 *Scientific researches*, 1802, James Gillray

SCIENCE

76 *Chemical Lectures*, 1810, Thomas Rowlandson

77 *Opening of the Glasgow and Garnkirk railway, 1832*

78 *Railway bridges on the Ancient Principle*, 1843

79 *Thurgarton station, Nottingham and Lincoln railway*, c. 1846

80 *Plate-layers on the Liverpool and Manchester railway*, 1831

81 and 82 *Navvies on the London and Birmingham railway*, c. 1857, J. C. Bourne

83 *Early stages of the excavation towards Euston*, J. C. Bourne

84 *Building the engine house, Camden Town*, J. C. Bourne

85 *Hampstead Road bridge*, J. C. Bourne

86 *Primrose Hill tunnel*, J. C. Bourne

88 *Box tunnel*, J. C. Bourne

87 *Kilsby tunnel*, J. C. Bourne

89 *No. 1 tunnel, Bristol,* J. C. Bourne

90 *Summit Tunnel, Manchester and Leeds railway, A. W. Tait*

91 *The Welwyn viaduct*, 1850

92 *The Wharncliffe viaduct, Great Western Railway*, J. C. Bourne

93 *Viaduct over the valley of the Erme at Ivybridge, 1848*

94 *Britannia tubular bridge over the Menai Straits, 1849*

95 *Britannia tubular bridge over the Menai Straits, 1849*

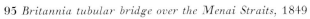

96 *John Cooke Bourne*

97 *Isambard Kingdom Brunel*

98 *The 'Great Eastern' on her launching cradles,* c. 1857

99 *Opening the Crystal Palace, 1851*

THE CRYSTAL PALACE

100 *The Crystal Palace, south transept in 1851.* Photograph by Fox Talbot

101 *The Crystal Palace exterior of the south transept* Photograph by Fox Talbot

102 *The east end of the Crystal Palace.* Photograph by Fox Talbot

103 *York station, 1877*

104 *St Pancras station*, c. 1866

105 *The Metropolitan railway near Paddington*, 1863

106 *St Hilda colliery, South Shields, c. 1844*

107 *Sheffield scythe tilters, 1856*

108 *The Forge*, 1849–59, James Sharples

110 *Be United and Industrious*, 1852, after James Sharples

109 *James Crossland and family*, 1847, James Sharples

112 *Iron and Coal*, 1861, William Bell Scott

111 *Charging retorts at the Beckton gasworks, 1878*

113

114